Business Issues, Competition and Entrepreneurship Series

PRIVATE EQUITY AND ITS IMPACT

BUSINESS ISSUES, COMPETITION AND ENTREPRENEURSHIP SERIES

Improving Internet Access to Help Small Business Compete in a Global Economy
Hermann E. Walker (Editor)
2009. ISBN: 978-1-60692-515-7

Multinational Companies: Outsourcing, Conduct, and Taxes
Loran K. Cornejo (Editor)
2009. ISBN 978-1-60741-260-1

Private Equity and its Impact
Spencer J. Fritz (Editor)
2009. ISBN 978-1-60692-682-6

Business Issues, Competition and Entrepreneurship Series

PRIVATE EQUITY AND ITS IMPACT

SPENCER J. FRITZ
EDITOR

Nova Science Publishers, Inc.
New York

LIBRARY OF CONGRESS CATALOGING-IN-PUBLICATION DATA
Available upon request

ISBN: 978-1-60692-682-6

Published by Nova Science Publishers, Inc. ✦ New York

CONTENTS

PREFACE

This book looks at the increase in leveraged buyouts (LBO) of U.S. companies by private equity funds prior to the slowdown in mid-2007 which has raised questions about the potential impact of these deals. Some praise LBOs for creating new governance structures for companies and providing longer term investment opportunities for investors. Others criticize LBOs for causing job losses and burdening companies with too much debt. This book addresses the effect of recent private equity LBOs on acquired companies and employment, the impact of LBOs jointly undertaken by two or more private equity funds on competition, the Securities and Exchange Commission's (SEC) oversight of private equity funds and their advisers, and regulatory oversight of commercial and investment banks that have financed recent LBOs. The U.S. Government Accountability Office (GAO) reviewed academic research, analyzed recent LBO data, conducted case studies, reviewed regulators' policy documents and examinations, and interviewed regulatory and industry officials, and academics. The GAO recommends that the federal financial regulators give increased attention to ensuring that their oversight of leveraged lending at their regulated institutions takes into consideration systemic risk implications raised by changes in the broader financial markets.

Chapter 1 - Academic research that GAO reviewed generally suggests that recent private equity LBOs have had a positive impact on the financial performance of the acquired companies, but determining whether the impact resulted from the actions taken by the private equity firms versus other factors is difficult. The research also indicates that private equity LBOs are associated with lower employment growth than comparable companies. However, uncertainty remains about the employment effect—in part because, as one study found, target companies had lower employment growth before being acquired. Further research may shed light on the causal relationship between private equity and employment growth, if any.

Private equity firms have increasingly joined together to acquire target companies (called "club deals"). In 2007, there were 28 club deals, totaling about $217 billion in value. Club deals could reduce or increase the number of firms bidding on a target company and, thus, affect competition. In analyzing 325 public-to-private LBOs done from 1998 through 2007, GAO generally found no statistical indication that club deals, in aggregate, were associated with lower or higher prices paid for the target companies, after controlling for differences in the targets. However, our results do not rule out the possibility of parties engaging in illegal behavior in any particular LBO. Indeed, according to securities filings and media reports, some large club deals have led to lawsuits and an inquiry into the practice by the Department of Justice.

Chapter 2 - The committee met, pursuant to notice, at 10 a.m., in room 2128, Rayburn House Office Building, Hon. Barney Frank [chairman of the committee] presiding.

Present: Representatives Frank, Waters, Maloney, Watt, Meeks, Moore of Kansas, Hinojosa, Clay, McCarthy, Baca, Lynch, Scott, Cleaver, Moore of Wisconsin, Davis of Tennessee, Klein, Wilson, Perlmutter, Boren; Bachus, Bak er, Pryce, Castle, Royce, Gillmor, Manzullo, Shays, Feeney, Hensarling, Barrett, Pearce, Neugebauer, Roskam, and Marchant.

The CHAIRMAN. This hearing of the Committee on Financial Services will come to order.

The subject of today's hearing is the question of private equity and specifically the effect that purchases of existing companies by private equity has on the workers and on the firms. There have been a number of concerns expressed about various new forms of activity in the economy, and this committee has had some hearings, and will have more, on the question of hedge funds.

Today, we are talking very specifically about private equity and one special area of concern. I will say, in general that I have not seen any argument that it is a matter for which public policy ought to be concerned as to whether people choose to own a company through a public shareholder method or privately. That seems to me to be a decision that ought to be left entirely up to the people who are making the investments, but we do have concerns about the impact on workers.

In: Private Equity and its Impact
Editor: Spencer J. Fritz, pp. 1-100

ISBN: 978-1-60692-682-6

Chapter 1

PRIVATE EQUITY: RECENT GROWTH IN LEVERAGED BUYOUTS EXPOSED RISKS THAT WARRANT CONTINUED ATTENTION*

United States Government Accountability Office

WHAT GAO FOUND

Academic research that GAO reviewed generally suggests that recent private equity LBOs have had a positive impact on the financial performance of the acquired companies, but determining whether the impact resulted from the actions taken by the private equity firms versus other factors is difficult. The research also indicates that private equity LBOs are associated with lower employment growth than comparable companies. However, uncertainty remains about the employment effect—in part because, as one study found, target companies had lower employment growth before being acquired. Further research may shed light on the causal relationship between private equity and employment growth, if any.

Private equity firms have increasingly joined together to acquire target companies (called "club deals"). In 2007, there were 28 club deals, totaling about $217 billion in value. Club deals could reduce or increase the number of firms bidding on a target company and, thus, affect competition. In analyzing 325 public-to-private LBOs done from 1998 through 2007, GAO generally found no statistical indication that club deals, in aggregate, were associated with lower or higher prices paid for the target companies, after controlling for differences in the targets. However, our results do not rule out the possibility of parties engaging in illegal behavior in any particular LBO. Indeed, according to securities filings and media reports, some large club deals have led to lawsuits and an inquiry into the practice by the Department of Justice.

Because private equity funds and their advisers typically claim an exemption from registration as an investment company or investment adviser, respectively, SEC exercises limited oversight of these entities. However, in examining some registered advisers to private

* This is an edited, excerpted and augmented edition of a GAO Report GAO-08-885, dated September 2008.

equity funds, SEC has found some control weaknesses but generally has not found such funds to pose significant concerns for fund investors. The growth in LBOs has led to greater regulatory scrutiny. SEC, along with other regulators, has identified conflicts of interest arising in LBOs as a potential concern and is analyzing the issue.

Before 2007, federal financial regulators generally found that the major institutions that financed LBOs were managing the associated risks. However, after problems with subprime mortgages spilled over to other markets in mid- 2007, the institutions were being exposed to greater-than-expected risk. As a result, the regulators reassessed the institutions' risk-management practices and identified some weaknesses. The regulators are monitoring efforts being taken to address weaknesses and considering the need to issue related guidance. While the institutions have taken steps to decrease their risk exposures, the spillover effects from the subprime mortgage problems to leveraged loans illustrate the importance of understanding and monitoring conditions in the broader markets, including connections between them. Failure to do so could limit the effectiveness and ability of regulators to address issues when they occur.

WHY GAO DID THIS STUDY

The increase in leveraged buyouts (LBO) of U.S. companies by private equity funds prior to the slowdown in mid-2007 has raised questions about the potential impact of these deals. Some praise LBOs for creating new governance structures for companies and providing longer term investment opportunities for investors. Others criticize LBOs for causing job losses and burdening companies with too much debt. This report addresses the (1) effect of recent private equity LBOs on acquired companies and employment, (2) impact of LBOs jointly undertaken by two or more private equity funds on competition, (3) Securities and Exchange Commission's (SEC) oversight of private equity funds and their advisers, and (4) regulatory oversight of commercial and investment banks that have financed recent LBOs. GAO reviewed academic research, analyzed recent LBO data, conducted case studies, reviewed regulators' policy documents and examinations, and interviewed regulatory and industry officials, and academics.

WHAT GAO RECOMMENDS

GAO recommends that the federal financial regulators give increased attention to ensuring that their oversight of leveraged lending at their regulated institutions takes into consideration systemic risk implications raised by changes in the broader financial markets. In line with the recommendation, the regulators acknowledged the need to factor in such implications into their approach to overseeing their regulated institutions' activities.

ABBREVIATIONS

BDC	business development company
CDF	cumulative distribution function
CD&R	Clayton, Dubilier & Rice
CSE	Consolidated Supervised Entity
DOJ	Department of Justice
EU	European Union
FRBNY	Federal Reserve Bank of New York
FSA	Financial Services Authority
IOSCO	International Organization of Securities Commissions
IPO	initial public offering
IRS	Internal Revenue Service
LBO	leveraged buyout
M&A	Merger and Acquisitions
ML	maximum likelihood
NAICS	North American Industry Classification System
NYSE	New York Stock Exchange
OCC	Office of the Comptroller of the Currency
OLS	ordinary least square
PDF	probability density function
PWG	President's Working Group on Financial Markets
SEC	Securities and Exchange Commission

September 9, 2008
The Honorable Byron L. Dorgan
Chairman
Subcommittee on Interstate Commerce, Trade, and Tourism
Committee on Commerce, Science, and Transportation
United States Senate

The Honorable Tim Johnson
Chairman
Subcommittee on Financial Institutions
Committee on Banking, Housing, and Urban Affairs
United States Senate

Over the past several years, an increase in buyouts of U.S. companies by private equity funds has rekindled controversy about the potential impact of these deals. Such funds borrow significant amounts from banks to finance their deals—increasing the debt-to-equity ratio of the acquired companies and giving rise to the term "leveraged buyouts" (LBO).[1] From 2000 through 2007, private equity funds acquired nearly 3,000 companies, with a value totaling more than $1 trillion. Helping to fuel the increase in LBOs has been a strong demand for private equity investments by pension plans and other institutional investors and relatively low borrowing rates, according to market observers. Some academics and others view such LBOs as revolutionizing corporate ownership by creating new funding options and corporate governance structures, as well as by providing investors with attractive, longer term investment opportunities. However, some labor unions and academics have a less favorable view—criticizing LBOs for harming workers, such as through job losses and lower benefits; providing private equity fund managers with, in effect, a tax subsidy; or burdening companies with too much debt.

The operations of private equity firms and the funds that they manage generally are subject to limited federal and state regulation, but the transactions done by the funds may be subject to a number of federal and state regulations depending on the nature of the transaction.[2] LBOs generally involve the takeover of a corporation. State corporation statutes impose broad obligations and specific procedural requirements on a corporation's board of directors with respect to the sale or change of control of a corporation. For example, directors have an obligation to act in the best interest of the corporation's shareholders, and the discharge of that duty may require taking steps to resist a takeover that they reasonably believe is contrary to the best interests of the corporation and its shareholders. Also, in certain circumstances, directors are required to maximize shareholder value and are precluded from considering the interests of any groups other than the shareholders.[3] Furthermore, takeover transactions that involve proxy solicitations, tender offers, or new securities offerings are subject to federal securities laws.[4] Under the Clayton Act, persons contemplating certain large takeover transactions must give advance notice of the proposed transaction to the Federal Trade Commission and the Antitrust Division of the U.S. Department of Justice and wait a designated time before consummating the transactions.[5]

Around mid-2007, the credit markets for LBOs contracted sharply and brought new LBO activity to a near standstill, especially for larger deals. This contraction has raised significant challenges for some banks because of their commitments to help finance pending LBOs but difficulties in finding investors to buy such debt. Nonetheless, market participants generally expect private equity-sponsored LBOs to continue to occur but at slower rate in light of the billions of dollars that private equity funds raised from investors in 2006 and 2007. Given that private equitysponsored LBOs are expected to continue to be an important part of the U.S. capital markets and your interest in the oversight of such activity, you asked us to address the following objectives:

- determine what effect the recent wave of private equity-sponsored LBOs had on acquired companies and employment, based largely on a review of recent academic research;
- analyze how the collaboration of two or more private equity firms in undertaking an LBO (called a club deal) could promote or reduce competition, and what legal issues have club deals raised;
- review how the Securities and Exchange Commission (SEC) has overseen private equity firms engaged in LBOs under the federal securities laws; and
- review how the federal financial regulators have overseen U.S. commercial and investment banks that have helped finance the recent LBOs.

In addition, we provide information on pension plan investments in private equity in appendix II and information on the tax treatment of private equity firm profits in appendix III.

We also present case studies to illustrate various aspects of five LBOs in appendixes IV through IX.

To address these objectives, we reviewed and analyzed relevant examinations and related guidance and documents from the Board of Governors of the Federal Reserve System (Federal Reserve), the Federal Reserve Bank of New York (FRBNY), the Office of the Comptroller of the Currency (OCC), and SEC. We reviewed academic research that included analysis of recent LBOs. We also analyzed merger-and-acquisition, syndicated loan, and related data from Dealogic, which compiles data on mergers and acquisitions, as well as the debt and equity capital markets. Dealogic estimates that it captures about 95 percent of private equity transactions from 1995 forward but is missing the value of some of the deals when such information is unobtainable. We assessed the procedures that Dealogic uses to collect and analyze data and determined that the data were sufficiently reliable for our purposes. We also analyzed relevant laws and regulations, regulatory filings, speeches, testimonies, studies, articles, and our reports. We interviewed staff representing the U.S. regulators identified above and the Federal Deposit Insurance Corporation, the Department of the Treasury, and the Department of Justice. We also selected and interviewed representatives from 2 large commercial banks and 3 large investment banks based on their significant role in helping to finance LBOs; 11 private equity firms of various sizes to obtain the views of small, medium, and large firms; 3 credit rating agencies that have analyzed leveraged loans or recent LBOs; a trade association representing private equity firms; 2 associations representing institutional investors that invest in private equity funds; 4 academics who have done considerable research on LBOs; 2 labor unions based on their concerns about private equity-sponsored LBOs; and a consulting firm that analyzed the private equity market. We selected five LBOs for in-depth case study to illustrate various aspects of such transactions that ranged in size and scope of the target companies, level and type of debt used to finance the transaction, or degree to which the news media focused on the transaction. We conducted this performance audit from August 2007 to September 2008 in accordance with generally accepted government auditing standards. Those standards require that we plan and perform the audit to obtain sufficient, appropriate evidence to provide a reasonable basis for our findings and conclusions based on our audit objectives. We believe that the evidence obtained provides a reasonable basis for our findings and conclusions based on our audit objectives. Appendix I provides a detailed description of our objectives, scope, and methodology.

Results in Brief

Academic research that we reviewed on recent LBOs by private equity firms suggests that the impact of these transactions on the financial performance of acquired companies generally has been positive, but these buyouts have been associated with lower employment growth at the acquired companies. The research generally shows that private equityowned companies outperformed similar companies across certain financial benchmarks, including profitability and the performance of initial public offerings (IPO), but determining whether the higher performance resulted from the actions taken by the private equity firms is often difficult due to some limitations in the academic literature. While some observers question whether private equity fund profits result less from operational improvements made by private equity firms and more from the use of lowcost debt by the firms, private equity executives told us that they use various strategies to improve the operations and financial performance of their acquired companies. Some evidence also suggests that private equity firms improve efficiency by better aligning the incentives of management with those of the owners. For example, private equity firms pay a higher share price premium for publicly traded companies with lower management ownership—indicating their expectation of having greater impact on performance in transactions where existing management may have less incentive to act in the interest of owners. Regarding the potentially broader impact of LBOs on public equity markets, a study found that roughly [6] percent of private equity-sponsored LBOs from 1970 to 2002 involved publicly traded companies, but 11 percent of private equity-owned companies were sold through IPOs during this period. This study suggests that the number of companies going public after an LBO exceeded the number of companies taken private by an LBO. Some critics contend that buyouts can lead to job reductions at acquired companies. Two academic studies found that recent private equity-sponsored LBOs were associated with lower employment growth than comparable companies. Nonetheless, uncertainty remains about the impact of such buyouts on employment, in part because, as one study found, target companies had lower employment growth than comparable companies before being acquired.

In the past several years, private equity firms increasingly have joined together to acquire target companies in arrangements called "club deals," which have included some of the largest LBOs. For example, of the almost 3,000 private equity-sponsored LBOs we identified as completed from 2000 through 2007, about 16 percent were club deals. However, with a value around $463 billion, these club deals account for about 44 percent of the roughly $1 trillion in total private equity deal value. Since 2004, club deals have grown substantially in both number and value, particularly club deals valued at $1 billion or more. According to various market participants, private equity-sponsored LBOs are the product of a competitive process. However, club deals could affect this process and increase or reduce the level of competition. Club deals could increase competition among prospective buyers by enabling multiple private equity firms to submit a joint bid in cases where the firms would not have the resources to independently submit a bid. Indeed, private equity executives told us the principal reason they formed clubs was that their funds did not have sufficient capital to make the purchases alone. Club deals also could reduce competition and result in lower prices paid for target companies if the formation of the club led to fewer firms bidding on target companies or bidder collusion. While club deals can be initiated by private equity firms, they also can be, and have been, initiated by the sellers, according to private equity executives we interviewed and securities filings we reviewed. To examine the potential effect that club deals may have on competition among private equity firms, we developed an econometric model to examine prices paid for target companies. Our analysis of 325 public-to-private LBOs done from 1998 through 2007 generally found no indication that club deals, in the aggregate, are associated with lower or higher prices for the target companies, after controlling for differences in targets. However, our results do not rule out the possibility of parties engaging in illegal behavior, such as collusion, in any particular LBO. Moreover, our analysis draws conclusions about the association, not causal relationship, between club deals and premiums. We also found that commonly used measures of market concentration generally suggest that the market for private equity-sponsored LBOs is predisposed to perform competitively and that single firms do not have the ability to exercise significant market power. Nevertheless, some large club deals have led to an inquiry into this practice by the Department of Justice's Antitrust Division, according to media reports and securities filings, and several shareholder lawsuits against private equity firms.

Because private equity funds and their advisers (private equity firms) typically claim an exemption from registration as an investment company or investment adviser, respectively, SEC exercises limited oversight of these entities. Private equity funds generally are structured and operated in a manner that enables the funds and their advisers to qualify for exemptions from some of the federal statutory restrictions and most SEC regulations that apply to registered investment pools, such as mutual funds. Nonetheless, some advisers to private equity funds are registered and thus are subject to periodic examination by SEC staff and other regulatory requirements. For example, about half of the 21 largest U.S. private equity firms have registered as advisers or are affiliated with registered advisers.6 From 2000 through 2007, SEC staff examined all but one of the private equity firms' advisers at least once. In the examinations we reviewed, SEC found some compliance control deficiencies, such as weak controls to prevent the potential misuse of inside information or to enforce restrictions on personal trades by employees. Despite such deficiencies, SEC and others have said that they generally have not found private equity funds to have posed significant concerns for fund investors. Since 2000, SEC has brought seven enforcement actions against private equity firms for fraud—five of which involved a pension plan investing money in private equity funds in exchange for illegal fees. An SEC official said that the Division of Investment Management has received more than 500 investor complaints in the last 5 years, but none involved private equity fund investors. Similarly, officials representing two institutional investor associations and two bar associations said that fraud has not been a significant issue with private equity firms. However, in light of the recent growth in LBOs by private equity funds, U.S. and foreign regulators, including SEC, have undertaken studies to assess risks arising from such transactions and have identified some concerns about potential market abuse and investor protection, which they are studying further.

Federal banking and securities regulators supervise the commercial and investment banks that financed the recent LBOs, and recent credit market problems have raised risk-management concerns. A small number of major commercial and investment banks have played a key role in financing recent LBOs: 10 U.S. and foreign commercial and investment banks originated around 77 percent of the nearly $634 billion in leveraged loans used to help finance U.S. LBOs from 2005 through 2007. Of these banks, four are national banks overseen by OCC; four are investment banks that have elected to be supervised on a consolidated basis by SEC as a consolidated supervised entity; and two are foreign banks.[7] Before the leveraged loan market began to experience problems in mid-2007, in the aftermath of problems that originated with subprime mortgages, OCC and SEC staff found through their examinations and ongoing monitoring that the major commercial and investment banks, respectively, generally had adequate controls in place to manage the risks associated with their leveraged finance activities. However, OCC, the Federal Reserve, and SEC raised concerns about weakening underwriting standards from 2005 through 2007. According to OCC and SEC staff, the major banks generally were able to manage their risk exposures by syndicating their leveraged loans, whereby a group of lenders, rather than a single lender, makes the loans. However, after the problems related to subprime mortgages unexpectedly spread to the leveraged loan market in mid-2007, the banks found themselves exposed to greater risk. The banks had committed to provide a large volume of leveraged loans for pending LBO deals but could no longer syndicate some of their leveraged loans at prices they originally anticipated. For example, four commercial banks at the end of May 2007 had more than $294 billion in leveraged finance commitments, and four major investment banks at the end of June 2007 had more than $171 billion in leveraged finance commitments. Since then, the commercial and investment banks have reduced their total loan commitments and had commitments at the end of March 2008 of about $34 billion and $14 billion, respectively. However, because the banks could not syndicate some of the loans as initially planned, the banks held on their balance sheets a considerable share of the loans they funded when the LBO deals closed. In light of such challenges, OCC, SEC, and other regulators, separately or jointly, have reviewed the risk-management practices of major commercial and investment banks and identified weaknesses at some banks. The regulators said that they plan to continue monitoring the efforts being taken by the banks to address risk-management weaknesses and are continuing to consider the need to issue related guidance.

Given that the financial markets are increasingly interconnected and in light of the risks that have been highlighted by the financial market turmoil of the last year, we recommend that the Federal Reserve, OCC, and SEC give increased attention to ensuring that their oversight of leveraged lending at their regulated institutions takes into consideration systemic risk implications raised by changes in the broader financial markets, as a whole.

We provided a draft of this report to the Federal Reserve, OCC, SEC, Treasury, and the Department of Justice and a draft of the case studies to the private equity firms we interviewed for the case studies. The Federal Reserve, OCC, and SEC provided written comments on a draft of this report; their comments are included in appendixes XI through XIII. In their written comments, officials from the three agencies generally agreed with our conclusions and, consistent with our recommendation, acknowledged the need to ensure that regulatory and supervisory efforts take into account the systemic risk implications resulting from the increasingly interconnected nature of the financial markets. To that end, they stated that they will continue to work closely with other regulators to better understand and address such risk. We also received technical comments from the Federal Reserve, SEC, OCC, Department of the Treasury, and the private equity firms, which we have incorporated into this report as appropriate.

BACKGROUND

A private equity-sponsored LBO generally is defined as an investment by a private equity fund in a public or private company (or division of a company) for majority or complete ownership. Since 2000, the number and value of LBOs of U.S. target companies completed by private equity funds have increased significantly, as shown in table 1. According to market observers, three major factors converged to spur this growth: (1) the increased interest in private equity investments by pension plans and other institutional investors; (2) the attractiveness of some publicly traded companies, owing to relatively low debt and inexpensively priced shares; and (3) the growth in the global debt market, permitting borrowing at relatively low rates. As discussed below, credit market problems surfacing in mid-2007 have led to a significant slowdown in LBOs by private equity funds.

Table 1. Number and Value of Private Equity LBOs with U.S. Targets, 2000–2007

Dollars in millions		
Year	Number of deals	Value of deals
2000	203	$29,019
2001	113	17,050
2002	143	27,811
2003	209	57,093
2004	326	86,491
2005	615	122,715
2006	804	219,052
2007	581	486,090
Total	2,994	$1,045,321

Source: GAO analysis of Dealogic data.

Note: Deals that were announced before December 31, 1999, but completed after that date are excluded from our totals.

As the private equity industry has grown, private equity-sponsored LBOs have become an increasingly significant subset of all merger-andacquisition activity—accounting for about 3 percent of the total value of U.S. mergers and acquisitions in 2000 but growing to nearly 28 percent in 2007. In recent years, large buyouts of publicly traded companies, valued in the tens of billions of dollars, have received considerable public attention. Such deals, however, are not representative of most private equity-sponsored LBOs. For example, among nearly 3,000 private equitysponsored LBOs we identified from 2000 through 2007, the median deal value was $92.3 million, according to Dealogic data.[8] In addition, LBOs of publicly traded companies (called "public-to-private" buyouts) accounted for about 13 percent of the total number of buyouts during this period but about 58 percent of the total value of the buyouts.

Private Equity-Sponsored LBOs Have Evolved Since the 1980s

Since the 1980s, private equity-sponsored LBOs have changed in a number of ways. Some LBOs in the 1980s were called "hostile takeovers," because they were done over the objections of a target company's management or board of directors. Few of the recent LBOs appear to have been hostile based on available data.[9] Two private equity executives told us that their fund investors, such as pension plans, typically do not want to be associated with hostile takeovers. In such cases, the private equity partnership agreements include a provision prohibiting the fund from undertaking certain acquisitions.[10] Another way in which the private equity-sponsored LBOs have changed is that the scope of LBOs has expanded to include a wider range of industries—not only manufacturing and retail—but also financial services, technology, and health care. In addition, private equity funds have expanded their strategies for enhancing the value of their acquired companies. In the 1980s, LBO funds sought to create value through so-called "financial and governance engineering," such as by restructuring a company's debt-to-equity ratio and changing management incentives. Later, the acquiring firms sought to improve operations to increase cash flow or profitability. Today, private equity firms often use a combination of these strategies. Finally, the size of private equity funds and buyouts has increased. For example, the 10 largest funds—ranging in size from about $8 billion to $21 billion—were created since 2005, according to a news media report. Similarly, 9 of the 10 largest buyouts in history were completed in 2006 or later.

Overview of an LBO Transaction by a Private Equity Fund

As illustrated in figure 1, a typical private equity-sponsored LBO of a target company and subsequent sale of the company takes place in several stages and over several years.

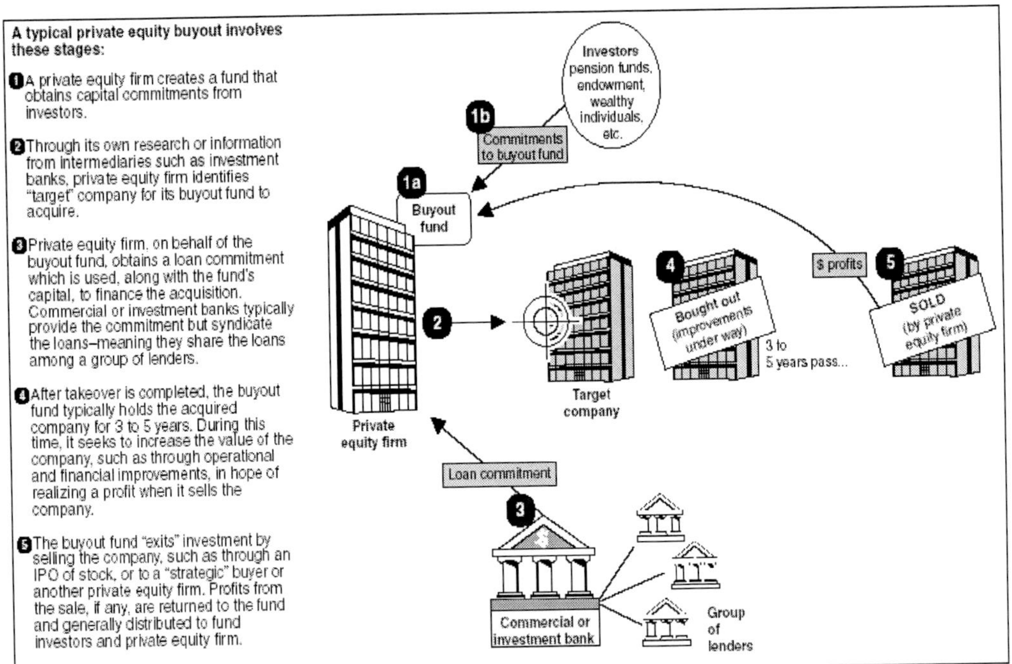

Sources: GAO analysis of information provided by private equity firms, investment banks, and commercial banks; Art Explosion (images).

Figure 1. The Stages of a Private Equity-Sponsored LBO.

In the first stage, a private equity firm creates a private equity fund and obtains commitments from investors (limited partners) to provide capital to its fund. Later, when the firm undertakes buyouts, it calls on the investors to provide the capital. Investors in private equity funds typically include public and corporate pension plans, endowments and foundations, insurance companies, and wealthy individuals. (See app. II for additional information on the investment in private equity by pension plans.) As shown in figure 2, private equity funds have increased their capital commitments from around $0.4 billion (inflation adjusted) in 1980 to nearly $185 billion (inflation adjusted) in 2007.

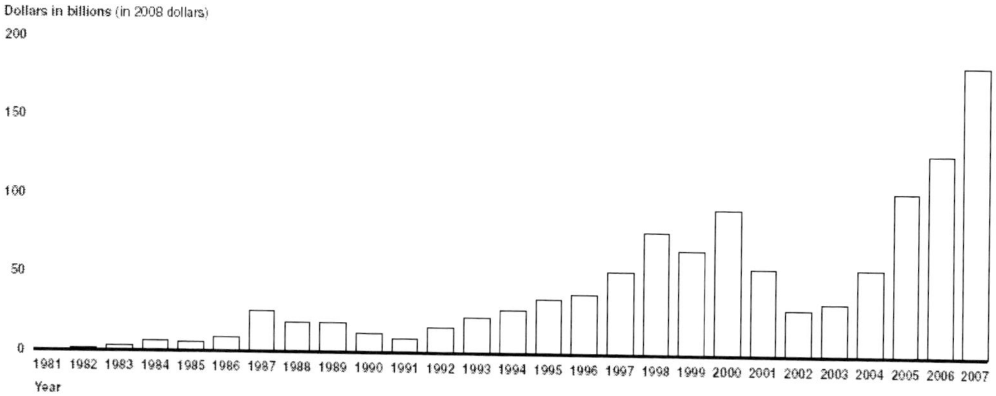

Sources: National Venture Capital Association and Thompson Financial.

Note: Capital commitments are defined as funds that private equity limited partnerships raise from their limited partners (the investors in private equity funds). The data include commitments made to buyout and mezzanine funds but not venture capital funds.

Figure 2. Inflation-Adjusted Capital Commitments to Private Equity Funds, 1980–2007.

In the second stage, the private equity firm identifies potential companies for its fund to acquire. According to private equity executives, their firms routinely research companies and industries to stay abreast of developments and to identify potential acquisitions. Moreover, they make regular contact with managers or owners of both potential targets and other companies. Two private equity executives told us it can take years of contacts before managers or owners might agree to sell. Further, private equity firms can spend significant amounts of time and money to research potential targets, including incurring costs for consulting and other professional fees. In addition to using their own contacts, private equity firms identify potential targets through investment banks, attorneys, and other such intermediaries. Companies interested in selling frequently hire investment banks or other advisers to help them sell their companies.

In the third stage, the private equity firm obtains a loan commitment, typically from commercial or investment banks, that it then uses to help finance its fund's acquisition of the target company. A loan commitment is a promise by the lender to make available in the future a specified amount of credit under specified terms and conditions. Loans are an essential component of an LBO because private equity firms typically contribute through their funds only a fraction of the capital needed to complete a takeover. The use of borrowed money, or debt capital, makes up the difference. Importantly, the legal agreements supporting the debt financing are often between the lender and target company, not the private equity firm. In 2000, private equity LBOs were financed, on average, with 41 percent equity and 59 percent debt, according to a consulting firm report.[11] By 2005, LBOs became more leveraged, with the average deal financed with 34 percent equity and 66 percent debt. Private equity executives told us they typically seek offers for loan commitments from multiple banks in an effort to obtain the best terms through competition. If its offer to buy a target company is accepted, a private equity firm will select one of the loan commitment offers, which the respective bank will fund at the time the acquisition is to be completed. LBO loans commonly are syndicated loans—meaning that they are shared by a group of banks and other lenders. The lead bank finds potential lenders and arranges the terms of the loan on behalf of the syndicate, which can include commercial or investment banks and institutional investors, such as mutual and hedge funds and insurance companies.[12] However, each lender has a separate credit agreement with the borrower for the lender's portion of the syndicated loan. Further, syndicated loans can be categorized as investment grade or leveraged loans.[13] Syndicated loans for LBOs typically are leveraged loans, reflecting the lesser creditworthiness of the borrowers.

In the fourth stage, after completing its buyout of the target company, the private equity firm seeks to improve the financial and operational performance of the acquired company. The aim is to increase the value of the company, so that the private equity firm can sell the company (fifth stage) at a profit and earn a return for its fund investors. (We discuss in detail how private equity firms seek to improve the performance of their acquired companies in the following section of this report.)

In the fifth stage, the private equity firm exits its fund's investment by selling its acquired company. Private equity funds typically hold an acquired company from 3 to 5 years before trying to realize their return. A private equity fund typically has a fixed life of 10 years, generally giving the private equity firm 5 years to invest the capital raised for its fund and 5 years to return the capital and expected profits to its fund investors. Executives told us they often have an exit strategy in mind when their firms buy a company. The executives identified the following options to exit their LBOs:

- make an IPO of stock;
- sell to a "strategic" buyer, or a corporation (as opposed to a financial firm);
- sell to another private equity firm; or
- sell to a "special purpose acquisition company," which is a publicly traded "shell" company that allows its sponsor to raise capital through an IPO for use in seeking to acquire an operating company within a fixed time frame.[14]

Research Suggests Recent LBOs Have Generally Had a Positive Impact on the Financial Performance of Acquired Companies, but LBOs Were Associated with Lower Employment Growth

Academic research on recent LBOs by private equity firms suggests that the impact of these transactions on the financial performance of acquired companies generally has been positive, but these buyouts have been associated with lower employment growth at the acquired companies. The research generally shows that private equity-owned companies outperformed similar companies across certain financial benchmarks, but it is often difficult to determine whether the higher performance resulted from the actions taken by the private equity firms. Private equity executives told us that they seek to improve the operations of their acquired companies through various strategies, but some observers question whether such strategies improve performance. Some evidence suggests that private equity firms improve efficiency by better aligning the incentives of management with those of owners. We also found some evidence that recent private equity-sponsored LBOs were associated with lower employment growth than comparable companies. However, uncertainty remains about the impact of such buyouts on employment, in part because, as one study found, target companies had lower employment growth than their peers before acquisition.

Private Equity-Owned Companies Usually Outperformed Similar Companies Based on Several Financial Benchmarks

Academic studies analyzing LBOs done in the 2000s suggest that private equity-owned companies usually outperformed similar companies not owned by private equity firms across a number of benchmarks, such as profitability, innovation, and the returns to investors in IPOs.[15] Recent research finding that private equity-owned companies generally outperformed other companies is consistent with prior research analyzing earlier LBOs.[16] However, it is often difficult to determine why the differences in economic performance occur. Specifically, because private equity firms choose their buyout targets, it is difficult to determine whether the performance of the acquired companies after the buyout resulted more from the characteristics of the chosen companies or actions of the private equity firms.[17] Executives of a private equity trade group told us that private equity firms typically choose their targets from among four general categories: (1) underperforming or declining companies; (2) "orphan" divisions of large corporations—that is, a division outside a company's core business that may be neglected as a result; (3) family businesses, where family owners are looking to exit; and (4) fundamentally sound businesses that nevertheless need an injection of capital to grow. The executives also said that private equity firms may specialize by industry. Other common limitations of academic studies are samples of buyouts that are small or not representative of all LBOs, resulting from the general lack of available data on private equity activities. Moreover, most empirical work on buyouts in the 2000s is based on European data because more data on privately held companies are available in Europe.[18]

Comparing private equity-owned companies to other companies of similar size in the same industry in the United Kingdom, one study found that operating profitability was higher at private equity-owned companies.[19] Similarly, two studies, one of U.S. LBOs and the other of European LBOs, found that growth in profitability was higher at companies owned by private equity firms.[20] A study of U.S. patents found that private equity-owned companies pursued more economically important innovations, as measured by how often the patents are cited by later patent filings, than similar companies.[21] This finding also suggests that private equity-owned companies are willing to undertake research activities that can require a large up-front cost but yield benefits in the longer term. An analysis of 428 IPOs of private equity-owned companies in the United States between 1980 and 2002 found that they consistently outperformed other IPOs and the stock market as a whole, over 3- and 5-year time horizons.[22] A study of the IPO market in the United Kingdom, covering 1992 to 2004, found that returns on the first day of the offering of 198 private equity-owned IPOs were on average lower than other IPOs, although 3-year returns (excluding the first day) were higher than other IPOs.[23] Regarding LBOs' potentially broader impact on public equity markets, critics have expressed concern about the loss of transparency when public companies are taken private, since the bought-out companies cease making securities filings required of publicly held companies.[24] However, one study of LBOs and their exits from 1970 to 2002 found that 6.3 percent of private equity-sponsored LBOs were public-to-private transactions, but 11 percent of the exits, or sales, of the acquired companies by private equity firms were accomplished through an IPO.[25] This study suggests that "reverse LBO" transactions resulted in more companies entering public markets during this period than exiting following private equity acquisitions.

Private Equity LBOs Seek to Enhance Performance through Techniques Such as Improving Management Incentives

According to the standard economic rationale for buyouts, LBOs enhance value because, among other things, the debt used to finance the buyout forces management to operate more efficiently, and private equity owners vary compensation schemes to better align management incentives with owners.[26] For example, greater debt can limit management's ability to undertake wasteful investments because free cash flow is committed to service the debt. Also, providing management with a higher ownership stake in the company can link its compensation more closely to shareholder returns.[27] Academic research analyzing the share price premium that private equity firms pay to shareholders over market prices in public-to-private buyouts is consistent with this view. Studies have shown that the buyout premium averages 20-40 percent over stock prices preceding a takeover. In theory, the premium paid over market prices should reflect the enhanced value private equity firms expect to realize after a buyout.[28] One study of UK buyouts estimated an average premium of 40 percent, and found that higher premiums were associated with lower recent share price performance, lower leverage, and lower management equity stakes at target companies.[29] A study of buyouts in European countries reported an average premium of 36 percent and also found that higher premiums were associated with lower recent share price performance at targets, as well as less concentrated ownership among external shareholders.[30] Finally, a study of U.S. buyouts done from 1995 through 2007 found average premiums of roughly 25 percent in public-toprivate LBOs.[31] Similarly, our analysis of public-to-private transactions from the Dealogic database determined that the average premium paid to shareholders in private equity-sponsored LBOs in the United States from January 2000 through October 2007 was about 22 percent.[32] Our analysis also corroborated studies of European buyouts in finding that lower premiums were associated with more concentrated ownership (in the form of management or external shareholders) in U.S. publicly traded companies prior to acquisition by private equity firms. On the whole, these results suggest that private equity buyers anticipate greater value enhancement in target companies when existing shareholders are more dispersed and thus have less incentive to monitor or improve performance.

Executives from private equity firms told us that improving the financial performance of their acquired companies is a key objective. The intent is to allow the companies, when later sold during the exit phase of the private equity cycle, to command a price sufficient to provide the desired returns to a private equity fund's investors. The executives told us they use strategies that include the following:

- formulating strategic plans to monitor progress and performance;
- retooling of manufacturing or other operations for greater efficiency;
- reducing the workforce to cut costs;
- acquiring other businesses that complement the acquired company's operations;

- reducing the cost of goods and supplies by consolidating purchasing;
- selling nonperforming lines of business; and
- developing new sources of revenue and improving marketing and sales for good, but under-supported, products.

We found that the private equity firms included in our case studies used some of these strategies in an effort to improve the financial performance of their acquired companies. For example, the private equity owners of Samsonite sought to reinvigorate the company's image and products, in part by creating a new label for higher priced luggage and implementing a high-end marketing campaign. (See app. IX for discussion of this buyout.) As another example, following their buyout of Hertz, the private equity firms involved sought not only to reduce costs by buying more cars for the company's fleet, rather than leasing them, but also to increase the company's share of the leisure car rental segment partly by creating selfservice kiosks for customers. (See app. VI for discussion of this buyout.) Also, to increase revenues, the private equity owners of Nordco acquired a competitor as an add-on acquisition. (See app. VIII for discussion of this buyout.)

According to the private equity executives, they typically do not become involved in the day-to-day management of the acquired companies; rather, they exercise influence at the board level, such as by setting policies and goals. For example, after the Hertz takeover, the lead private equity firm installed one of its partners as the Chairman of the board of directors. However, executives said they will replace an acquired company's senior management, if necessary. As owners of private companies, the executives said they can make strategic decisions that might be more difficult for public companies, given their focus on quarterly earnings performance. ShopKo's new private equity owners, for instance, planned to spend about $70 million annually—up from about $35 million in the year before the takeover—to remodel the stores. (See app. VII for discussion of this buyout.) Overall, the executives said that boosting their companies' performance rests more on improving operations and less on financial engineering, such as the use of debt to leverage returns and the tax deductibility of interest on such debt.

Altering compensation schemes is another important strategy for improving financial performance, according to the private equity executives we interviewed. Executives of one private equity firm told us that aligning incentives is a primary strategy they use to boost the performance of their companies. The firm has acquired companies that were divisions of larger companies, but the incentives of the division management were tied to the performance of the companies, not to the divisions. According to the executives, the key is providing management with equity ownership in a specific area over which managers have control. They note that when incentives are properly aligned, managers tend to work harder and improve profitability. Similarly, in the Nordco buyout, the private equity firm has sought to give the management team an opportunity to own a significant portion of the company and expects management to own 30 percent of the company by the time it exits the investment.

Another area that has received considerable attention has been the use of debt by private equity firms. Overall, several executives told us that boosting their companies' performance rests more on improving operations and less on financial engineering, but we did not independently assess such assertions. Private equity executives told us debt financing plays an important role in private equity transactions, but it is not in their interest to overburden a target company with debt. According to the executives, if an acquired company cannot meet its debt payments, it risks bankruptcy; in turn, the private equity fund risks losing the equity it has invested. If that happens, the private equity fund will be unable to return profits to its limited partner investors. Moreover, such a failure would cause reputation damage to the private equity firm, making it harder for the firm to attract investors for its successor funds. While default rates on loans associated with private equity have remained at historically low levels, one credit rating agency found that being acquired by a private equity fund increases default risk for some firms.[33] However, the extent to which LBO and other firms will suffer financial distress under the current credit cycle remains to be seen.

Some market observers question how and the extent to which private equity firms improve their acquired companies. For example, a credit rating agency acknowledged that private equity firms are not driven by the pressure of publicly reporting quarterly earnings but questioned whether the firms are investing over a longer horizon than public companies.[34] A labor union agreed, saying even if a private equity firm planned to hold an acquired company from 3 to 5 years, that period would not be long enough to avoid pressure to forego long-term investment and improvements. The rating agency also questioned whether there was sufficient evidence to support claims that private equity returns were driven by stronger management rather than by the use of the then readily available, low-cost debt to leverage returns. Similarly, a recent study estimates that private equity firms do not earn their income primarily by enhancing the value of their companies.[35] The study, based on one large investor's experience with, among other investments, 144 private equity buyout funds, estimated that private equity firms earned about twice as much income from management fees as from profits realized from acquired companies.

Private Equity-Sponsored LBOs Were Associated with Lower Employment Growth, but Causation Is Difficult to Establish

Our review of academic research found that recent private equity LBOs are associated with lower employment growth than comparable companies, but a number of factors make causation difficult to establish. Labor unions have expressed concern about the potential for a buyout to leave the acquired company financially weakened because of its increased debt and, in turn, to prompt the private equity firm to cut jobs or slow the pace of job creation. At the same time, job cuts may be necessary to improve efficiency. One study of private equity LBOs in the United Kingdom found that the acquired companies have lower wage and employment growth than non-LBO companies.[36] Research on U.S. buyouts in the 1980s also found that LBOs were associated with slower employment growth than their peers.[37] In addition, a comprehensive study of roughly 5,000 U.S. buyouts from 1980 to 2005 found that private equityowned "establishments" (that is, the physical locations of companies) had slower job growth than comparable establishments in the 3 years after an LBO, but slightly higher job growth in the fourth and fifth years.[38] The net effect of these changes is lower employment growth than comparable establishments in the 5 years after the LBOs.[39] Furthermore, private equityowned companies undertake more acquisitions and divestitures and are more likely to shut down existing establishments and open new ones. The researchers noted that these results suggest private equity owners have a greater willingness to restructure the company and disrupt the status quo in an effort to improve efficiency. However, the study also found that target establishments were underperforming their peers in employment growth prior to acquisition. This suggests that LBO targets are different from non-LBO companies prior to acquisition, making it difficult to attribute differences in employment outcomes after acquisition to private equity.[40] Further uncertainty is due to the limited number of academic studies of the impact of recent buyouts on employment and difficulty faced by the studies in isolating the specific impact of private equity.

Private equity executives told us that a chief concern generally is improving efficiency, not necessarily job creation. For example, executives from one private equity firm said that following an acquisition, the acquired company eliminated 300 jobs after a $100 million spending reduction in one department. Although jobs were lost, the executives said it is important to realize that the goal was to produce an overall stronger company. Executives from another private equity firm told us that following an acquisition, employment fell when it closed some outlets. But at the same time, jobs were created elsewhere when new outlets were opened. One private equity executive told us that while his firm is sympathetic to calls to do such things as offer health insurance to workers at acquired companies, "market economics" sometimes stands as a barrier, because to do so would produce unacceptably lower investment returns. This challenge, however, is not unique to private equity-owned companies. As illustrated by our case studies, strategies implemented after a buyout can lead to either employment growth or loss. Of the five buyouts we studied, two experienced job growth, while three experienced job losses (see apps. V through IX). As noted previously, the LBOs we selected were not intended to be a representative sample of all LBOs.

Club Deals Have Raised Questions about Competition, but Our Analysis of Such Deals, in the Aggregate, Shows No Negative Effect on Prices Paid

In the past several years, private equity firms increasingly have joined together to acquire target companies in arrangements called club deals, which have included some of the largest LBOs. Some have expressed concern that club deals could depress acquisition prices by reducing the number of firms bidding on target companies. However, others have posited that club deals could increase the number of potential buyers by enabling firms that could not individually bid on a target company to do so through a club. In addition, sellers of target companies, as well as potential buyers, can initiate club deals. In an econometric analysis of publicly traded companies acquired by public equity firms, we generally found no indication that club deals, in the aggregate, were associated with lower or higher per-share price premiums paid for the target companies, after controlling for differences among target companies. (A premium is the amount by which the per-share acquisition price exceeds the then-current market price; private equity buyouts of public companies typically take place at a premium.) We also found that commonly used measures of market concentration generally suggest that the market for private equitysponsored LBOs is predisposed to perform competitively and that single firms do not have the ability to exercise significant market power. Nevertheless, some large club deals have been the object of several recent shareholder lawsuits and, according to media reports and securities filings, have led to inquiries by the Department of Justice's Antitrust Division.

Club Deals Have Grown Substantially in Recent Years, Especially Those Involving Large LBOs

In recent years, private equity firms increasingly have joined to acquire companies through LBOs, resulting in some of the largest LBO transactions in history.[41] These club deals involve two or more private equity firms pooling their resources, including their expertise and their investment funds' capital, to jointly acquire a target company. From 2000 through 2007, we identified 2,994 private equity-sponsored LBOs of U.S. companies, based on Dealogic data, of which 493, or about 16 percent, were club deals. These club deals accounted for $463.1 billion, or about 44 percent, of the $1.05 trillion in total LBO deal value we identified. As shown in table 2, club deals have grown substantially both in number and value since 2004, particularly club deals involving companies valued at $1 billion or more. Between 2000 and 2007, there were 80 club deals valued at $1 billion or more—accounting for about 16 percent of the total number of all club deals but almost 90 percent of the total value of the club deals. These large club deals peaked in 2007, with 28 deals valued at about $217 billion. Among the club deals we identified, the number of private equity firms collaborating on a transaction ranged from two to seven.

Table 2. Number and Value of Club Deals, 2000–2007

Dollars in billions					
	All club deals		Club deals valued at $1 billion or more		
Year	Number	Value	Number	Percentage of all club deals	Value
2000	47	$8.8	2	4.3%	$4.2
2001	37	7.9	2	5.4	3.0
2002	34	10.1	2	5.9	4.4
2003	37	18.9	5	13.5	10.4
2004	68	30.8	13	19.1	22.4
2005	97	64.6	11	11.3	56.1
2006	110	100.8	17	15.5	92.9
2007	63	221.2	28	44.4	217.4
Total	493	$463.1	80	16.2%	$410.8

Source: GAO analysis of Dealogic data.

According to private equity executives, the principal reason they formed clubs to buy companies was that their funds did not have sufficient capital to make the purchase alone or were restricted from investing more than a specified portion of their capital in a single deal. For example, an executive of a large private equity firm told us that, under its agreements with limited partners, the fund may invest no more than 25 percent of its total capital in any one deal, which equated to a limit of $750 million for its then-current fund. Another executive said his firm stops short of such formal limits. For example, even though its per-investment limit in a recent fund also was $750 million, the executive said, the firm limited its investment in one acquisition to $500 million because that was thought to be more prudent. Because of these constraints, the firms needed to partner with other private equity firms to make recent acquisitions requiring several billion dollars in equity.[42] Other factors leading private equity firms to pursue club deals, according to executives and academics, include the benefits of pooling resources for the pre-buyout due diligence research that private equity firms perform, which can be costly, and of getting a "second opinion" about the value of a potential acquisition. Several private equity executives told us that club deals promote competition because they enable bids to be made that would not otherwise be possible.

Although more prevalent in recent years, club deals may not always be the preferred option for private equity firms. According to an academic we interviewed, this is largely due to control issues. The academic said that private equity firms joining a club may have to share authority over such matters as operating decisions, which they otherwise would prefer not to do. Executives of a large private equity firm agreed, saying that their firm ordinarily has one of its partners serve as the Chairman of the board of directors in an acquired company. They said that in a club deal, this could be a contentious point. An executive of a midsize private equity firm told us that his firm was offered, but declined, a minority stake in a technology company buyout because his firm prefers to be in control. A consultant told us that private equity firms are finding club deals less attractive and, as a result, turning more frequently to other arrangements, such as soliciting additional limited partners, including sovereign investors, to coinvest in deals, rather than coinvesting with another private equity firm. Table 3 shows the 10 largest completed club deal LBOs of U.S. target companies since 2000. As shown, these buyouts have involved companies in a range of industries. Overall, reflecting their large value, club deal transactions represent 6 of the 10 largest LBOs done since 2000.

The extent to which private equity firms were involved in club deals for large LBOs is shown in figure 3, which depicts the relationships among the firms involved in the 50 largest U.S. LBOs from 2000 through 2007. These LBOs had a total value of around $530 billion and involved 33 private equity firms. Of the 50 LBOs, 31 were club deals. Most (31 of the 33) of the private equity firms were involved in these club deals. For example, as shown in the figure, Goldman Sachs Capital Partners (upper left corner) entered into club deals that involved 14 other private equity firms, including Apollo Advisors, Blackstone Group, and CCMP Capital. Moreover, it entered into more than one club deal with some of the other firms, such as Blackstone Group.

Private equity executives with whom we spoke had differing opinions on the future trend in club deals. One executive said that private equity funds will continue to face constraints in acquiring large companies alone, suggesting a continued role for club deals. Some noted that private equity firms have been raising larger funds from limited partner investors and thus should be able to acquire larger target companies alone. Credit market conditions will also play an important role, some executives said, because as long as credit is in relatively tight supply due to the problems in the credit markets, it will be difficult to get the debt financing necessary to support large club deals.

Table 3. The 10 Largest Club Deals and Their Private Equity Firm Sponsors

Dollars in billions			
Target company (industry)	Value	Private equity sponsors	Completion date
TXU Corp. (utility)	$43.8	TPG Capital LP (Texas Pacific) Goldman Sachs Capital Partners Kohlberg Kravis Roberts & Co.	October 2007
HCA Inc. (health care)	32.7	Bain Capital Partners LLC Kohlberg Kravis Roberts & Co. Merrill Lynch Private Equity	November 2006
Alltel Corp. (communications)	27.9	Goldman Sachs Capital Partners TPG Capital LP (Texas Pacific)	November 2007
Harrah's Entertainment Inc. (gaming)	27.4	TPG Capital LP (Texas Pacific) Apollo Advisors LP	January 2008
Kinder Morgan Inc. (energy)	21.6	AIG Global Investment Group Inc Carlyle/Riverstone Global Energy & Power Carlyle Group Inc. Goldman Sachs Capital Partners	May 2007
Freescale Semiconductor Inc. (electronics/I ntegrated circuits)	17.6	Carlyle Group Inc. TPG Capital LP (Texas Pacific) Blackstone Group LP Permira Ltd	December 2006
Hertz Corp. (car and equipment rental)	15.0	Carlyle Group Inc. Clayton Dubilier & Rice Inc Merrill Lynch Private Equity	December 2005
Univision Communications Inc. (Spanish language media)	13.6	Saban Capital Group Inc Thomas H Lee Partners Madison Dearborn Partners LLC TPG Capital LP (Texas Pacific) Providence Equity Partners Inc.	March 2007
SunGard Data Systems Inc. (software and information technology services)	11.8	TPG Capital LP (Texas Pacific) Blackstone Group LP Goldman Sachs Capital Partners Silver Lake Partners LP Providence Equity Partners Inc. Bain Capital Partners LLC Kohlberg Kravis Roberts & Co.	August 2005
Biomet Inc. (medical products)	$11.4	TPG Capital LP (Texas Pacific) Blackstone Group LP Goldman Sachs Capital Partners Kohlberg Kravis Roberts & Co.	September 2007

Source: GAO analysis of Dealogic data.

Note: Includes transactions completed through first week of April 2008.

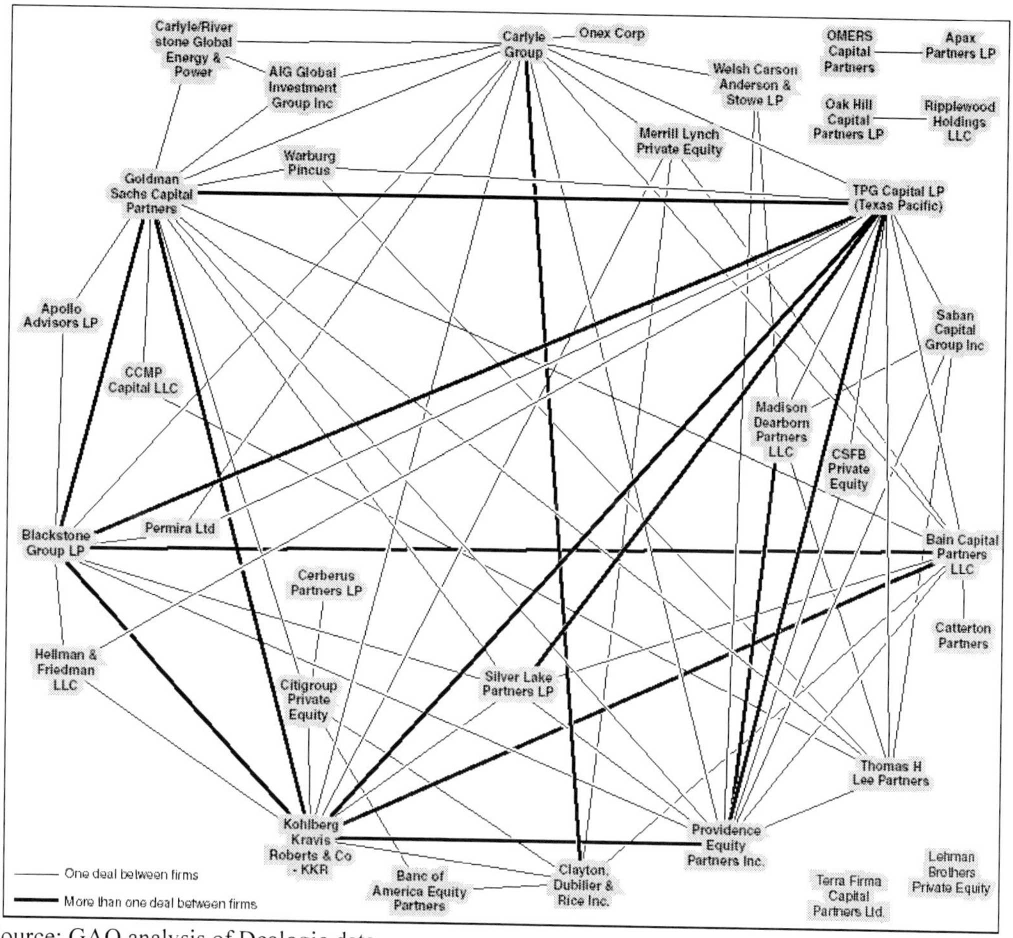

Source: GAO analysis of Dealogic data.

Figure 3. Club Deal Ties among Private Equity Firms Involved in the 50 Largest LBOs, 2000–2007.

LBOs Commonly Involve a Competitive Process and Club Deals Could Support or Undermine this Process

Private equity firms commonly acquire target companies through a competitive process in which interested parties bid on the target companies, according to academics, executives of private equity firms, and commercial and investment bank officials.[43] For example, two private equity executives said that selling companies or their advisers use an auction process to try to increase the companies' sale price. The nature and formality of the process can vary from deal to deal, depending on the level of interest in the target company and other factors. For example, sellers might solicit bids from any interested buyer or ask only select would-be buyers to bid. After an initial round of offers, bidders judged to be more capable of working together or bringing a deal to completion might be invited to submit revised offers. Additionally, even when the parties have agreed on the principal terms of a buyout transaction, executives said that the agreement may include a "go-shop" provision that allows the seller to seek a better offer from other potential buyers within a certain period.[44] In general, the auction process and go-shop provision seek to produce higher sales prices for sellers and to allow sellers to fulfill legal duties to obtain best prices for their shareholders.[45] Those involved in the process also note that sellers need not ultimately accept even the highest bids for their companies, if they believe prices offered are inadequate.

For LBOs involving an auction process, club deals can be formed by either buyers or sellers. First, private equity firms can form clubs on their own before making an offer to buy a target company. For example, executives of one firm told us that they might approach other firms with whom they have dealt effectively in a prior deal or who would bring advantageous experience or skill to the particular deal. An executive of another firm cited geographic or industry experience that a partner could bring. Second, the target company or its advisers can play a role in organizing private equity firms into clubs to bid on the company. For instance, in the private equity-sponsored LBO of retailer Neiman Marcus, the company's adviser organized bidders into four clubs after receipt of an initial round of proposals. According to the company, it formed the bidders into clubs because of the size of the transaction and to maximize competition among the competing groups. (See app. V for additional details about this LBO.)

Private equity executives said that sellers or their advisers can influence the formation of bidding clubs by controlling the flow of information. Before bidding on a target company, potential buyers typically want detailed information about the company's operations and finances. Sellers may provide this information under a nondisclosure agreement, which bars the potential buyers from discussing such information with others. Executives from private equity firms told us that by using this control of information as a lever, sellers sometimes encourage potential buyers to form clubs for several reasons. A seller may realize that the deal size is too large for one private equity firm to undertake alone. Also, negotiating the sale of a company can be time-consuming and distracting, so management of the target company may wish to limit the number of offers it entertains. Sellers also might encourage club deals among particular buyers for strategic purposes; that is, to increase the price paid to acquire their companies. For example, a seller might pair up a private equity firm offering a lower bid with another firm offering a higher bid. The expectation is that as bidding goes forward, prices offered will go up from earlier bids. Thus, if the starting point for a new round of bids begins at a higher price, the seller would expect to receive more.

The recent growth of club deals, particularly the larger ones, has given rise to questions and concerns about joint bidding's potential effect on buyout competition. If each private equity firm that is part of a club deal could and would bid independently on a target company, but instead chooses to bid jointly, this could reduce price competition. In an auction process, a greater number of bidders, all else being equal, should lead to a higher purchase price. Thus, if club deals lead to fewer bidders participating in an auction for target companies, then such deals could result in lower prices paid for target companies than would otherwise be true. Even if joint bidding does not reduce the number of potential bidders for a particular target company, club deals could still lead to lower prices paid for target companies. For example, bidders could collude, such as by agreeing on which bidder will submit the highest offer and potentially win the auction and allowing the losing bidder to join in later on the LBO.

Our Analysis Indicates that Public-to-Private Club Deals, in Aggregate, Generally Are Not Associated with Lower or Higher Prices Paid for Target Companies, and the Private Equity Marketplace Is Predisposed to Perform Competitively

To examine the potential effect club deals may have on competition among private equity firms, we developed an econometric model to examine prices paid for target companies in a subset of all private equity deals—that is, those transactions where the target company is publicly traded.[46] We selected these transactions because pricing and other information necessary for the analysis was publicly available. We examined these transactions as a group, while incorporating individual characteristics associated with each acquisition. The analysis generally found no statistically meaningful negative or positive relationship between the price paid for a target company and whether the buyout was the product of a club deal.[47] That is, public-to-private club deals, in the aggregate, generally are not associated with lower or higher per share price premiums, once important characteristics of target companies are factored into the analysis. Thus, to the extent that potentially anticompetitive effects of such club deals would be reflected in the acquisition price, we do not find evidence of such an effect in the aggregate. However, our results do not rule out the possibility that, in any particular transaction, parties involved could seek to engage in illegal behavior, such as bid-rigging or other collusion. We caution that we draw conclusions about the association, not casual relationship, between clubs deals and premiums. Accordingly, our results showing no association between club deals and price paid should not be read as establishing that club deals necessarily caused acquisition prices to be higher or lower. To the extent that the nature of the firms and transactions we examined differ from the overall population of club deals, our results may not generalize to the population. (See app. X for details on our methodological and data limitations.)

For our econometric model, we initially identified 510 “public-to-private” U.S. buyouts from 1998 through 2007, in which private equity firms acquired publicly held companies. By number, this type of transaction represents about 15 percent of all deals but accounts for about 58 percent of total reported deal value. We examined price paid using the premium paid over a target company’s prebuyout stock price. Premiums are common in buyouts, because it is the premium over current stock price that helps persuade current owners to sell. By itself, the size of this premium can vary significantly among buyouts overall, as well as for club versus nonclub deals, depending on how it is measured. For example, comparing a publicly held target company’s stock price 1 day before announcement of a buyout to the final price paid shows that the premium in club deal acquisitions is slightly smaller—by roughly 1 percent—than for other buyouts (fig. 4). On the other hand, using stock price 1 month before announcement shows that the premium paid in club deals is significantly larger—about 11 percent higher.[48] Neither of these differences is statistically significant in our econometric models run on the full sample.[49]

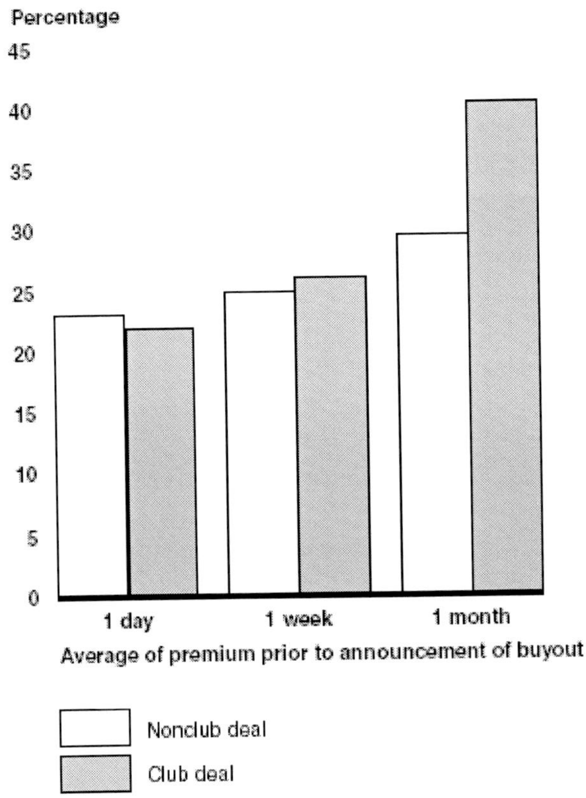

Source: GAO analysis of Dealogic data.

Note: "Premium, 1 Day" is the premium offered based on a target company's share price 1 day before announcement of a buyout; "Premium, 1 Week" is the premium offered based on share price 1 week before announcement; "Premium, 1 Month" is the premium offered share price 1 month before announcement.

Figure 4. Premium Paid for Target Companies in Public-to-Private Buyouts.

Academic research in this area is limited, but our finding that club deals are not associated with lower per share price premiums in the aggregate is consistent with two other studies done on U.S. data.[50] However, our results are inconsistent with another recent study that found large club deals before 2006 led to lower premiums paid for target companies.[51] This study also found that target companies with high institutional ownership did not experience the same effect, suggesting that such institutional investors are able to counter the potentially negative price effect of club deals. Moreover, we also found evidence, consistent with the literature, that larger companies, companies with larger debt burdens, and companies with large block and managerial holders of equity, received smaller premiums upon takeover.[52].

Given concerns about the potential exercise of market power in private equity transactions, we also employed two commonly used measures of market concentration to assess the potential for anticompetitive behavior in the private equity marketplace generally; that is, among buyouts of both publicly and privately held target companies. One of these measures is known as the Four-Firm Concentration Ratio. It is the sum of the market shares by the four largest participants. A four-firm concentration ratio of less than 40 percent generally indicates "effective competition," although it does not guarantee competition prevails. Markets are considered tight oligopolies if a four-firm concentration ratio exceeds 60 percent.[53] For the private equity marketplace, we estimate the concentration ratio at about 32 percent, below the 40 percent threshold.

The second measure of market concentration we employed is the Herfindahl-Hirschman Index, which the Federal Trade Commission and the U.S. Department of Justice (DOJ) use to assess market concentration and the potential for firms to exercise market power. The index is calculated as the sum of the squares of each participant's market share.[54]

According to guidelines issued by DOJ, Herfindahl-Hirschman Index values of below 1,000 indicate an unconcentrated marketplace, which is more inclined to perform competitively. For the private equity marketplace, we estimate the index value at 402.

We note that the private equity marketplace is likely even less concentrated, and more inclined to perform competitively, than our analyses indicate. Both concentration measures are sensitive to the definition of the "market," and we have assumed that the marketplace is comprised only of private equity firms as potential buyers. In actuality, nonprivate equity buyers, often called "strategic" purchasers, also can seek to acquire companies. Were such buyers reflected in our analyses, the market shares of the private equity firms would be lower, producing lower calculations of market concentration.

Some Large Club Deals Reportedly Have Attracted the Interest of the Department of Justice and Have Prompted Lawsuits against Some Private Equity Firms

Beginning in October 2006, news media reports said that DOJ's Antitrust Division sent letters of inquiry to a number of large private equity firms, asking them to voluntarily provide information about their practices in recent high-profile club deals.[55] As of May 2008, DOJ staff told us they could not disclose any details of their activities and neither confirmed nor denied the agency's inquiry. At least one private equity firm, Kohlberg, Kravis, Roberts & Co., disclosed receipt of a DOJ letter related to the inquiry in a registration statement filed with SEC.

Beyond the reported DOJ inquiry, we identified four shareholder lawsuits that have been filed in connection with private equity firms' club deals. In their respective complaints, shareholders of target companies acquired by a consortium of private equity firms alleged generally that the private equity firms acted in concert to fix the price paid for the target companies at below competitive prices and in violation of federal antitrust laws.

One of these cases has been dismissed and, in another, an antitrust claim stemming from the club deal was dismissed.[56]. Two other cases filed in federal district court, Davidson v. Bain Capital Partners, LLC, and Dahl v. Bain Capital Partners, LLC, were recently consolidated into a single action.[57] The consolidated case was pending as we completed this report.

SEC Exercises Limited Oversight of Private Equity Funds, but It and Others Have Identified Some Potential Investor-Related Issues

Because private equity funds and their advisers generally have qualified for exemptions from registration under the federal securities laws, SEC exercises limited oversight of these entities. Nonetheless, several advisers to some of the largest private equity funds are registered, and SEC routinely has examined these advisers and found some compliance control deficiencies. At the same time, SEC and others historically have not found private equity funds or their advisers to raise significant concerns for fund investors—in part evidenced by the limited number of enforcement actions SEC has brought against such funds or their advisers. Nonetheless, in light of the growth in LBOs by private equity funds, U.S. and foreign regulators have undertaken studies to assess risks posed by such transactions and have identified some potential market abuse and investor protection concerns that they are studying further.

Private Equity Funds and Their Advisers Typically Qualify for an Exemption from Registration with SEC

Private equity funds typically are organized as limited partnerships and structured and operated in a manner that enables the funds and their advisers (private equity firms) to qualify for exemptions from some of the federal statutory restrictions and most SEC regulations that apply to registered investment pools, such as mutual funds.[58] For example, SEC staff told us that private equity funds and their advisers typically claim an exemption from registration as an investment company or investment adviser, respectively.[59] Although certain private equity fund advisers may be exempt from registration, they remain subject to antifraud (including insider trading) provisions of the federal securities laws.[60] In addition, private equity funds typically claim an exemption from registration of the offer and sale of their partnership interests to investors.[61]

Because private equity funds and their advisers typically claim an exemption from registration as an investment company or investment adviser, respectively, SEC exercises limited oversight of private equity funds and their advisers. SEC's ability to directly oversee private equity funds or their advisers is limited to those that are required to register or voluntarily register with SEC. For example, funds or advisers exempt from registration are not subject to regular SEC examinations or certain restrictions on the use of leverage and on compensation based on fund performance and do not have to maintain their business records in accordance with SEC rules.

A number of investment companies serving to facilitate venture capital formation also are engaged in LBOs, like traditional private equity funds. These companies have elected to be regulated under the Investment Company Act as business development companies (BDC), which are investment companies, or funds, operated primarily for the purpose of investing in eligible portfolio companies and that offer to make significant managerial assistance to such portfolio companies.[62] BDCs are permitted greater flexibility than registered investment companies in dealing with their portfolio companies, issuing securities, and compensating fund managers.[63] However, BDCs must have a class of their equity securities registered with SEC and thus are required to file periodic reports with SEC. Moreover, BDCs are subject to SEC examinations. In 2004, a number of private equity firms created or planned to create BDCs. For example, Apollo Management created the most significant BDC during that period, raising around $900 million. According to data provided by SEC staff, 76 investment companies had elected to be classified as BDCs as of June 2007. However, around 50 of them were active, and they held about $19.5 billion in net assets. In comparison, a consulting firm estimated that U.S. private equity funds had $423 billion of assets under management at the end of 2006.[64]

SEC Examinations of Registered Advisers to Private Equity Funds Have Identified Deficiencies in Some Compliance Controls

Private equity fund advisers that are registered with SEC are subject to the same regulatory requirements as other registered investment advisers. These advisers are required to maintain books and records and are subject to periodic examinations by SEC staff. They also must provide current information to both SEC and their investors about their business practices, disciplinary history, services, and fees but are not required to report specifically whether they advise a private equity fund exempt from registration under the Investment Company Act. As a result, SEC staff do not know which and, in turn, how many, of the registered advisers advise exempt private equity funds. The SEC staff said that they can determine whether a registered adviser advises a private equity fund when examiners go on-site to do an examination and through other information sources, such as an adviser's Internet site.

Using publicly available sources, we compiled a list of 21 of the largest private equity firms based on their assets under management and amount of capital raised from investors. From this list, SEC staff identified 11 private equity firms that were registered as investment advisers or affiliated with registered investment advisers during the period from 2000 through 2007. During this period, SEC examiners conducted 19 routine examinations involving 10 of the 11 firms.[65] We reviewed 17 of the examinations.[66] In each of these examinations, SEC examiners identified one or more deficiencies. In 6 examinations, they found internal control weaknesses related to preventing the potential misuse of material nonpublic or insider information. In 4 examinations, they found that the adviser had weak controls related to monitoring or enforcing restrictions on personal trades by employees. Less commonly found deficiencies included the adviser using testimonials to endorse its private equity fund, weaknesses in its marketing materials, or lack of a contingency plan. These types of deficiencies are not unique to private equity firms that are registered investment advisers, according to SEC staff, and none of the deficiencies involved abuses that warranted referring them to SEC's Division of Enforcement. Nonetheless, SEC examiners sent the advisers a deficiency letter after completing the examinations, and SEC staff said that the advisers responded in writing about how they would address the deficiencies.

From 2000 through 2007, SEC examiners also did 7 "sweep examinations" that included 4 of the 11 private equity firms' registered advisers, but it did not conduct any cause examinations of the registered advisers.[67] We reviewed 6 of the sweep examinations.[68] In 4 of the examinations, SEC examiners found deficiencies concerning internal control weaknesses, including a failure to obtain clearance for personal trades by employees. In 2 of these examinations, SEC staff sent the advisers a deficiency letter; in the other 2 examinations, SEC staff told us that examiners discussed the deficiencies with the advisers. SEC staff did not find any deficiencies in its other two sweep examinations.

Growth in Private Equity-Sponsored LBOs Has Led to Greater Regulatory Scrutiny

SEC and others generally have not found private equity funds or their advisers to have posed significant concerns for fund investors. In a 2004 rule release, SEC stated that it had pursued few enforcement actions against private equity firms registered as investment advisers.[69] In commenting on the 2004 SEC rule, officials from committees of the American Bar Association and Association of the Bar of the City of New York noted that enforcement actions involving fraud and private equity firms have not been significant. In addition, an SEC official told us that the Division of Investment Management had received more than 500 investor complaints in the past 5 years but none involved private equity fund investors. In reviewing SEC enforcement cases initiated since 2000, we identified seven cases that involved investments in private equity funds (excluding venture capital funds) and fraud. Five of the cases involved officials associated with a pension plan who invested the plan's money in private equity funds in exchange for illegal fees paid to them by the private equity firms. In one of the other two cases, SEC alleged that a private equity firm official misappropriated money that was meant to be invested in the firm's private equity funds. In the other, SEC alleged that a private equity firm official engaged in insider trading based on information received about a potential acquisition.

Officials from a labor union told us that one of their areas of concern regarding private equity funds was the level of protection provided to fund investors, particularly pension plans. They said that general partners (or private equity firms) must be accountable to investors, particularly in terms of their fiduciary duties to investors and protections against conflicts of interest. An association representing private equity fund limited partners, such as pension plans, found that the vast majority of members responding to an informal survey had not encountered fraud or other abuse by a general partner and viewed the funds as treating them fairly. Although the vast majority of survey respondents viewed themselves as sophisticated and able to protect their interests, they identified areas where funds needed to improve, such as fees, valuation of fund assets, and timeliness in reporting fund performance. An official from another association representing institutional investors, including public, union, and corporate pension plans, told us that its members generally do not see a need to subject private equity funds, or their advisers, to greater regulation. Additionally, the official was not aware of any cases of a private equity fund adviser defrauding investors. In a recent report, we found that pension plans with which we spoke, some of which had been investing in private equity for more than 20 years, indicated that these investments had met their expectations and, as of late 2007 and early 2008, planned to maintain or increase their private equity allocation.[70] Nevertheless, we also found that pension plans investing in private equity face challenges beyond those associated with traditional investments, such as stocks and bonds. The challenges included the variation of performance among private equity funds, which is greater than for other asset classes, and the difficulty of gaining access to funds perceived to be top performers, as well as valuation of the investment, which is difficult to assess before the sale of fund holdings.

In light of the recent growth in private equity-sponsored LBOs, some regulators have undertaken efforts to identify potential risks raised by the activity and assess the need for additional regulation. For instance, the UK Financial Services Authority (FSA) issued a private equity study in November 2006, and a technical committee of International Organization of Securities Commissions (IOSCO), which included SEC, issued a study in November 2007.[71] In its study, FSA raised concerns about, among other things, the potential for market abuse (for example, insider trading) to result from the leakage of price-sensitive information concerning private equity transactions. It noted that a main cause of the increased potential for information leaks in the private equity market is the number of institutions and people involved in private equity deals, especially ones involving publicly held companies. FSA further noted that the development of related products traded in different markets, such as credit derivatives on leveraged loans, increases the potential for this abuse.[72] The IOSCO technical committee also raised concerns about the potential for market abuse in its study. It stated that market abuse, such as insider trading, which is not limited to the private equity industry, remains a key priority for IOSCO and individual regulators. In that regard, the committee noted that the issue is relevant to other ongoing work by IOSCO but not to its further work on private equity.

In their reports, the regulators also identified potential concerns raised by private equity transactions that related to the protection of fund investors. FSA stated that conflicts of interest may arise between fund management and fund investors even though fund management seeks to align its interests with the interests of fund investors by investing its capital in the fund. It stated that both sets of interests may become misaligned in a number of situations, such as if management is allowed to coinvest with the fund in a particular deal. The IOSCO technical committee also commented that private equity transactions, along with other merger-and- acquisition activities, can present conflicts of interest for a number of parties, including private equity firms, fund investors, and target companies. For example, it noted that when management is participating in a buyout, it may not have an incentive to act in the best interests of existing shareholders by recommending a sale at the highest possible price. According to the committee, where public companies are involved, regulators and investors (including fund investors and public shareholders) emphasize the controls that firms have in place to ensure that potential conflicts do not undermine investor confidence. In that regard, the committee is pursuing additional work to analyze conflicts of interest that arise in private equity transactions, as they relate to the public markets, and policies and procedures used to manage such conflicts.

Recent Credit Events Raised Regulatory Scrutiny about Risk- Management of Leveraged Lending by Banks

A small number of commercial and investment banks have played a key role in providing leveraged loans to help finance the recent U.S. LBOs. Before the problems related to subprime mortgages spread to the leveraged loan market in mid-2007, the regulators generally found that the major commercial and investment banks had adequate risk-management practices but noted some concerns, such as weakening of underwriting standards and significant growth in leveraged loan commitments. In general, the major banks managed their risk exposures by providing the loans through a group of lenders rather than by themselves, but after the problems surfaced in mid-2007, the banks were no longer able to do so, exposing them to greater risk. In light of this situation, regulators have reviewed the risk-management practices of commercial and investment banks and identified some weaknesses. As the regulators continue to ensure that their respective institutions correct identified riskmanagement weaknesses, it will be important for them to evaluate periodically whether their guidance responds to such identified weaknesses and to update their guidance, as appropriate.

Major Commercial and Investment Banks Have Played a Key Role in Financing U.S. LBOs

A small number of major commercial and investment banks have helped to finance the majority of recent LBOs in the United States. Under their loan commitments, banks usually agree to provide "revolvers" (or revolving lines of credit) and term loans to private equity funds when their LBO transactions close.[73] A revolver is a line of credit that allows the borrower to draw down, repay, and reborrow a specified amount on demand. A term loan is a loan that the borrower repays in a scheduled series of repayments or a lump-sum payment at maturity. Although banks fund the term loans when the LBO transactions are completed, the revolvers usually are not funded at that time but rather are saved to meet future financing needs. As discussed in the background, loans issued to finance LBOs are typically syndicated—provided by a group of lenders—and categorized as leveraged, rather than investment-grade, loans.

Banks and other lenders provided, in total, nearly $2.7 trillion in syndicated, leveraged loans in the U.S. market from 2005 through 2007, according to Dealogic. Of this total, around $1.1 trillion, or 42 percent, was used to finance transactions sponsored by private equity funds. More specifically, private equity funds used nearly $634 billion, or 56 percent, of the leveraged loans to finance a total of 956 LBOs and the remainder for other purposes, such as the refinancing of companies held in the funds' investment portfolios.[74] Table 4 shows that 10 commercial and investment banks arranged and underwrote nearly $489 billion, or 77 percent, of the U.S. syndicated leveraged loans used to finance 700 private equitysponsored LBOs from 2005 through 2007[75]. Four were U.S. commercial banks—JP Morgan Chase, Citibank, Bank of America, and Wachovia; four were U.S. investment banks (or broker-dealers)—Goldman Sachs, Lehman Brothers, Merrill Lynch, and Morgan Stanley; and two were foreign banks.

Table 4. Top 10 Commercial and Investment Banks Providing Syndicated Leveraged Loans for LBOs by Private Equity Funds, U.S. Market, 2005–2007

Dollars in billions			
Commercial or investment bank	Deal value	Number of deals	Market share based on deal value
JP Morgan Chase	$95.3	272	15.0%
Goldman Sachs	58.3	129	9.2
Citigroup	56.2	107	8.9
Credit Suisse	54.9	189	8.7
Bank of America	49.6	192	7.8
Deutsche Bank	47.4	103	7.5
Lehman Brothers	40.2	95	6.4
Merrill Lynch	33.5	151	5.3
Morgan Stanley	28.9	61	4.6
Wachovia	24.4	122	3.9
Subtotal	488.7	700	77.1
Total	$633.8	956	100.0%

Source: GAO analysis of Dealogic data.

Before 2007, Federal Banking Regulators Generally Found Risk Management for Leveraged Financing to Be Satisfactory

The banking regulators have been addressing risk-management for leveraged financing for two decades and, before the credit market problems in mid-2007, a key concern was underwriting standards. Since the LBO boom in the 1980s, the Federal Reserve and OCC periodically have issued regulatory guidance on financing LBOs and other leveraged transactions. For example, in 1989, the regulators jointly defined the term "highly leveraged transaction" to establish consistent procedures for identifying and assessing LBOs and similar transactions.[76] In guidance that they jointly issued in 2001, the regulators stated that banks can engage in leveraged finance in a safe and sound manner, if pursued within an appropriate risk-management structure.[77] According to the guidance, such a risk-management structure should include a loan policy, underwriting standards, loan limits, a policy on risk rating transactions, and internal controls.

OCC is responsible for supervising national banks, which include the four U.S. commercial banks that played a key role in financing recent LBOs. According to OCC staff, they have continued to supervise the financing of LBOs by these banks through examinations and ongoing, on-site monitoring. Moreover, each of these banks is a subsidiary of a bank or financial holding company supervised by the Federal Reserve.[78] Because of the complexity of leveraged transactions and restrictions on commercial bank finance activities, various parts of a leveraged financing package may be arranged through the bank, its subsidiaries, or its holding company. According to OCC examiners, OCC works with the Federal Reserve to assess a banking organization's total participation in and exposure to leveraged finance activities.

OCC examiners told us that each year they have examined the leveraged lending activities of the four banks as part of their ongoing supervision. In large banks, most examination-related work is conducted throughout a 12- month supervisory cycle. The objectives of the examinations covering the banks' leveraged lending activities included assessing the quantity of risk and quality of risk management, reviewing underwriting standards, and testing compliance with regulatory guidance. To meet these objectives, examiners, among other things, sampled and reviewed loans and related documentation, reviewed management reports, and interviewed bank staff. OCC examiners told us that they also monitor the banks' risk management of their leveraged lending activities on an ongoing basis throughout the year. For example, they meet with bank managers from various bank operations on a regular basis to discuss issues such as portfolio trends, market conditions, underwriting practices, and emerging risks. In addition, they periodically review management reports to identify changes in portfolio performance, composition, and risk and audit reports to assess the effectiveness of the programs and identify deficiencies requiring attention.

We reviewed 17 examinations that OCC examiners conducted between 2005 and 2007 that included some aspects of the leveraged finance activities at two major banks. Each of the examinations generally covered different portfolios that included leveraged loans, such as special credits, North American leveraged loans, and syndicated credits. The examiners found that underwriting standards for leveraged loans had been easing every year since at least 2005, evidenced by increased leverage, liberal repayment schedules on term loans, and erosion of loan covenants.[79] However, the examiners generally found the quality of risk management at the two banks to be satisfactory for the processes reviewed, at least until mid-2007. For one of the banks, examiners noted that bank management understood the key risks and implemented appropriate strategies and controls to manage those risks. For instance, the bank retained a relatively small percentage of its leveraged loans. Likewise, examiners at the other bank noted that underwriting and distribution volume in leveraged loans was significant and increasing, but the bank retained a small position in leveraged loans. Nevertheless, in 2006 and 2007 internal documents that outlined planned examinations and other supervisory activities, examiners at one bank identified a key risk—the potential for investor demand for leveraged loans to slow and adversely affect the bank's ability to syndicate loans and manage risk by retaining only small positions in leveraged loans. The examiners noted that they would continue to monitor the bank's leveraged lending activities through ongoing monitoring and examinations, and they conducted such examinations in subsequent years.

The Federal Reserve and OCC also supervised the financing of LBOs by the major banks through other types of reviews and surveys. Each year, they jointly review shared national credits, which include syndicated leveraged loans.[80] In 2006, the review found that the volume of leveraged loans rose rapidly, in part because of the rise in mergers and acquisitions. It also found that strong market competition had led to an easing of underwriting standards in leveraged loans, evidenced partly by minimum amortization requirements and fewer maintenance covenants. The 2007 review continued to find weakened underwriting standards in leveraged loans, and regulators stated in their joint press release that banks should ensure that such standards are not compromised by competitive pressures.[81] Furthermore, the review noted that banks had a backlog of leveraged loan commitments that could not be distributed without incurring a loss and may need to be retained by the banks. Similarly, in OCC's 2006 and 2007 survey of underwriting practices, the regulator also found that banks were easing their credit standards for leveraged loans and cautioned them about their weakening standards.[82] Finally, in the Federal Reserve's 2006 and 2007 "Senior Loan Officer Opinion Survey on Bank Lending Practices," responding banks generally reported that the share of loans related to mergers and acquisitions, including LBOs, on their books was fairly small.[83] For example, in 2007, around 85 percent of the large banks responding to the survey said that LBO loans accounted for 20 percent or less of the syndicated loans on their books.

SEC Began to Supervise Financing of LBOs by Investment Banks around 2005

As noted earlier, four of the major underwriters of leveraged loans used to help finance LBOs are investment banks (broker-dealers), all of which have elected to be supervised by SEC under its Consolidated Supervised Entity (CSE) program.[84] SEC's supervision of CSEs extends beyond the registered broker-dealers to their unregulated affiliates and holding companies. SEC staff said that the CSEs usually originate their leveraged loans in affiliates outside of their registered broker-dealers to avoid capital charges that otherwise would be assessed under SEC's capital rules. Between December 2004 and November 2005, selected broker-dealers agreed to participate in the CSE program, and SEC has been responsible for reviewing unregulated affiliates of the broker-dealers.[85]

According to SEC staff, they reviewed guidance issued by, and talked to, federal bank regulators in developing their approach to supervising the securities firms' leveraged lending. SEC staff said that they focus on credit, market, and liquidity risks associated with the leveraged lending activities of the CSEs to gain not only a broad view of the risks but also insights into each of the different areas, because these risks are linked. For example, under their approach, SEC staff can monitor how a firm's credit risk exposure from its leveraged loan commitments can increase the firm's liquidity risk if the firm cannot syndicate its leveraged loans as planned. Because management of these three risks generally involves different departments within a firm, the staff said that they routinely meet with the various departments within each firm that are responsible for managing their firm's credit, market, and liquidity risk exposures. They also said that they review risk reports and other data generated by the firms.

In fiscal year 2006, SEC reviewed the leveraged lending activities across each of the CSEs. As part of the review, SEC analyzed the practices and processes of leveraged lending, management of the risks associated with leveraged lending, and the calculation of capital requirements for loan commitments. SEC found that the CSEs, like the major commercial banks, used loan approval processes and loan syndications to manage their risks. According to an SEC official, the review generally found that the firms were in regulatory compliance but identified areas where capital computation and risk-management practices could be improved. Moreover, the SEC official said four firms modified their capital computations as a result of feedback from the leveraged loan review. Like other consolidated supervisors overseeing internationally active institutions, SEC requires CSEs to compute capital adequacy measures consistent with the Basel standards.[86]

2007 Market Events Increased Risk Exposures of Banks that Financed LBOs and Raised Some Concerns about Systemic Risk that Warrant Regulatory Attention

Before June 2007, the major commercial and investment banks were able to use an "originate-to-distribute" model to help manage the risks associated with their leveraged finance, according to OCC and SEC staff. Under this model, a bank or group of banks arrange and underwrite a leveraged loan and then syndicate all or some portion of the loan to other institutions, rather than holding the loan on their balance sheets.[87] Leading up to June 2007, strong demand by nonbank institutions (such as collateralized loan obligations, insurance companies, mutual funds, and hedge funds) that invest in leveraged loans fostered the growth of the leveraged loan market.[88] According to officials representing four major banks, they typically were able to syndicate their leveraged loans when the LBO deals closed. As a result, the banks generally were able to limit their leveraged loan exposure to the amount that they planned to hold when they initially committed to make the loans. The bank officials said that their banks typically held portions of the pro rata loans, not the longer term and, thus, potentially more risky institutional loans.[89] In addition, the bank officials said that, before mid-2007, high-yield bond offerings used to help finance some LBOs normally were completed by the time the deals were closed. This eliminated the need for the banks to provide bridge loans for those LBOs, according to the bank officials.

After June 2007, investor concerns about the credit quality of subprime mortgages spread to other credit markets, leading to a sudden and significant decline in demand for leveraged loans. Not expecting market liquidity to change so suddenly, the major banks were left with a large number of unfunded loan commitments for pending LBO deals. The four major commercial banks had more than $294 billion in leveraged finance commitments at the end of May 2007, and the four major investment banks had more than $171 billion in commitments at the end of June 2007. When market conditions changed, the banks were no longer able to syndicate some of their leveraged loans at prices they had anticipated when the LBO deals closed. The banks also had to fund some of the bridge loans for such deals. As a result, the banks held on their balance sheets considerably more loans than originally planned, including leveraged loans intended to be syndicated to institutional investors. For the major commercial banks, the amount of leveraged loans that exceeded the amount that they planned to hold increased from around zero at the end of May 2007 to around $62 billion at the end of December 2007. Similarly, the total amount of leveraged loans held by the major investment banks increased from almost $9 billion to around $59 billion from June to December 2007. Because the decrease in demand for syndicated loans caused prices to decline, the banks had to mark down some of their leveraged loans and loan commitments to reflect the lower market prices, resulting in substantial reductions to earnings.[90] For example, a credit rating agency estimated that the major U.S. banks suffered around $8 billion in losses (before fees and hedges) on their leveraged loans and loan commitments in the third quarter of 2007.

Since then, the major banks have made progress in reducing the number of unfunded leveraged loan commitments but continue to face challenges reducing their loan holdings. First, the major commercial banks have reduced their leveraged finance commitments from about $294 billion to about $34 billion from the end of May 2007 through the end of March 2008. Likewise, the major investment banks have reduced their commitments from about $171 billion to about $14 billion from the end of June 2007 through the end of March 2008.

According to a credit rating agency, the banks have been able to slowly reduce their commitment volume, as liquidity gradually has returned to the leveraged finance market, and as some LBO deals have been cancelled, restructured, or repriced. Second, the banks are continuing to work to reduce their holdings of leveraged loans. At year-end 2007, the commercial banks held about $62 billion more in leveraged loans than they planned to hold but had reduced the amount to around $53 billion at the end of March 2008. During the same period, the total amount of leveraged loans held by the investment banks decreased from around $59 billion to around $56 billion. Bank officials told us that they are continuing to look for market opportunities to syndicate or otherwise sell their leveraged loans. Additionally, the banks can, and some do, manage their leveraged loan risk exposures through hedging, such as with credit derivatives.

During the third quarter of 2007, federal bank examiners and a credit rating agency assessed the exposures of banks to their leveraged loans and commitments under various market scenarios. Such analyses generally indicated that the banks had sufficient capital to absorb potential losses. In March 2008, OCC noted that the major commercial banks continued to be well capitalized, despite adding a sizeable amount of leveraged loans onto their balance sheets and taking significant write-downs on these and other assets. Importantly, the default rate for leveraged loans has remained at a historically low level to the benefit of banks holding leveraged loans. However, in January 2008, a credit rating agency forecasted that the default rate for U.S. leveraged loans will increase to approximately 3 percent from its current 0.1 percent by the end of 2008, in part driven by the weaker economy.[91]

Although the regulators consistently told us that individual banks were not exposed to significant risk from their leveraged lending activities, some broader concerns about systemic risk have arisen. In its June 2006 study on private equity, FSA stated that market turbulence and substantial losses among private equity investors and lenders potentially raised systemic risk. It noted that such risk could be greater if leveraged debt positions were concentrated and could not be exited during a turbulent market. Although the originate-to-distribute model has served to disperse risk, it also has made it more difficult to determine which financial institutions or investors have concentrated leveraged debt exposures. Federal bank regulators told us that they know the amount of leveraged loans held by banks and nonbank investors through their review of shared national credits. However, they said that although they know the concentrated leveraged debt exposures of their supervised banks, they lack data to determine whether, if any, of the nonbank investors have such exposures. The regulators said that it would be difficult to collect and track such data because leveraged loans could be traded or securitized, such as through collateralized loan obligations. Moreover, they said that it is unclear whether the benefits of collecting such information would exceed the costs, which could be high—in part because it is unclear what they could do with the information with respect to nonbank investors. In its November 2007 report on private equity, an IOSCO committee highlighted the potential for a large and complex default, or a number of simultaneous defaults in private equity transactions, to create systemic risk for the public debt securities markets. To assess this risk, the committee plans to do a survey of the complexity and leverage of capital structures employed in LBOs across relevant IOSCO jurisdictions. Because the survey would include issues of interest to banking regulators, the technical committee recommended that the survey be done under the Joint Forum, which postponed making a decision until a related study on leveraged finance of LBOs was completed (which was issued in July 2008).

Although the commercial and investment banks have taken steps to decrease their leveraged lending exposures, the unexpected increase in risk faced by these banks illustrates one of the ways in which problems in one financial market can spill over to other financial markets and adversely affect market participants. Accordingly, it highlights the importance of understanding and monitoring the conditions in the broader markets, particularly potential connections between markets. Should regulators fail to fully understand and consider such interconnections and their potential systemic risk implications, the effectiveness of regulatory oversight and the regulators' ability to address such risk when market disruptions that have potential spillover effects occur could be limited.

Pursuant to Recent Credit Market Problems, Regulators and Others Have Raised Concerns about the Risk Management of Leveraged Finance

As a result of the recent credit market problems, financial regulators and others have conducted a number of special studies on leveraged lending or raised specific concerns. Based on a special review of the leveraged finance activities of four banks, FRBNY examiners reported in September 2007 that the banks needed to improve their risk-management practices. Confirming the findings of earlier examinations, FRBNY examiners found that the banks generally had a robust credit risk approval process for evaluating individual deals, but underwriting standards had weakened in response to competitive market conditions. The examiners noted that the banks used the same standards to underwrite loans held by banks and loans that the banks traditionally would syndicate because of their more risky characteristics. According to the examiners, the banks could have worked through their pipeline of leveraged finance commitments if liquidity had declined gradually, but the sudden shock highlighted the negative impact of weakened underwriting standards and certain riskmanagement practices. Although the examiners found that the banks had recently changed some of their risk-management controls and were continuing to review their controls for any additional changes that might be appropriate, they concluded that the banks needed to set or improve limits on their pipeline commitments and test such exposures under different market scenarios. Although the examiners noted that such risk- management controls are not addressed in detail in the 2001 regulatory guidance on leveraged finance (discussed earlier), they recommended waiting until the leveraged finance market adjusted to the current market events to revisit the guidance.

In an October 2007 speech, the Comptroller of the Currency said that he asked examiners to encourage the major banks to underwrite their leverage loans in a manner more consistent with the standards they would use if they held the loans. He said that the originate-to-distribute model has led banks to move too far away from the underwriting standards they would have used if the banks held onto the loans. The Comptroller said that the banks need to strengthen their standards, but the standards need not be identical to what they would be if banks held the loans. He noted that there are legitimate differences in risk tolerances that are useful in matching willing lenders with risky borrowers. Nonetheless, he said that the banks should have risk-management systems to measure, monitor, and control underwriting differences between syndicated loans and loans to be held in their loan portfolios. In its 2008 survey of underwriting practices, OCC found that underwriting standards for leveraged loans changed significantly. According to OCC, since the disruption in financial markets that began last summer, most banks have responded to investor concerns and the negative economic outlook by tightening underwriting terms, particularly those relating to pricing, covenants, and maximum allowable leverage.

In a March 2008 policy statement, the President's Working Group on Financial Markets (PWG), working with FRBNY and OCC, issued its findings on the cause of the recent market turmoil and recommendations to help avoid a repeat of such events.[92] According to PWG, the financial markets have been in turmoil since mid-2007, which was triggered by a dramatic weakening of underwriting standards for U.S. subprime mortgages. This and other developments, such as the erosion of market discipline on the standards and terms of loans to households and businesses, revealed serious weaknesses in the risk-management practices at several large U.S. and European financial institutions. Such weaknesses included weak controls over balance sheet growth and inadequate communications within the institutions. These weaknesses were particularly evident in the risk management of the syndication of leveraged loans and other business lines. As a result, some institutions suffered significant losses, and many experienced balance sheet pressures, according to PWG. For example, some firms were left holding exposures to leveraged loans that were in the process of being syndicated. PWG made a broad array of recommendations to reform the mortgage origination process and certain rating processes, as well as to strengthen risk-management practices and enhance prudential regulatory policies. With respect to leveraged finance, the PWG recommendations included that (1) financial institutions promptly identify and address any weaknesses in risk-management practices revealed by the turmoil, (2) regulators closely monitor the efforts of financial institutions to address risk-management weaknesses, and (3) regulators enhance guidance related to pipeline risk management for firms that use an originate-todistribute model.

Finally, in May 2008, consistent with the PWG recommendation about riskmanagement practices, OCC examiners completed a special review of the leveraged lending activities of four banks, prompted partly by the large losses from their leveraged loan positions. The review's objectives included comparing the risk-management practices across the banks, assessing bank compliance with the 2001 regulatory guidance (discussed above), and assessing the management systems used by banks to identify, monitor, and control for underwriting differences between loans held by the banks and loans sold to other institutions. Based on their preliminary results, OCC examiners generally found that the banks needed to improve aspects of their risk-management framework governing their leveraged finance syndications. In particular, the examiners found that the banks did not fully comply with the regulatory guidance for managing the risks associated with their loan syndications. For example, the banks lacked formal policies for managing syndication failures. According to the OCC examiners, the banks are documenting lessons learned to reassess their risk-management practices and making changes. In turn, OCC is identifying best practices to communicate to the banks.

In July 2008, Federal Reserve, OCC, and SEC staff told us that they are continuing to monitor their respective financial institutions and work with other regulators to address issues raised by the ongoing market turmoil. The Federal Reserve staff said that they were still reviewing and analyzing the risk-management weaknesses uncovered over the past year to ensure that any revised guidance issued was sufficiently comprehensive and appropriately targeted. OCC staff told us that they intend to provide additional guidance on leveraged lending through a supplement to the agency's existing guidance and will work with the

Federal Reserve and others to determine whether the 2001 interagency guidance on leveraged lending needs to be revised. SEC staff told us that they do not plan to issue any written guidance, but if the federal bank regulators develop additional guidance for their commercial banks or holding companies, SEC will review the guidance and, to the extent it is relevant to its investment banks, discuss such guidance with the investment banks.

CONCLUSIONS

Academic research on recent LBOs by private equity funds generally suggests that these transactions have had a positive impact on the financial performance of acquired companies. However, it is often difficult to determine whether the impact resulted from the actions taken by the private equity firms or other factors, due to some limitations in academic literature. Research also indicates that private equity LBOs are associated with lower employment growth, but uncertainty remains about the employment effect. In that regard, further research may shed light on the causal relationship between private equity and employment growth, if any. Our econometric analysis of a sample of public-to-private LBOs generally found no indication that club deals, in aggregate, are associated with higher or lower prices paid for the target companies, after controlling for differences in targets. But, our analysis does not rule out the possibility of parties engaging in illegal behavior in any particular LBO.

SEC generally has not found private equity funds to have posed significant concerns for fund investors. However, in light of the recent growth in LBOs, U.S. and foreign regulators have undertaken studies to assess risks arising from such transactions and have identified some concerns about potential market abuse and investor protection, which they are studying further. As a result of the recent financial market turmoil, federal financial regulators reassessed the risk-management practices for leveraged lending at the major financial institutions and identified weaknesses. PWG, working with OCC and FRBNY, has reviewed weaknesses in markets, institutions, and regulatory and supervisory practices that have contributed to the recent financial market turmoil. It has developed a broad array of recommendations to address those weaknesses, some of which apply to leveraged lending. As U.S. financial regulators continue to seek to ensure that their respective institutions address risk-management weaknesses associated with leveraged lending, it will be important for them to continue to evaluate periodically whether their guidance addresses such weaknesses and to update their guidance in a timely manner consistent with the PWG and other relevant recommendations.

Although the leveraged loan market comprises a relatively small segment of the financial markets and has not raised the systemic risk concerns raised by subprime mortgages and related structured financial products, it shares similar characteristics and includes elements that could contribute to systemic risk. First, the major players in the leveraged loan market include some of the largest U.S. commercial and investment banks. Second, the use of the originate-to-distribute model by such financial institutions played a part in the erosion of market discipline and easing of underwriting standards for leveraged loans. Third, the current financial market turmoil—triggered by weakening underwriting standards for subprime mortgages—revealed risk-management weaknesses in the leveraged lending activities of the financial institutions and exposed them to greater-than-expected risk when market events caused them to hold more leveraged loans on their balance sheets. This situation increased the vulnerability of these institutions because of the other challenges they were facing due to the broader turmoil in the financial markets. Finally, while the originate-to-distribute model provides a means by which to transfer risk more widely among investors throughout the system, it can reduce transparency about where such risk ultimately resides when held outside regulated financial institutions and whether such risk is concentrated. Such concentrations could directly or indirectly impact regulated institutions.

Recent events involving leveraged loans underscore the potential for systemic risk to arise not only from the disruption at a major regulated institution but also from the transmission of a disruption in a financial market to other financial markets. Consequently, it is important for regulators not to focus solely on the stability of their financial institutions but also to understand how markets are interconnected and how potential market changes could ultimately affect their regulated institutions. While financial institutions have taken steps to decrease their leveraged lending exposures, the unexpected increase in such exposures due to the spread of problems with subprime mortgages to other credit markets illustrates the importance of understanding and monitoring the conditions in the broader markets, including potential connections between markets. Failure of regulators to understand and fully consider such interconnections within the broader markets and their potential systemic risk implications can limit their regulatory effectiveness and ability to address issues when they occur.

Recommendation for Executive Action

Given that the financial markets are increasingly interconnected and in light of the risks that have been highlighted by the financial market turmoil of the last year, we recommend that the heads of the Federal Reserve, OCC, and SEC give increased attention to ensuring that their oversight of leveraged lending at their regulated institutions takes into consideration systemic risk implications raised by changes in the broader financial markets, as a whole.

Agency Comments and Our Evaluation

We provided a draft of this report to the Secretary of the U.S. Department of the Treasury, Chairmen of the Federal Reserve and SEC, the Comptroller of the Currency, and the U.S. Attorney General for their review and comment. We also provided draft appendixes on the case studies to private equity firms we interviewed for our LBO cases studies: TPG; Clayton, Dubilier & Rice; Carlyle Group; Sun Capital Partners; Riverside Company; and Ares Management.

We received written comments from the Federal Reserve, SEC, and OCC, which are presented in appendixes XI, XII, and XIII, respectively. In their written comments, the three federal financial regulators generally agreed with our findings and conclusion and, consistent with our recommendation, acknowledged the need to ensure that regulatory and supervisory efforts take into account the systemic risk implications resulting from the increasingly interconnected nature of the financial markets. Recognizing that no one regulator can effectively address systemic risk by itself, the regulators said that they will continue to work closely with other regulators, such as through the PWG, to better understand and address such risk. They also discussed examinations, surveys, and other actions that their agencies have taken to address risks from leveraged financing, many of which we discuss in the report. Finally, the Federal Reserve noted that it, in coordination with other U.S. and international regulators, is undertaking a number of supervisory efforts to address various firmwide risk-management weaknesses that were identified over the past year through "lessons learned" exercises. We also received technical comments from staff of the Federal Reserve, SEC, OCC, the Department of the Treasury, and the private equity firms, which we have incorporated into this report as appropriate. The Secretary of the U.S. Department of the Treasury and the U.S. Attorney General did not provide any written comments.

As agreed with the office of the Chairman, Subcommittee on Interstate Commerce, Trade, and Tourism, Committee on Commerce, Science, and Transportation, U.S. Senate, unless you publicly announce the contents of this report earlier, we plan no further distribution until 30 days from the report date. At that time, we will send copies of this report to the other interested members of Congress; the Secretary, U.S. Department of the Treasury; Attorney General, U.S. Department of Justice; Chairman, Federal Reserve; Comptroller of the Currency; and Chairman, SEC. We also will make copies available to others upon request. In addition, the report will be available at no charge on the GAO Web site at http://www.gao.gov.

If you or your staff have any questions regarding this report, please contact me at (202) 512-8678 or williamso@gao.gov. Contact points for our Offices of Congressional Relations and Public Affairs may be found on the last page of this report. GAO staff who made major contributions to this report are listed in appendix XIV.

Orice M. Williams
Director, Financial Markets and
Community Investment

Appendix I: Objectives, Scope, and Methodology

As agreed with your staff, the report's objectives are to

- determine, based largely on academic research, what effect the recent wave of private equity-sponsored leveraged buyouts (LBO) has had on acquired companies and employment;
- analyze how the collaboration of two or more private equity firms in undertaking an LBO (called a club deal) could promote or reduce competition, and what legal issues have club deals raised;
- review how the Securities and Exchange Commission (SEC) has overseen private equity firms engaged in LBOs under the federal securities laws; and
- review how the federal financial regulators have overseen U.S. commercial and investment banks that have helped finance the recent LBOs.

Determining the Effect of Recent LBOs on Acquired Firms and Employment

To analyze what effect the recent wave of private equity-sponsored LBOs has had on the acquired companies and their employment, we reviewed and summarized academic studies that included analysis of LBOs completed in 2000 and later. Based on our searches of research databases (EconLit, Google Scholar, and the Social Science Research Network), we included 17 studies, both published and working papers, all written between 2006 and 2008. Most empirical work on buyouts in the 2000s is based on European data, as more data on privately held firms are available in Europe. Due to similar levels of financial development, we included studies based on European data because they should be instructive for understanding U.S. buyouts and the private equity market. However, there are some structural differences between the U.S. and European economies, such as differences in shareholder rights in the legal systems of many countries in continental Europe, which may lead to differences in LBOs. Based on our selection criteria, we determined that these studies were sufficient for our purposes. However, the results should not necessarily be considered as definitive, given the methodological or data limitations contained in the studies individually and collectively. We also interviewed four academics who have done research on LBOs by private equity funds and had two academics review a summary of our literature review. We also reviewed academic studies analyzing LBOs done before 2000 and other studies on the subject by trade associations, a labor union, and consultants. However, we limited our discussion in this report to the academic literature in an effort to focus our review on independent research. In addition, we interviewed executives from 11 private equity firms that ranged from small to large in size, as well as officials from a trade association representing private equity firms, two labor unions, and a management consulting firm that analyzed the private equity market. We reviewed and analyzed regulatory filings and other documents covering companies recently acquired by private equity funds through LBOs. Finally, we selected five LBOs for in-depth case study. (See app. IV for additional information on our case study methodology.)

Assessing the Impact of Club Deals on Competition

To analyze how the collaboration of two or more private equity funds jointly engaged in an LBO (called a club deal) may promote or reduce price competition, we identified and analyzed club deals completed from 2000 through 2007 using data from Dealogic, which compiles data on mergers and acquisitions, as well as on the debt and equity capital markets.[93] Dealogic estimates that it captures about 95 percent of private equity transactions from 1995 forward but is missing the value of some of the deals when such information is unobtainable. We assessed the procedures that Dealogic uses to collect and analyze data and determined that the data were sufficiently reliable for our purposes. We also reviewed academic studies on club deals and various articles on the subject by attorneys and the news media. We reviewed several complaints filed on behalf of shareholder classes in connection with club deals and interviewed attorneys in three of the lawsuits. We also interviewed an antitrust attorney not affiliated with any of the cases. We did our own analysis of the potential effect that club deals may have had on competition among private equity firms by using an econometric model to examine the prices paid for target companies in a subset of private equitysponsored LBOs done from 1998 through 2007. (See app. X for additional information about our econometric analysis of club deals.) We also employed two commonly used measures of market concentration to assess competition in the private equity marketplace generally. We performed data reliability assessments on all the data used in our analyses. Finally, we interviewed staff from the Department of Justice's Antitrust Division and SEC, as well as officials representing seven private equity firms and two academics to discuss the impact of club deals.

Reviewing SEC's Oversight of Private Equity Fund Advisors and Funds

To review how SEC has been overseeing private equity firms and funds engaged in LBOs, we reviewed the federal securities laws and regulations applicable to such entities, as well as articles on the subject. We also reviewed and analyzed examinations of registered advisers to private equity funds conducted by SEC from 2000 through 2007, as well as enforcement actions taken by SEC against private equity funds or their advisers for fraud over the same period. We also reviewed various studies conducted by SEC, the U.K. Financial Services Authority, International Organization of Securities Commissions (IOSCO), a labor union, and us.[94] Finally, we interviewed staff from SEC's Division of Investment Management and Office of Compliance, Inspections, and Examinations, as well as officials from two labor unions, two associations representing institutional investors, and an association representing private equity funds to gather information on SEC oversight and investor-related issues.

Reviewing Financial Regulatory Oversight of Bank LBO Lending Activity

To review how the federal financial regulators have been overseeing U.S. commercial and investment banks helping to finance the recent LBOs, we analyzed 2005-2007 data on LBOs, syndicated leveraged loans, and highyield bonds from Dealogic. We also analyzed data on leveraged finance commitments and leveraged loans obtained from the Office of the Comptroller of the Currency (OCC) and SEC, as well as from regulatory filings and news releases made by the banks. We reviewed regulatory guidance and other material, such as speeches, testimonies, or news releases, issued by the Board of Governors of the Federal Reserve System, OCC, and SEC covering the leveraged lending activities of commercial banks and reviewed examinations of such activities conducted by the Federal Reserve Bank of New York (FRBNY), OCC, and SEC from 2005 to mid-2008. We also reviewed studies on leveraged finance or LBOs by us, academics, credit rating agencies, and regulators, including the U.K. Financial Services Authority, President's Working Group on Financial Markets (PWG),[95] Senior Supervisors Group,[96] and IOSCO. Finally, we interviewed officials representing two commercial banks, three investment banks, three credit rating agencies, as well as staff from the Federal Deposit Insurance Corporation, the Board of Governors of the Federal Reserve System, FRBNY, OCC, and SEC to discuss risk management and regulatory oversight of leveraged lending.

Addressing Pension Plan Investments and Taxation on Private Equity Fund Profits

To address pension plan investments in private equity (discussed in app. II), we obtained and analyzed survey data of private-sector and publicsector defined benefit plans on the extent of plan investments in private equity from three private organizations: Greenwich Associates, Pensions & Investments, and Pyramis Global Advisors. We identified the three surveys through our literature review and interviews with plan representatives and industry experts. The surveys varied in the number and size of plans surveyed. Although the information collected by each of the surveys is limited in some ways, we conducted a data reliability assessment of each survey and determined that the data were sufficiently reliable for purposes of this study. These surveys did not specifically define the term private equity; rather, respondents reported allocations based on their own classifications. Data from all three surveys are reflective only of the plans surveyed and cannot be generalized to all plans.

To determine the federal income tax rules generally applicable to returns paid on partnerships interests in a typical private equity fund (discussed in app. III), we reviewed and analyzed sections of the federal tax code applicable to limited partnerships. We also reviewed and analyzed studies, articles, and material on the subject by academics, trade associations, private equity firms, federal agencies, and other interested parties. We identified and reviewed legislative and other proposals to revise the current tax treatment of private equity funds or their managers. We also attended various forums discussing the subject. Finally, we interviewed staff from the Department of the Treasury, two academics, and two labor unions to obtain an understanding of the relevant tax issues.

We conducted this performance audit from August 2007 to September 2008 in accordance with generally accepted government auditing standards. Those standards require that we plan and perform the audit to obtain sufficient, appropriate evidence to provide a reasonable basis for our findings and conclusions based on our audit objectives. We believe that the evidence obtained provides a reasonable basis for our findings and conclusions based on our audit objectives.

Appendix II: Pension Plan Investments in Private Equity

Many pension plans invest in private equity funds, and such investment is not a recent phenomenon. As we recently reported, the majority of plans we interviewed began investing in private equity more than 5 years before the economic downturn of 2000 to 2001, and some of these plans had been investing in private equity for 20 years or more.[97] We also reported that pension plans invest in private equity primarily to attain long-term returns in excess of returns from the stock market in exchange for greater risk, and most plans we interviewed said these investments had met expectations for relatively high returns. To a lesser degree, pension plans also invest in private equity to further diversify their portfolios.

Two recent surveys of public-sector and private-sector pension plans indicated that many plans invest in private equity.[98] As shown in table 5, Greenwich Associates found that about 43 percent of its surveyed plans invested in private equity in 2006, and Pyramis found that 41 percent of its surveyed plans had such investments.[99] Both surveys also show that a larger percentage of public-sector plans than private-sector plans invested in private equity. Separately, the Greenwich Associates survey found that investment in private equity was most common among collectively bargained plans (arrangements between a labor union and employer), with 12 out of 17 such surveyed plans investing in private equity.

Table 5. Extent of Defined Benefit Plan Investments in Private Equity

	Greenwich Associates (2006)	Pyramis Global Advisors (2006)
Sample	164 public-sector plans 420 private-sector plans, including 17 collectively bargained plans (All plans had $250 million or more in total assets.)	90 public-sector plans 124 private-sector plans (All plans had greater than $200 million in total assets.)
Percentage of plans which invest in private equity:		
All plans	43%	41%
Public sector	51%	44%
Private sector	40%	38%
Private sector: collectively bargained	71%	n/a

Sources: Greenwich Associates and Pyramis Global Advisors, 2006.
Note: The total assets of plans surveyed by Greenwich Associates were $3.6 trillion.

According to Greenwich Associates, the percentage of pension plans investing in private equity increased from about 39 percent to 43 percent from 2004 through 2006. For larger plans surveyed by Pensions & Investments, the percentage of plans investing in private equity grew from 71 percent to 80 percent from 2001 through 2007.

As shown in figure 5, Greenwich Associates survey found that the percentage of pension plans investing in private equity increased as the size of the pension plans increased, measured by their total assets. For example, 16 percent of midsize plans—those with $250 to $500 million in total assets—invested in private equity, but about 71 percent of the largest plans—those with $5 billion or more in assets—invested in private equity. Similarly, the Pensions & Investments survey found nearly 80 percent of the large funds invested in private equity in 2007. Survey data on plans with less than $200 million in assets are not available.[100]

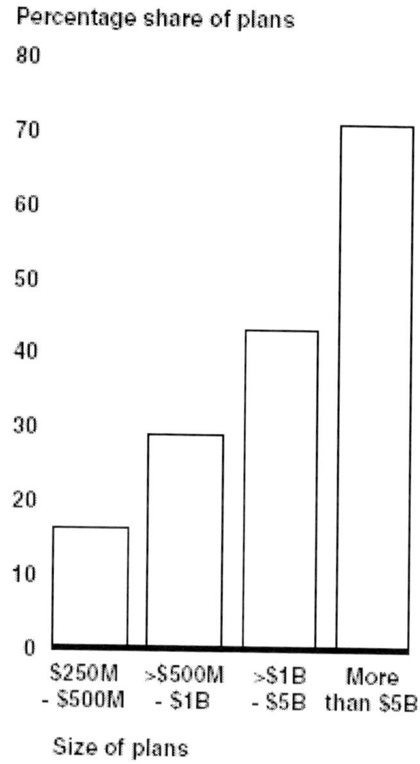

Note: The figure above includes public-sector and private-sector plans (excluding collectively bargained plans). Information on the investments of collectively bargained plans by size of total assets was not available.

Source: Greenwich Associates, 2006.

Figure 5. Pension Plans with Investments in Private Equity by Size of Total Plan Assets.

Although many public-sector and private-sector pension plans invest in private equity, such plans typically have allocated a small percentage of their total assets to private equity. According to the Pensions & Investments survey, large pension plans allocated, on average, percent of their total plan assets to private equity in 2007. Likewise, the Pyramis survey, which included midsize to large-size plans, found plans allocated, on average, 5 percent of their total plan assets to private equity in 2006. Although the majority of plans investing in private equity have small allocations to such assets, a few plans have relatively large allocations, according to the Pensions & Investments survey. [101] Of the 106 plans that reported investing in private equity in 2007, 11 of them had allocations of 10 percent or more; of those, only 1 plan had an allocation of about 20 percent.

For a more complete discussion of pension plan investments and private equity, see *Defined Benefit Pension Plans: Guidance Needed to Better Inform Plans of the Challenges and Risks of Investing in Hedge Funds and Private Equity* (GAO-08-692).

APPENDIX III: OVERVIEW OF TAX TREATMENT OF PRIVATE EQUITY FIRMS AND PUBLIC POLICY OPTIONS

The tax treatment of private equity fund profits received by private equity firms has raised a number of public policy questions. For managing private equity funds, private equity firms generally receive an annual management fee and a share of fund profits. Under current law, the management fee typically is taxed as "ordinary" income for the performance of services. The share of fund profits typically is taxed at a preferential rate for longterm capital gains. Some argue that the share of profits should be taxed as ordinary income for the performance of services. Others, however, maintain that the current approach is appropriate. Reflecting the debate, there have been a number of congressional and other proposals to change the tax treatment.

Private Equity Firms Receive Two Types of Income, and They Are Taxed Differently

Private equity firms generally receive two types of income for managing the funds they establish to undertake buyouts of target companies. These two types of income are taxed differently, so how income is classified is a significant driver of tax liability. First, in serving as general partners, firms receive an annual management fee based on the amount of fund assets under management. According to an industry trade group, firms historically have set their management fee at 2 percent of the assets under management but recently have been lowering the fee, as the size of private equity funds has grown and raising fund capital has become more competitive. Private equity firms receive the fee for performing services for the fund partnership (not in their capacity as partners), and the fee is intended to finance their day-to-day operations. The management fee received by a private equity firm generally is taxed as ordinary income and subject to a federal marginal tax rate ranging up to 35 percent.

Second, private equity firms, as the general partners of the funds, also receive a share of the funds' profits, called carried interest. This carried interest typically represents a right, as a partner, to share in 20 percent of the future profits of the fund.[102] The concept of carried interest is not new; it has been employed since at least the 1930s in a number of industries. Because private equity funds typically are organized as partnerships, partnership tax rules determine the tax treatment of the distributive share of the income from the carried interest.[103] Under current tax law, partnerships are "pass-through entities," meaning that income passes through the partnership to the partners without being taxed at the partnership level.[104] When income earned by a partnership is passed through to the individual partners, it is taxed based on the nature of the income from the underlying activity. While taxation of private equity profits may be a new issue today, partnership taxation rules are well established. Upon receipt of carried interest—that is, the grant of the right to a share of future profits—a private equity firm becomes a partner in the fund and pays tax in the same manner as other fund partners on its distributive share of the fund's taxable income.[105] Thus, if the fund earns ordinary income, or a short- or long-term capital gain, each partner's distributive share includes a portion of that income. In other words, carried interest is not automatically subject to long-term capital gains treatment. But the typical nature of private equity firms' activities—selling investment assets held for several years—means carried interest received by private equity firms commonly is taxed as a long-term capital gain. As such, it is subject to a preferential federal tax rate of 15 percent.[106]

Tax Treatment of Carried Interest as a Capital Gain Is Subject to Debate

According to academics and others, categorizing carried interest as entirely ordinary income or capital gains can be difficult, especially as it reflects a combination of capital assets and labor in the form of expertise applied to those assets. In short, private equity firm managers use investor capital to acquire assets in the form of portfolio companies and then apply their expertise to increase the value of the companies. Table 6 highlights conceptual difficulties in making clear distinctions among types of income, by comparing income earned by a traditional employee and a fund's general partner, based on characteristics such as effort, capital contributed, and compensation risk.

Table 6. Comparison of Income Earned by an Employee and General Partner by Effort, Capital, and Risk

	Traditional employee	Private equity general partner
Effort	Applies effort to earn wages.	Applies effort to make a leveraged buyout investment pay off.
Capital	Applies effort not to own capital assets, but instead to capital assets owned by employer.	Contributes little equity (on the order of low single-digit percentages) and largely applies effort to capital contributed by others (limited partner investors).
Risk	Level of compensation often not assured, such as with sales commissions and contingent income.	Significant portion of compensation not assured, because it depends on nonguaranteed investment returns.

Source: David A. Weisbach, professor of law, University of Chicago, September 19, 2007, forum on taxation of carried interest sponsored by the American Enterprise Institute, Washington, D.C.

Whether the private equity firm's distributive share from the carried interest should be viewed as ordinary income for the performance of services, and hence subject to a higher tax rate, has been the subject of debate. Some academics and others, including labor union executives and some in the private equity and venture capital industries, have criticized allowing capital gains treatment to carried interest on a number of grounds.[107] These reasons include that such treatment

- is inconsistent with the theory of capital gains because private equity firms provide services similar to asset management when they select, acquire, and oversee acquired companies; therefore, income from these activities should be treated like that of an ordinary employee performing services;

- represents an unfair subsidy to wealthy individuals because it allows private equity managers whose earnings can be millions of dollars per year to pay a lower marginal rate than many lower-income workers earning ordinary income;
- is inappropriate to the extent that private equity involves risking of time and effort, but not money, since private equity firms contribute only a small portion of total capital invested in a buyout fund; and
- is inconsistent with the nature of the private equity business because the general partners are sophisticated enterprises that compete for the same employee talent as investment banks and provide services analogous to investment banking/financial services, where income is taxed as ordinary income.

By contrast, private equity executives and others, including some academics and other business executives, say capital gains treatment is appropriate and thus oppose treating carried interest as ordinary income because

- carried interest represents an ownership interest in assets held for longterm investment that involves risk-taking by private equity firms; because risk-taking is a goal of the preferential treatment for capital gains, it is appropriate for carried interest to be taxed at the lower rate;
- private equity firms are creating new ventures and not being compensated for services;
- private equity firms' portfolio companies hold capital assets and pass their gains to the private equity partnerships, which is not a performance of services;
- the notion of capital gains taxation is not based on separating returns to labor and returns to capital; instead, if there is a capital asset, and its value grows through someone's effort, then that is a capital gain. For example, the owner of a business may supply labor to the venture, causing the value of the business to grow and upon sale of the business, any gains generally would be entitled to capital gains treatment; and
- capital gains treatment mitigates effects of "double taxation" of private equity activities, because portfolio companies already pay corporate taxes before passing any gains to the private equity partnerships owning them. Supporters of the capital gains approach also say that changing the treatment would have negative consequences. They said that investment and innovation will be discouraged, the supply of capital would decline, productivity would suffer, U.S. competitiveness in international capital markets would be undermined, and tax avoidance activities will increase. Tax avoidance occurs when the nature of activity is changed to lessen or eliminate tax liability.[108]

Several Bills Have Been Introduced and Other Ideas Suggested to Change the Tax Treatment of Private Equity Firms' Income

As the taxation of carried interest became a higher profile issue beginning in 2007, a number of legislative proposals to change the tax treatment of private equity firms' income were introduced in the 110th Congress. These proposals fall into two categories: Tax treatment of carried interest, and treatment of the limited case in which a private equity firm is a publicly traded partnership.

The carried interest proposals generally have similar provisions. H.R. 2834 (introduced June 22, 2007) would eliminate capital gains treatment in favor of an ordinary income approach. Specifically, this bill would treat income received by a partner from an "investment services partnership interest" as ordinary income. It would define "investment services partnership interest" as any partnership interest held by a person who provides services to the partnership by

- advising as to the value of specified assets, such as real estate, commodities, or options or derivative contracts;
- advising as to investing in, purchasing, or selling specified assets;
- managing, acquiring, or disposing of specified assets; or
- arranging financing with respect to acquiring specified assets.

The sponsor of the legislation said that he and others were concerned that capital gains treatment is inappropriately being substituted for the tax rate applicable to wages and earnings. He added that investment managers are essentially able to pay a lower tax rate on their income because of the structure of their investment firm. Under this proposed legislation, the capital gains rate would continue to apply to the extent that the managers' income represents a reasonable return on capital they have actually invested in a partnership.

H.R. 3970 (introduced October 25, 2007) would also treat carried interest as ordinary income; specifically, it would treat partnership income earned for providing investment management services as ordinary income.[109] H.R. 6275 (introduced June 17, 2008) would, among other things, treat net income and losses from investment services partnership interests as ordinary income and losses. The Joint Committee on Taxation estimated the ordinary income treatment would raise $25.6 billion from 2008 through 2017.

Bills addressing publicly traded partnerships arise from a limited number of private equity firms and hedge funds that have made initial public offerings of stock. They would change the tax treatment of such partnerships that provide investment advisory and related asset management services. S. 1624 (introduced June 14, 2007) would treat as a corporation for income tax purposes publicly traded partnerships that derive income or gains from providing services as investment advisers (as defined by the Investment Advisers Act of 1940) or asset management services. That is, they would pay the corporate income tax on their earnings, rather than pass those earnings through to be taxed only as the partners' individual income.[110]

The sponsor and another senator said that, if a publicly traded partnership earns profits by providing financial services, that kind of business should be taxed as a corporation. Otherwise, creative new structures for investment vehicles may blur the lines for tax treatment of income. The sponsor said that the law must be clear and applied fairly, or there is risk of eroding the corporate tax base.

Another bill, H.R. 2785 (introduced June 20, 2007), is identical to S. 1624. According to the sponsor, the proposal is a matter of fairness. He said that a loophole in current law allows some of the richest partnerships in the world to take advantage of American taxpayers. Also, such partnerships enjoy a competitive advantage over corporations that pay taxes.

There has been some concern expressed about legislative proposals to change the current tax treatment of private equity profits. For example, some senators have questioned targeting carried interest, according to news reports. Likewise, a leading national business association has said that a change in private equity taxation, as part of a larger change in partnership taxation in general, would reduce the productivity of American workers and the ability of U.S. companies to compete in global markets.

In addition to formal legislative proposals, others, in seminars and during congressional testimony, have cited other possible ways to tax carried interest. Such ideas include the following:

- Taxing carried interest when granted. Under current law, when a person receives a profits interest in the partnership—such as, when the private equity firm general partner receives a 20 percent share of the fund's profits—the Internal Revenue Service (IRS) does not treat receipt of that interest as a taxable event to the extent the firm received the profits interest for providing services to the fund in a partner capacity or in anticipation of becoming a partner.[111] Under the proposal, the initial grant of the carried interest to the general partner would be assigned a value and that value would be subject to taxation as ordinary income. However, according to commentary we reviewed, it can be difficult to value a profit interest in a partnership when it is received, and the process is vulnerable to manipulation.
- An election method, in which the general partner would choose between the loan method or all profits being taxed as ordinary income.

APPENDIX IV: CASE STUDY OVERVIEW

To illustrate various aspects of private equity buyouts, we created case studies of five private equity transactions, ranging from small to large and covering a variety of industries. The purpose of this appendix is to explain how the case studies are structured and what information is being provided. Each of the cases discussed in appendixes V through IX provides information on the following:

- a summary of the transaction;
- a time line of significant events;
- an overview of notable aspects of the acquisition;
- background on the target company and the private equity firms involved;
- details of the takeover;
- post-buyout strategy and implementation;
- results following the buyout; and
- as available, details of the private equity firm(s)' exit, or sale of interest in the acquired company.

Table 7 lists the private equity buyouts we selected for these case studies.

Table 7. Companies Selected for Private Equity Buyout Case Studies

Private equity buyout	Private equity firms involved	Industry	Selected to illustrate
Neiman Marcus Group, Inc.	TPG, Warburg Pincus	High-end retailing	Highly leveraged (high level of debt used to undertake transaction)
Hertz Corp.	Clayton, Dubilier & Rice, Carlyle Group, Merrill Lynch Global Private Equity	Auto and equipment rental	Large transaction drawing public attention
ShopKo Stores, Inc.	Sun Capital Partners	Regional discount retail chain	Target company with broad operations
Nordco, Inc.	Riverside Company	Manufacturer of railroad "maintenance of way" equipment	Small transaction
Samsonite Corp.	Ares Management, Bain Capital, Teachers' Private Capital (Ontario Teachers' Pension Plan)	Luggage and travel items	Less common method of financing transaction

Source: GAO.

These transactions are intended to be illustrative of various features of private equity transactions, and not representative of all such buyouts. We judgmentally selected these cases from among 2,994 buyouts we identified for the 2000-07 period from Dealogic data. We selected five LBOs for indepth case study based on the size and scope of the target company, amount and type of debt used to finance the transaction, or degree to which the news media focused on the transaction. These case studies illustrate, among other factors: post-buyout changes in employment; financing methods and extent of borrowings; pre-buyout competition among bidders; formation of "clubs" among bidders to make joint acquisitions; strategies for improving operations post-buyout; and methods by which private equity firms exit, or divest, their investments.

Our analysis is based on publicly available information, including company news releases, news articles, and filings with SEC, as well as interviews with private equity firm executives. We requested comments on the case studies from private equity firms involved in the transactions, and incorporated technical comments received, as appropriate.

APPENDIX V: NEIMAN MARCUS GROUP, INC., CASE STUDY

Overview

The Neiman Marcus buyout illustrates a number of aspects of how private equity deals can work: a target company that, after evaluating its business, sought out a buyer itself; an acquisition in which the new owners have not made significant operational changes; use of a financing method in which the company may pay interest that it owes or take on additional debt; and creation of bidding teams of potential buyers at the behest of the seller. Figure 6 provides an overview of the LBO transaction, including a time line of key events.

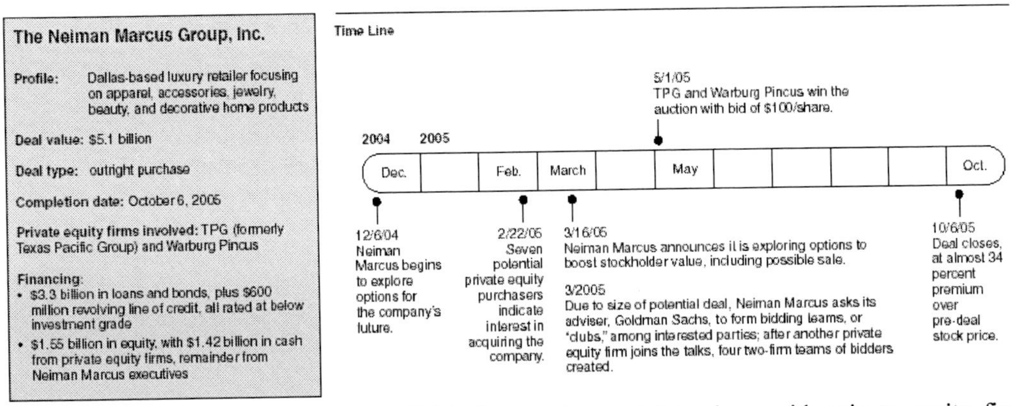

Sources: GAO analysis of publicly available information and interviews with private equity firm executives.

Figure 6. Overview and Time Line of the LBO of Neiman Marcus.

Background

As of July 2005, just before the buyout, Neiman Marcus operated 35 Neiman Marcus department stores, 2 Bergdorf Goodman department stores, and 17 Last Call clearance centers. The retailer also sells by catalog and online.

TPG is a Forth Worth, Texas-based, private investment firm with more than $50 billion under management. TPG typically looks to invest in companies that are market leaders and have a defensible competitive position, long-term growth potential, and experienced management. Other TPG investments include J. Crew Group, Burger King, MGM, and Harrah's Entertainment. New York-based Warburg Pincus, with $19 billion invested in nearly 500 companies, says it looks to invest in companies with strong management and then work with them to formulate strategy, implement better financing, and recruit talented executives. Previous Warburg Pincus investments include BEA Systems, Coventry Health Care, and Knoll.

The Acquisition

In late 2004, Neiman Marcus stock was trading at alltime highs. Given improved operating results and relative strength of the financial markets at the time, the Neiman Marcus board decided to explore options for the company's future. This was part of a regular evaluation of long-term alternatives, including whether the company should remain independent. At the time, some directors believed there might be an uncommon opportunity for stockholders to realize significant investment gains, so the board engaged Goldman Sachs as an adviser to assist in considering alternatives. In early 2005, the board authorized

Goldman Sachs to contact potential buyers, based on demonstrated ability to complete large transactions, ability to preserve confidentiality, and interest in the retail industry. Seven private equity firms responded. Given the size of any potential buyout transaction, the board asked Goldman Sachs to arrange the bidders into teams, or "clubs," as they are sometimes known, to make joint offers. After an eighth firm entered the mix, Goldman Sachs formed four teams of private equity firms. The company's board evaluated bids from the teams on factors such as price, strength of financing commitment letters, and advantages or disadvantages to Neiman Marcus shareholders. A ninth bidder eventually joined the process as well.

The team of TPG and Warburg Pincus won the auction with a $100 per share bid, valuing the company at about $5.1 billion. The $100 bid was an almost 34 percent premium over the closing price of Neiman Marcus stock on the last trading day before the company announced it was exploring strategic alternatives. At the time, the buyout was the third-largest deal done since 2000. TPG executives said that several factors made Neiman Marcus an attractive acquisition. TPG believed Neiman Marcus management to be exceptional, with a stellar track record. TPG also believed Neiman Marcus to be a unique asset—having prime locations in all major metropolitan areas, a widely known and respected brand name, a highly loyal customer base, and a leadership position in the luxury retail industry. TPG saw Neiman Marcus as having superior customer service, good relationships with top designers, and a disciplined growth strategy. From the customer side, TPG thought demographic trends among Neiman Marcus's affluent customer base showed potential for significant growth. TPG executives were confident that Neiman Marcus's sales force could continue to produce higher average transaction sizes, repeat visits, and increased customer loyalty. Finally, TPG saw Neiman Marcus's Internet and direct sales businesses, which were fast-growing and highly profitable, as channels to tap into affluent customers beyond the geographic range of its traditional stores. (Warburg Pincus executives did not respond to GAO requests for comment.)

Strategy and Implementation

Based on the company's attributes, TPG viewed Neiman Marcus as an investment that would not require major changes in strategy or operations but instead would rely on the growth strategy and operating plans already in place. TPG executives said they plan to increase value by increasing the company's earnings and repaying debt by using free cash flow. TPG and Warburg Pincus have kept Neiman Marcus's pre-buyout management in place and are not involved in day-today management of the company.

Results

Revenues are up, profits are down, and the company has expanded since the buyout. Neiman Marcus has opened five Neiman Marcus stores, and it has also opened seven additional Last Call clearance centers. The company has launched a new brand of store, called CUSP, aimed at younger, fashion-savvy customers. Employment has increased by about 11 percent since the buyout, from 16,100 to 17,900 employees.

As part of its expansion, Neiman Marcus's capital expenditures reached $502 million during fiscal years 2005 through 2007, compared with $369.2 for fiscal years 2001 through

2003. New store construction, store renovations, and the expansion of distribution facilities account for the bulk of these expenditures. The company has also pared some of its operations, selling its credit card business, as was planned before the buyout, and also divesting its interest in two private companies—Kate Spade for $121.5 million and Gurwitch Products for $40.8 million.

Revenues reached a record $4.4 billion for fiscal 2007, an increase of 8.9 percent from fiscal 2006. Comparable store revenues increased 6.7 percent in fiscal year 2007, following an increase in comparable revenues of 7.3 percent in fiscal year 2006.

Meanwhile, although the company has moved to pay down debt used to finance the buyout, Neiman Marcus says it remains highly leveraged. In fiscal year 2005, before the buyout, net interest expense was $12.4 million. Post-buyout, for fiscal year 2007, net interest expense increased more than 20-fold, to $259.8 million. At the end of 2007, outstanding debt was almost $3 billion. Net income fell from $248.8 million in fiscal year 2005, before the acquisition, to $56.7 million the following fiscal year and $111.9 million for fiscal year 2007. Earnings from operations, however, are up, the company said.

The Neiman Marcus deal also featured a $700 million financing feature known as a payment-in-kind, high-yield bond. This arrangement allows the company to make a choice each quarter: pay interest to its bondholders in cash or in the form of additional bonds. But if the company decides to exercise the payment-in-kind option, it pays a higher interest rate—threequarters of a percentage point—payable in additional bonds for that interest period. This gives the company the ability to ease its debt servicing burden in the short-term but at the cost of greater overall indebtedness. To date, Neiman Marcus has not used this feature. To protect itself against debt costs, Neiman Marcus has entered into interest rate swaps, which have the effect of fixing the interest rate on a portion of its variable rate debt.

Exit

The private equity firms continue to own the company, and TPG executives declined to discuss specifics of any exit strategy.

APPENDIX VI: HERTZ CORP. CASE STUDY

Overview

The Hertz buyout is one of the largest private equity deals. It drew criticism in the media and from union members, after the company's new owners paid themselves $1.3 billion in dividends not long after the transaction closed and ultimately financed the payments by selling stock to the public. The company has realized hundreds of millions of dollars in improved financial results annually, but also has cut thousands of jobs as it has sought to make operations more efficient. Figure 7 provides an overview of the LBO transaction, including a time line of key events.

Hertz Corporation

Profile: Rents cars and equipment globally

Deal value: $14.9 billion

Deal type: outright purchase

Completion date: December 21, 2005

Private equity firms involved: Clayton, Dubilier & Rice; the Carlyle Group; Merrill Lynch Global Private Equity

Financing:

- $2.3 billion in equity
- $5.8 billion in corporate loans and bonds rated below investment grade
- $6.8 billion in asset-backed securities rated investment grade

Time Line

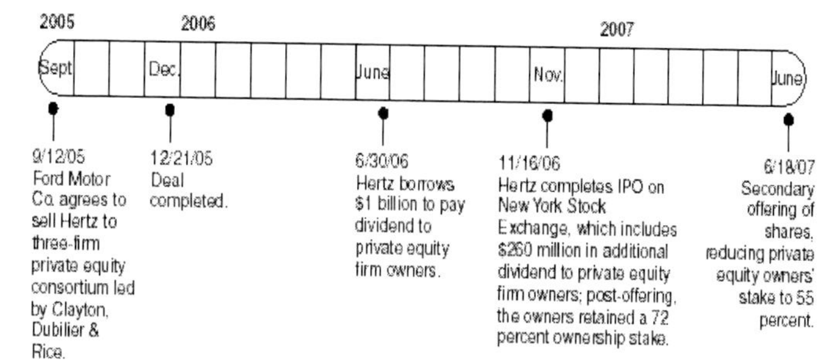

Sources: GAO analysis of publicly available information and interviews with private equity firm executives.

Figure 7. Overview and Time Line of the LBO of Hertz Corp.

Background

Hertz says it is the world's largest general use car rental company, with approximately 8,100 locations in about 145 countries. Hertz also operates an equipment rental company with about 380 locations worldwide, although car rentals accounted for 80 percent of 2007 revenues. Ford Motor Co. had purchased an ownership stake in Hertz in 1987 and purchased the company outright in 1994.

CD&R executives said that the firm emphasizes making operational improvements in companies it acquires. The firm has long had an interest in multilocation service businesses, they said, as evidenced by investments including Kinko's and ServiceMaster. The Carlyle Group is one of the biggest private equity firms and says it has demonstrated expertise in the automotive and transportation sectors. Its investments include Dunkin' Brands, AMC Entertainment, Inc., and Grand Vehicle Works, which provides products and services to truck fleets and recreational vehicle users. Merrill Lynch Global Private Equity is the private equity arm of Merrill Lynch & Co.

The Acquisition

In 2000, CD&R began exploring acquisition targets in the car rental industry. It analyzed a number of firms before targeting Hertz because of its industry-leading position. In addition to having strong brand recognition, Hertz was the leader in airport rentals, and its equipment rental division provided diversification. CD&R also had an interest in "corporate orphans," that is, units of large corporations that are not part of the company's core operations, and thus may not receive sufficient management attention. CD&R viewed Hertz as such an orphan, with significant room for improvement as a result.

Beginning in 2002, CD&R regularly approached Ford about acquiring Hertz, CD&R executives said. They explained that Ford was skeptical about CD&R's ability to finance the acquisition and operation of Hertz, which is capital-intensive due to its large holdings of cars and equipment. By 2005, Ford was experiencing difficulty in its core auto manufacturing business and decided to divest Hertz. Ford took a two-track approach to doing that, simultaneously pursuing an initial public offering (IPO) of Hertz, as well as a bidding process for the outright sale of the company.

Given the size of the potential deal, CD&R needed partners, executives said. Like many other private equity firms, CD&R has restrictions on how much it can invest in a single entity and buying Hertz on its own would have meant exceeding this "concentration" limit. Thus, CD&R partnered with two other firms—the Carlyle Group and Merrill Lynch Global Private Equity. Carlyle officials said they too had been interested in Hertz for some time and were attracted by the strong brand and orphan status. The two firms agreed to a partnership, with CD&R as the lead firm with operational control. Both firms had worked previously with Merrill Lynch's private equity fund, and they invited the company to join the two firms.

In September 2005, after several rounds of bidding, Ford agreed to sell Hertz to the consortium. CD&R executives described the bidding process as difficult and competitive, with two other groups of leading private equity firms participating. Ford's investment bankers managed the process and pitted the competing bidders not only against each other but also against the prospect of an IPO. During bidding, CD&R stressed to Ford that a direct sale would provide a higher price, more certainty, and more cash than an IPO. Eventually, Ford went for the private sale, in a deal valued at $14.9 billion, which included $5.8 billion of corporate debt and $6.8 billion of debt secured by the company's vehicle fleet. At the time, it was the second largest leveraged buyout ever done. The private equity firms invested $2.3 billion, with each contributing an approximately equal amount, to acquire ownership of all of Hertz's common stock.

Strategy and Implementation

Even before acquiring Hertz, CD&R had identified three main areas for improving Hertz's operations: the offairport market segment, high expenses in European rental car operations, and widely varying performance among individual branch locations. According to CD&R executives, Hertz had significantly increased its number of off-airport locations, for example, but was losing money. So the firm decided to close some poorly performing offices. In Europe, CD&R identified overhead expenses, such as sales and administrative costs, which were several times higher than in the United States and thus would be a target for change.

After the buyout, the consortium helped Hertz management develop operational and strategic plans and implemented a new management compensation method, according to Carlyle executives. The plans included, for example, efforts to increase market share in the leisure segment and to improve buying and managing of vehicles. Carlyle executives said hiring a new chief executive in mid-2006 was critical to implementing the plans. The new Chief Executive Officer came to Hertz with a background in process improvement and industrial management after working at General Electric Co. and serving as the Chief Executive of auto parts supplier Tenneco.

To target price-sensitive and leisure customers, Hertz began offering discounts to customers making online reservations and using self-service kiosks. Carlyle executives said that to reduce the cost of its fleet, Hertz increased the share of cars that it buys, rather than leases, from manufacturers. (Owning is cheaper, because with a lease, the manufacturer must be compensated for the residual risk of disposing of a rental car once its service lifetime is up.) As part of efforts to increase efficiency, Hertz relied on employees to generate ideas. For example, workers identified ways to improve cleaning and processing of rental cars upon their return, Carlyle executives said. Changes in compensation were designed to better align the interests of management and shareholders. For example, Hertz provided more than 300 employees an opportunity to own stock in the company, based on revenue growth, pretax income, and return on capital.

Results

Hertz's financial performance has improved in some areas since the buyout. Revenues have continued to grow steadily, as they did under Ford's ownership, with an increase of 16 percent from 2005 to 2007. Cash flow, as measured by a common industry benchmark of earnings before interest, taxes, depreciation, and amortization, grew by about 25 percent, from $2.8 billion in 2005 to $3.5 billion in 2007. Hertz's operational improvements can be seen in its direct operating expenses as a percentage of revenues, which declined from 56 percent in 2005 to 53 percent in 2007.

Net income, however, fell below preacquisition levels, although it is growing. In 2005, net income was $350 million, but this declined to $116 million in 2006, before improving to $265 million in 2007. The lower earnings reflect higher interest payments stemming from debt used to finance the acquisition. In September 2005, before the acquisition was completed, Hertz's total debt was $10.6 billion, and this balance increased to $12.5 billion by the end of 2005, after the deal closed. Consequently, net interest expense rose from $500 million in 2005 to $901 million in 2006 and $875 million in 2007. These amounts represented 6.7 percent, 11.2 percent, and 10.1 percent of revenue, respectively. At the same time, however, Hertz's new owners have used the increased cash flow to pay down the debt. As a result, total debt decreased by $555 million from 2005 to 2007.

To help cut costs, Hertz has reduced its workforce by about 9 percent since the end of 2005. After the private equity consortium acquired Hertz in late 2005, the company had about 32,100 employees, with 22,700 in the United States. By the end of 2007, total employment had decreased to about 29,350, with 20,550 in the United States. Most of the reduction came following job cuts announced in 2007 that the company said were aimed at improving competitiveness. It said the reductions were aimed at eliminating unnecessary layers of management and streamlining decision making. According to CD&R, 40 percent of the lost jobs came in the equipment rental business, which fluctuates with the construction cycle. Further workforce cuts are planned, as Hertz has said the company has completed agreements to outsource functions including procurement and information technology by the end of the third quarter of 2008.

In June 2006, 6 months after the acquisition, Hertz borrowed $1 billion to pay its private equity firm owners a dividend. Five months later, Hertz made an IPO of stock, raising $1.3 billion, and used the proceeds to repay the $1 billion loan and to make another $260 million dividend payment to the private equity firms. The dividends drew criticism, such as in the media and from union members, for their size, and the IPO, coming less than a year after the acquisition, drew criticism as a "quick flip" transaction. For example, *Business Week* magazine, in an article describing what it called private equity firms' "slick new tricks to gorge on corporate assets," singled out dividend payments as a "glaring" sign of excess and cited the $1 billion Hertz dividend.

Carlyle and CD&R executives said a desire to return funds to the private equity firms' limited partners and uncertainty whether the IPO would actually be completed as planned, spurred the June dividend. Banks were willing to loan money at attractive rates to fund the dividend, they said. As for the timing of the IPO, the executives explained that Hertz's performance turned out to be better than expected, while at the same time, market conditions were attractive. It can often take 3 years or more to exit a buyout through an IPO and subsequent secondary equity offerings, one executive said, because public investors are often unable or unwilling to purchase more than a portion of the shares held by private equity owners in a single offering. This long horizon, coupled with Hertz's financial performance, convinced the private equity firms to proceed with the IPO.

Hertz's stock debuted at $15 per share, peaked near $27, and more recently has been in the $13 range. The decline has generally been in line with the performance of other large, publicly traded car rental companies.

Exit

After the IPO, the three firms retained an ownership stake in the company of 72 percent, which Carlyle and CD&R executives said demonstrated that there was no "quick flip." In June 2007, the firms completed a secondary offering of their Hertz shares, selling $1.2 billion worth of shares, and leaving them with a 55 percent ownership stake. Executives of one of the firms said three or four more such offerings are likely.

Appendix VII: ShopKo Stores, Inc., Case Study

Overview

The ShopKo transaction is a deal involving a relatively large employer, a competitive bidding process that produced a significantly higher purchase price, and insider ties that forced the Chairman of the board to not participate in the sale. Figure 8 provides an overview of the LBO transaction, including a time line of key events.

ShopKo Stores, Inc.

Profile: Wisconsin-based regional discount retail chain focusing on casual apparel, housewares, and health and beauty items; many stores also have optical centers and pharmacies

Deal value: $1.2 billion ($879 million in cash plus assumption of debt)

Deal type: outright purchase

Completion date: December 28, 2005

Private equity firm involved: Sun Capital Partners

Financing:
- $675 million in loans classified as noninvestment according to Dealogic
- Approximately $205 million in equity investment grade

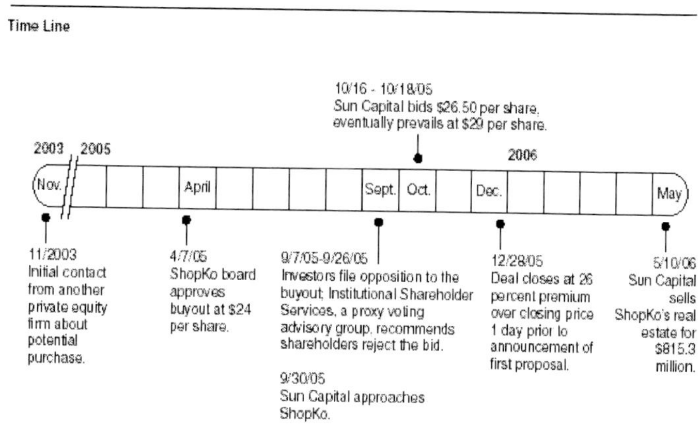

Sources: GAO analysis of publicly available information and interviews with private equity firm executives.

Figure 8. Overview and Time Line of the LBO of ShopKo Stores, Inc.

Background

ShopKo is a Green Bay, Wisconsin-based discount retail chain in the same category as Kohl's, Target, or Wal-Mart. At the time the deal closed, ShopKo had 356 stores under its ShopKo, Pamida, and ShopKo Express Rx brand names in 22 states in the Midwest, Mountain, and Pacific Northwest regions. Founded in 1961, ShopKo merged into SuperValue, a wholesale grocer, in 1971. In 1991, SuperValue divested ShopKo via an IPO of stock, and ShopKo became an independent public company. In fiscal year 2000, ShopKo sales reached $3.5 billion, and the company was on the Fortune 500 list. Four years later, however, sales had fallen to $3.2 billion, and the company was experiencing its fourth straight year of declining same-store sales. (Same-store sales are a common benchmark for retail sales comparisons, so that the baseline of comparison remains the same.)

Sun Capital, with about $10 billion in equity capital, targets its buyout efforts on companies that are important in their markets but which are underperforming or distressed. Other Sun Capital acquisitions include Bruegger's Bagels, Wickes Furniture, and Mervyn's department stores.

The Acquisition

Several factors contributed to ShopKo's declining sales and set the stage for the Sun Capital buyout. In January 2001, ShopKo had begun a reorganization that closed 23 stores and associated distribution centers. ShopKo also faced heavy competition from national retailers. For fiscal year 2004, ShopKo reported that Wal-Mart was a direct competitor in 97 percent of ShopKo's markets; for Target, the figure was 75 percent, and for Kmart, 70 percent. In addition, ShopKo was testing alternative store layouts in remodeled stores and attempting to identify its core customer— which it came to define as mothers with family income between $45,000 and $50,000 a year—and to develop a merchandising strategy around that customer. In late 2003, the private equity firm Goldner-Hawn approached ShopKo about buying the company, and an agreement was reached in April 2005. But some shareholders objected, saying ShopKo's board had not fully investigated its options and that the proposed deal undervalued the company. These other options considered by ShopKo's board, included continuing current operations, seeking out strategic buyer(s), and recapitalizing the company but keeping it publicly owned. Amidst the controversy, two large shareholders—a hedge fund and a real estate investment firm—individually approached Sun Capital about possible interest in participating in a ShopKo buyout. ShopKo fit Sun Capital's focus on underperforming companies. Sun Capital also believed ShopKo had shown resilience in the face of its competition, primarily from Target and Wal-Mart. In addition, Sun Capital thought that ShopKo had strength in its pharmacy and optical business lines; that the chain had strong brand recognition and loyalty among its customers, and that it was beginning to see success in shifting its merchandise mix. However, Sun Capital executives said they were initially hesitant to participate in bidding for ShopKo because the company had already agreed to a buyout with Goldner-Hawn. In the end, Sun Capital executives said they decided to join the bidding for ShopKo because it appeared Sun Capital could pay more, for a deal it judged to be worth more, and because the Goldner-Hawn deal appeared to have what Sun Capital executives called an "insider flavor." This was because ShopKo's nonexecutive Chairman had talked with Goldner-Hawn about potentially becoming an investor in the private equity fund purchasing ShopKo and about post-buyout employment at ShopKo as well. (This conflict caused the Chairman, as well as another director, to recuse themselves from lengthy deliberations on sale of the company.) After the shareholder complaints raised in opposition to the Goldner-Hawn deal, Sun Capital believed the ShopKo board would welcome its offer. Sun Capital's winning bid of $29 per share was 21 percent better than Goldner-Hawn's initially accepted offer of $24 per share, and it boosted the deal value by $160.8 million.

Strategy and Implementation

Following the buyout, Sun Capital began a makeover of ShopKo operations. Sun Capital describes its approach to managing its portfolio companies as more hands-on than most private equity firms. It designates an operating partner who holds weekly calls and monthly meetings with company management. According to Sun Capital executives, these meetings help to monitor the acquired company's health, coach its management, and identify areas for efficiencies and cost savings.

ShopKo consolidated its vendors, making it a more important customer to each vendor. In addition, Sun leveraged its portfolio's purchasing power to acquire higher quality goods at a lower cost with better credit terms, Sun Capital executives said. For example, ShopKo was able to realize what executives said were large savings in the cost of prescription drugs. The company overhauled its marketing, launching a broadcast television and radio advertising campaign that included back-to-school ads for the first time in many years. Before the buyout, ShopKo's promotions revolved around local newspaper circulars. To capitalize on its in-store pharmacies, which executives say is a key strength, ShopKo began buying small, independent drugstores and transferring their business to ShopKo.

Sun Capital executives say they plan to spend approximately $70 million annually—up from about $35 million planned for fiscal year 2005, before the takeover—to continue the remodeling of ShopKo and Pamida stores, an initiative started before the buyout. In addition, ShopKo is opening its first new store in 6 years. These moves bring capital expenditures back up to 2004 levels.

Operationally, ShopKo reorganized its five regional management offices into 14 district groups. The aim was to provide better and faster communication between store managers and field management. Sun Capital recruited a new Chief Executive Officer but retained most ShopKo management. In addition, Sun Capital decided to operate ShopKo and Pamida as separate entities. This was because Sun Capital believed the ShopKo and Pamida customer bases were sufficiently different —chiefly, with Pamida's being more rural. Shortly after the acquisition, Sun Capital sold off ShopKo's real estate holdings, leasing the properties back from the new owners, in an $815.3 million deal that at the time was the biggest retail sale-leaseback in U.S. history. Previously, ShopKo owned both the land and buildings at about half its stores. Sun Capital executives said the real estate deal allowed Sun Capital to retire debt used to finance the buyout and to operate ShopKo with reasonable debt ratios and ample liquidity. Using the real estate proceeds to pay down initial debt was planned at the time of the buyout, Sun Capital executives said.

Results

Sun Capital executives declined to provide information on postbuyout revenue and income, but they said that revenue has been relatively level, after being on the decline before the takeover. Sun Capital executives say they believe they have put ShopKo in a better position to compete against national competitors like Target and Wal-Mart, by leveraging Sun Capital's retailing experience and sourcing capabilities, and by allowing ShopKo to focus on improving the business away from the demands of the public marketplace. ShopKo is expanding again, and remodeling efforts are paying off, with sales at remodeled stores up 5 percent compared with a base level for stores that have not been remodeled, which executives say is a significant difference.

Given pre-buyout store closings, Sun Capital judged corporate and administrative staffing to be excessive when it took control. As a result, there were a small number of layoffs in these areas after the deal closed. Overall, before the buyout, the company employed approximately 22,800— 17,000 at ShopKo stores and 5,800 at Pamida stores. Today, ShopKo employs approximately 16,000. Sun Capital executives declined to provide a figure for Pamida. Overall, jobs have been lost due to store closures but are being added as new stores open. Given the geographic spread of ShopKo stores, company employment is dispersed as well, and generally, no single store is a major employer within its market area.

Exit

Sun Capital plans to hold ShopKo in its portfolio for the immediate future. Eventually, according to executives, an IPO of stock is the most probable exit strategy, as there does not appear to be a strategic buyer. Sun Capital executives believe the Pamida division, which has been established as a separate internal unit, will have more exit options than the ShopKo division because of Pamida's particular customer base.

APPENDIX VIII: NORDCO, INC., CASE STUDY

Overview

The Nordco buyout illustrates several elements of the private equity market: a smaller deal; a buyout in which the seller was another private equity firm; and pursuit of an add-on strategy in which the acquired firm serves as a platform for subsequent purchases that build the size of the company. Figure 9 provides an overview of the LBO transaction, including a time line of key events.

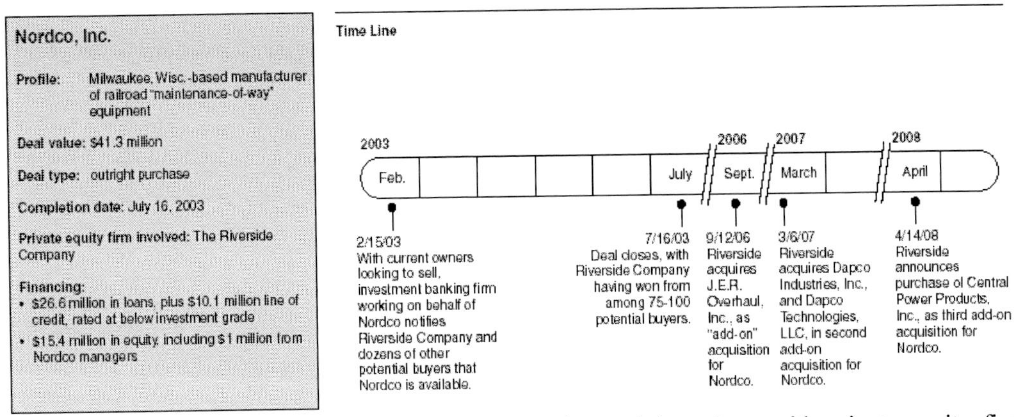

Sources: GAO analysis of publicly available information and interviews with private equity firm executives.

Figure 9. Overview and Time Line of the LBO of ShopKo Stores, Inc.

Background

When acquired by the Riverside Company (Riverside), Nordco designed and built railroad "maintenance-of-way" equipment for the North American freight, transit, and passenger railroad markets, such as equipment used for tie and rail replacement and right-of-way clearing. Although a supplier of heavy machinery, Nordco's strategy is to avoid burdensome capital expenditures by outsourcing component production and then doing only assembly work itself.

Riverside makes acquisitions in what it calls the small end of the middle market, focusing on industry-leading companies valued at under $150 million. Riverside has about $2 billion under management, and its previous investments include American Hospice, a Florida-based hospice care provider with centers in four states; GreenLine Foods, an Ohio provider of packaged green beans; and Momentum Textiles, a California contract textile supplier.

The Acquisition

As a smaller firm, Riverside executives said that it does not rely on referrals from prominent Wall Street firms to identify its buyout targets. Instead, it works with a variety of sources, including smaller investment banks and brokers. Among Riverside's contacts was a Minneapolis investment bank that alerted Riverside executives, among others, that Nordco's then-current owners, another private equity firm, were selling. Riverside executives met with Nordco management before Riverside decided to submit a bid. Because of the investment bank's promotional efforts, there was strong competition for the acquisition, Riverside executives said. Although small, Riverside considers thousands of buyout opportunities. In 2007, the company reviewed 3,500 opportunities, which executives said they quickly reduced to only about 1,200. Riverside personnel visited 400 would-be targets, with the company ultimately buying 28 of them, or 0.8 percent of the original group.

Financing for the Nordco deal included a feature where one lender receives some of the interest it was due as an increase in its outstanding balance rather than cash. This allowed Riverside to offer a higher overall return, which the lender demanded, but without diverting cash from earnings to pay the interest due.

Strategy and Implementation

While considering Nordco an attractive acquisition target, Riverside executives nonetheless had some concerns about Nordco's ability to increase revenues internally. For instance, Nordco management had been projecting revenue growth of about 5 percent to 6 percent annually, which a Riverside executive told us was "kind of underwhelming." Thus, from the beginning, Riverside's strategy in acquiring Nordco was to boost revenue by using Nordco as a vehicle for making add-on acquisitions that would increase the size of the company.

In line with this strategy, Riverside acquired J.E.R. Overhaul Inc., another maintenance-of-way company, in September 2006 as an add-on to Nordco in a $12 million deal. J.E.R. makes replacement parts used to rebuild equipment, which can then be rented out. Nordco was already in the replacement-part business, and J.E.R. copied parts made by Nordco and others. Besides expanding Nordco's business, the J.E.R. deal also allowed Nordco to eliminate the copying of its parts by a competitor. J.E.R. also had expertise in rebuilding equipment made by Nordco competitors, meaning that Nordco could thus gain intelligence about other makers' machines. In March 2007, Riverside made a second add-on acquisition: $14.1 million for Dapco Industries, Inc., and Dapco Technologies, LLC, two related companies active in rail inspection, including ultrasonic testing of rails. With the Dapco companies holding 10 patents, Riverside found their technology to be attractive. In April 2008, Riverside announced its third add-on buyout for Nordco: $45.5 million for Central Power Products, Inc., one of only three U.S. makers of railcar movers, and whose innovation is the use of rubber tires for traction instead of steel wheels.

While the initial acquisition of Nordco was highly competitive, Riverside approached the smaller, add-on companies directly. Beyond building the core business, the add-on acquisitions were part of another post-takeover strategy for Nordco: build revenues by providing services, in an effort to achieve a more diversified, and hence steadier, stream of sales as a way to buffer the cyclicality of the capital equipment marketplace, executives said.

Riverside's strategy for Nordco has also included emphasizing new product development, which had lagged, and making manufacturing more efficient. According to Riverside executives, apart from seeking to improve operational efficiency, a key element has been to give the management team an opportunity to own a significant portion of the company, on the theory of aligning managers' interests with the company's. Riverside executives said they expect that by the time the company sells Nordco, management will own about 30 percent of the business.

Results

Revenue and employment have grown steadily since the acquisition, even after factoring out the growth attributable to the acquisitions. Excluding the most recent add-on acquisition, combined revenues grew from $39.1 million in 2002 to $100.2 million in 2007, with net income up from $2.6 million to $4.2 million For the same period, employment more than doubled, from 106 to 283. For only Nordco, revenues grew from $39.1 million in 2002 to $77.8 million in 2007, with net income level at about $2.6 million. Employment increased from 106 to 158. Riverside's initial concern about Nordco's internal growth turned out to be unfounded, because actual sales growth has been about 20 percent annually in recent years, versus the 5 percent to 6 percent once forecast.

Riverside executives say they are pleased by the developments, which they say have relied upon standard practices, such as planning and executing well, rather than novel or unique methods. A union representing many employees complimented the new owners for the job they have done. A union official told us that new management has invested significantly; been hands-off on daily operations; hired new managers without purging the old; and negotiated a contract with comparatively generous benefits. The official added that in contract negotiations, the company initially made aggressive antiunion proposals on such matters as organizing activity and insurance benefits but quickly withdrew most of them. Overall, union members, who are affiliated with the United Steelworkers, traded off changes in work rules in return for an otherwise favorable contract that won overwhelming approval. The official said that if the union is concerned about anything, it is that the company still has room to improve its efficiency, which is something workers want for the sake of long-run job security.

Exit

Riverside executives said they do not yet have a definite exit strategy. But in this case, a "strategic" buyer, that is, one interested in the company specifically for what it does, versus another private equity firm, seems more likely, they said. The railroad industry is large, and a number of players would have the necessary capital, the executives said. Riverside had identified several possible buyers even before it closed on the Nordco deal.

APPENDIX IX: SAMSONITE CORP. CASE STUDY

Overview

The Samsonite transaction illustrates the use of a recapitalization—an alternate financing structure for LBOs—by a team of three private equity firms to acquire a controlling interest in the company. After owning the company for 4 years, the team sold out to another private equity firm. Figure 10 provides an overview of the LBO transaction, including a time line of key events.

Samsonite Corporation

Profile: Massachusetts-based designer and manufacturer of travel luggage and other baggage products

Deal value: $106 million

Deal type: recapitalization, a change in a corporation's capital structure, such as exchanging bonds for stock

Completion date: July 31, 2003

Private equity firms involved: Ares Management LLC, Bain Capital, Teachers' Private Capital (Ontario Teachers' Pension Plan)

Financing:

- $106 million in cash, invested in convertible preferred stock; with earlier holdings, total ownership reached 56 percent of voting stock

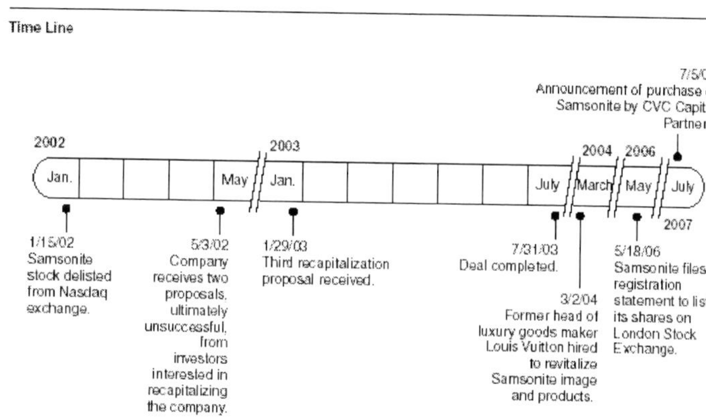

Sources: GAO analysis of publicly available information and interviews with private equity firm executives.

Figure 10. Overview and Time Line of the LBO of Samsonite Corp.

Background

In 2003, Samsonite had a well-known brand name but was on the verge of bankruptcy, as the company sought to save a business burdened by debt and hurt by a post-9/11 travel slowdown. Samsonite was best known for its hard-sided, durable suitcases and was responsible for innovations including lightweight luggage and wheeled suitcases. Today, Samsonite generates most of its revenues from outside North America, with Europe accounting for more than 40 percent of its $1.07 billion in sales for fiscal year 2007.

Ares Management was the lead private equity firm in the acquisition. Based in Los Angeles, Ares Management was founded in 1997 and has offices in New York and London. The firm has invested in a number of retail and consumer product companies, including General Nutrition Centers, Maidenform Brands, and National Bedding (Serta). Bain Capital is an investment firm whose activities include private equity, venture capital, and hedge funds. Its private equity investments include Toys "R" Us, Burger King, Dunkin' Brands, and Staples. Teachers' Private Capital is the private equity arm of the Ontario Teachers' Pension Plan, which invests pension fund assets of 271,000 active and retired teachers in Ontario, Canada. Its investments include General Nutrition Centers, Shoppers Drug Mart Corp., and Easton-Bell Sports.

The Acquisition

In 2002, Samsonite directors were trying to find a solution to growing financial pressure stemming from indebtedness. In a 1998 recapitalization, Samsonite had issued $350 million of notes at 10.75 percent interest and $175 million of preferred stock at a dividend rate of almost 14 percent, in order to buy back common stock and refinance existing debt. As a result, large, debt-related and dividend payments were burdening the company. In October 2002, a potential investment deal proposed several months earlier fell apart. In February 2003, Samsonite announced it was pursuing a new recapitalization investment from the Ares Management-led group. Ares Management executives said that they became interested in the travel industry after its downturn following the 9/11 attacks and also were aware of Samsonite because of a prior investment in the company. Samsonite's brand was attractive to Ares Management, executives said, but the firm was also aware of the company's debt service burden and potential for bankruptcy.

Ares Management formed a three-firm team and offered Samsonite a cash investment in conjunction with a restructuring of Samsonite's debt and preferred stock. Ares Management executives said they brought in partners because the deal was too large to handle alone. Ares Management first approached the largest investor in its private equity fund, the private equity arm of the Ontario Teachers' Pension Plan, which agreed to join. Because a large portion of Samsonite's sales came from Europe, Ares Management sought to include an investor located in that region. To that end, executives brought in a fund managed by the European private equity group of the investment firm Bain Capital.

After several months of negotiations, Samsonite announced in May 2003 that an agreement had been reached. The three private equity firms invested $106 million (with each firm investing a little over $35 million), in return for a new series of Samsonite preferred stock. Samsonite used the proceeds, in part, to repay existing debt. Samsonite also exchanged its existing preferred stock for a combination of the new preferred stock and common stock. Building on a prior investment stake held by Ares Management, the three-firm consortium used this transaction to gain control of about 56 percent of the company's outstanding voting shares.

Holdings of existing common shareholders, who approved the deal, were diluted from 100 percent to about a 3 percent stake of outstanding voting shares. Ares Management executives said that common shareholders had faced losing everything in a bankruptcy, while the recapitalization left them with a smaller share of a more valuable company.

Strategy and Implementation

The consortium's revitalization strategy was to focus on reducing the debt load while seeking to improve marketing and product quality. According to Ares Management executives, troubled businesses struggling to service high debt loads often reduce spending on marketing and product development in favor of simply focusing on survival. Samsonite's restructuring of its finances lowered its interest and dividend payments, providing more cash for marketing and other activities, the executives said. Other efforts focused on improving product sourcing and distribution.

In early 2004, Samsonite's new owners hired the former President and Chief Executive of luxury goods maker Louis Vuitton to reinvigorate the company's image and products. He moved to reposition Samsonite as a premium lifestyle brand, rather than simply as a commodity provider of luggage. Especially in the United States, the Samsonite brand had suffered in recent years, although it was still strong in Europe and Asia. The company created a new label—the Samsonite Black Label—for the higher-priced, and higher-margin, segment of the market, while establishing a sister brand, American Tourister, as the company's lowerpriced product. The new Chief Executive also focused on a high-end marketing campaign by using business and entertainment celebrities to sell the products. The company hired a noted designer to produce a new line of luggage. Another element of the strategy was an expansion of retail activities by opening stores in fashionable locations such as Bond Street in London and Madison Avenue in New York City. Spending on advertising grew steadily from $37 million in the company's 2004 fiscal year to $67.5 million in the 2007 fiscal year.

Results

Since the acquisition, Ares Management achieved its goals of boosting revenues and margins, with both measures steadily improving from fiscal year 2003, before the acquisition, through fiscal year 2007. Annual revenue grew by about 42 percent, from $752 million to $1.07 billion, and gross profit margin widened from 43 percent to 51 percent. Over the same period, the company was profitable in fiscal years 2004 and 2006. But it suffered losses in fiscal years 2005 and 2007, due in part to higher expenses in redeeming preferred shares and retiring debt. Ares Management executives said net income has been hurt by one-time charges, such as for restructuring and a computer system, that did not reflect Samsonite's operating performance.

Although Ares Management executives said they wanted to cut Samsonite's debt burden, it went up. Six months before the three private equity firms acquired Samsonite, the company had $423 million in longterm debt. This amount declined to $298 million at January 2006 but then increased to $490 million for 2007.

While owned by the group of private equity firms, Samsonite's global employment dropped by about 7 percent, as the company laid off workers following factory closings and relocations. In January 2003, 6 months before the firms acquired the company, Samsonite employed 5,400 people. In each year since then, according to federal securities filings, the employment level has been at about 5,000. In 2007, about 1,300 of those employees were in North America. Ares Management executives said they could not provide figures for U.S. employment. They also said Samsonite's mix of workers has changed, as manufacturing employees were reduced in number, largely in Europe, but employees were added in marketing, distribution, product development, and retail.

In recent years, Samsonite has continued a pre-buyout trend to outsource its manufacturing from company-owned factories to third-party vendors in lower-cost regions, mostly in Asia. In fiscal year 2007, Samsonite purchased 90 percent of its soft-sided luggage and related products from vendors in Asia, while most of its hard-sided luggage was manufactured in company-owned facilities. Because of the shift, Samsonite has sold or closed several of its remaining manufacturing facilities, in France, Belgium, Slovakia, Spain, and

Mexico. Samsonite has also revamped domestic operations. In May 2006, the company announced it would close its former headquarters in Denver, Colorado; relocate Denver distribution functions to Jacksonville, Florida; and consolidate corporate functions in a Mansfield, Massachusetts, headquarters office.

Exit

Initially, the three firms in the consortium were looking to exit their Samsonite investment through an IPO of stock, but eventually pursued another option. In early 2006, Samsonite, whose stock had been delisted from the Nasdaq exchange in 2002, began exploring a listing on the London Stock Exchange. In 2007, Samsonite began marketing the planned offering in Europe. But, in May 2007, several private equity firms approached one of Samsonite's private equity owners, Bain Capital, about acquiring the company. As a result, Samsonite's consortium of owners decided to open up an auction for the company, while still continuing with plans for the stock offering. The auction attracted a number of bidders, with CVC Capital Partners, a Luxembourg-based private equity firm, emerging as the winning bidder.

The buyout was completed in October 2007. Terms of the deal were $1.1 billion in cash, plus assumption of debt that valued the transaction at $1.7 billion. Samsonite directors and the three private equity owners, whose holdings had grown to about 85 percent of the company, approved the deal unanimously. The private equity firms received about $950 million, according to a securities filing. An Ares Management executive said the company believed it had re-energized the Samsonite brand.

Appendix X: Econometric Analysis of the Price Impact of Club Deals

The presence of club deals (collaboration of two or more private equity firms in a buyout) in the leveraged buyout market has raised concerns about the potential for anticompetitive pricing. For example, the Department of Justice's Antitrust Division has reportedly launched an inquiry into this practice by some large private equity firms. While club deals could enhance competition by enabling private equity firms to bid together for companies they otherwise could not buy on their own, these deals could also reduce competition by reducing the number of firms bidding on target companies and fostering a collusive environment. If joint bidding by private equity firms facilitates collusion, the share price premium over market prices that private equity firms pay to shareholders should be lower in club deals than in nonclub deals. To investigate the relationship between club deals and the premium, we constructed a sample of public-to-private U.S. buyouts by private equity firms using Dealogic's Merger and Acquisitions (M&A) database. The sample initially contained observations on 510 public-to-private transactions involving U.S. target companies from 1998 through 2007.[112] Of these transactions, 325 had the requisite premium data for further analysis. We employed standard econometric modeling techniques, including Heckman's two-stage modeling approach to address potential selection bias issues. While the results suggest that, in general, club deals are not associated with lower or higher premiums, we caution that our results should not be taken as causal: that is, they should not be read as establishing that club deals necessarily caused acquisition prices to be higher or lower. To the extent that the nature of the firms and transactions we examined differ from the overall population of club deals, our results may not generalize to the population. This appendix provides additional information on the construction of our database, econometric model, additional descriptive statistics, and limitations of the analysis.

Data Sample Was Created Using the Dealogic Database with Additional Fields from SEC's Edgar, LexisNexis and Audit Analytics

To construct the database used to estimate the econometric model, we compiled transaction data and the associated demographic and financial data on the buyout firms and target companies from Dealogic's M&A Analytics Database for deals completed from 1998 through February 1, 2008. The database captures worldwide merger and acquisition activity covering a range of transactions, including buyouts, privatizations, recapitalizations, and acquisitions. Using the database, we were able to identify 510 buyouts of publicly traded, U.S. companies by private equity firms—some of which were transactions undertaken by a consortium of firms (club deals). Because each transaction included financial information on the target company and private equity acquirer(s), as well as other details regarding the deal, we were able to construct a set of variables to explain the variation in the premium across transactions. We augmented our set of variables with information from SEC's Edgar database, Audit Analytics, and LexisNexis. We used the Edgar database to collect data on managerial and beneficial holdings of equity[113] for each of the target companies in our sample since the existing literature has shown that the presence of these shareholders is associated with the premium paid by buyout firms. Similarly we used Audit Analytics—an online intelligence service maintained by Ives Group, Incorporated—to extract data on audit opinions dating back to 2000. As a result, we were able to include information on the risk characteristics (going concern opinions) of the target companies as an additional control variable in the resultant econometric model focusing on the 2000-2007 period. Finally, we included stock price data for the target firms using the Historical Stock Quote database in LexisNexis. Company filings with SEC are the principal source for data on managerial and beneficial equity holdings. Moreover, we have used Audit Analytics data in recent reports and, as a result, have performed various checks to verify the reliability of the data. For this performance audit, we also conducted a limited check of the accuracy of the LexisNexis data by ensuring that the stock prices for a random subset of the companies matched the stock price data contained in the Dealogic database.

From our sample of 510 U.S. "public-to-private" transactions, we deleted deals that did not have the requisite premium data, leaving us with 325 private equity buyouts for our initial econometric analysis. These transactions span multiple industries but are clustered in specific areas of the economy—as defined by two-digit North American Industry Classification System (NAICS) codes, namely manufacturing, information, finance and insurance, professional, scientific and technical services, accommodation and food services, and wholesale trade. These six sectors of the economy account for 209 of the 325 public-to-private transactions involving private equity firms. Table 8 reports the descriptive statistics on the resultant sample and illustrates that club deals, on average, are larger and can differ from single private equity deals along a number of other dimensions.

Because some transactions in our sample resulted in the private equity firm holding less than 100 percent of the target company, we identified whether the target company filed a Form 15 (which notifies SEC of a company's intent to terminate its registration) to determine whether the company actually went private. Transactions that resulted in the private equity firm(s) holding less than a 100 percent stake in the company, and where no Form 15 was filed for the company around the time the transaction was completed, were excluded from the econometric model.

Table 8. Descriptive Statistics of the Sample (Averages), 1998–2007

	Single firm private equity deals N=242	Club deals N=83	All deals N=325
Percentages			
Premium pre bid, 1 day	23.2%	22.0%	22.9%
Premium pre bid, 1 week	25.0	26.1	25.3
Premium pre bid, 1 month	29.6	40.6	32.4
Management holdings	24.0	19.8	22.9
Beneficial holdings	28.1	27.0	27.8
Target debt equity ratio	-183.1	126.3	-101.8
Target current ratio	286.5	201.4	264.0
Target cash ratio	72.3	42.7	64.6
Target debt ratio	60.2	53.3	58.4
Concentration ratio	1.8%	8.3%	3.4%
Dollars in millions			
Deal value	$1,257.3	$4,091.6	$1,974.6
Target earnings	70.4	280.9	125.5
Target market capitalization	776.1	2,847.5	1,300.3
Target net cash flow	1.3	-13.5	-3.8
Target sales revenue	816.1	2,224.7	1,184.8
Target total assets	1,134.8	2,911.0	1,599.7
Target long-term debt	434.5	1070.3	604.2
Target gross profit	338.8	1,004.3	529.7
Target long-term liabilities	$631.4	$1,362.0	$827.6

Sources: GAO analysis of Dealogic and SEC data.

Notes: N is the number of observations. Target refers to the company taken private by the private equity firm(s). The concentration ratio is the aggregate market share of the private equity firm(s) involved in the transaction. See table 9 for a full definition of the variables.

Econometric Modeling Procedures

Our econometric methodology exploits standard ordinary least squares (OLS) and maximum likelihood (ML) procedures to investigate the following questions:

- What attributes of the target company or deal characteristics increase the probability that the transaction will be a club deal (multiple private equity firms will join together to acquire the target company)?
- When other important factors influencing shareholder premiums are accounted for—including controlling for differences in club and nonclub deals—are companies taken private in club deals associated with lower premiums than those paid to shareholders of companies that are taken private by a single firm?

While obtaining an answer to the second question is our explicit goal, the first question is critical to producing valid estimates of the impact of club deals on the share premium. Because club deals are not randomly selected by private equity firms and instead can be deliberate choices, ignoring these company selection effects potentially introduces bias into our OLS regression estimates. To control for selection bias in club deal transactions, a two-stage selection model is estimated. This analysis uses the widely accepted two-stage Heckman approach.[114] The first stage is a club deal selection Probit model (estimated using ML) used to estimate the probability of a target company being acquired in a club deal. From the Probit parameter estimates, we derive inverse Mills ratios,[115] which are then used as an additional explanatory variable in the second stage model, a share premium regression estimated by OLS. The Heckman selection model is estimated as follows:

$$\text{Probit: } z_i = \theta + Mi\beta + \varepsilon_{1i} \quad (1)$$

where z = the dependent variable (a dummy variable indicating whether or not the transaction is a club deal).

M = a matrix of explanatory variables that varies across transactions. These are variables that help capture the characteristics of the public target company, characteristics of the deal as well as time and industry dummies.

θ= constant term.

ε_i = a random disturbance term (residual).

$$\text{OLS:} yi = \theta + Xi\beta + Ci\sigma + \lambda i\alpha + \varepsilon\, 2i \quad (2)$$

where y = the dependent variable (premium paid to shareholders of the target company).

X = a dummy variable indicating whether or not the transaction is a club deal.

C = a matrix of explanatory variables that varies across transactions. These are variables that help capture the characteristics of the public target company, characteristics of the deal as well as time and industry dummies.

λ= the inverse Mills ratio constructed from equation (1).

The selection model can only be estimated if the Probit and OLS equations have elements that are not common, thus satisfying the identification condition. However, the Probit is identified even without the addition of variables to the equation that are not present in the OLS equation. This is true because even though the inverse Mills ratios are functions of the same variables, they are nonlinear functions of the measured variables, given the assumption of normality in the Probit model.[116] In our case, in addition to variables specific to equation 2 required for identification, we were also able to exploit variables unique to equation 1 as well.

Variables Included in the Model

As shown in table 9, the dependent variable in all of our OLS econometric models is the shareholder premium, which is calculated as the logarithm of the final price offered by the acquiring firm(s) divided by the target company's share price 1 day before the announcement. Published research suggests that under this specification, the premium incorporates the informational value of any announcement made during the going-private process, such as amended bid prices, bidder competition, and the identification of the acquiring party.[117] We use the premium based on the price 1 day before the announcement since this measure is lower for club deals than for single private equity transactions. However, we also use the premium calculated as the logarithm of the final price offered by the acquiring firm(s) divided by the share price 1 month before the announcement in some models as a sensitivity test.

The primary variable of interest is the dummy variable, which indicates whether or not a given public-to-private transaction is a club deal (Club). Club is used to determine whether club deals are associated with lower premiums within the methodological framework laid out above. This variable is also used as the dependent variable in the first-stage Probit model. Because some club deals involve more and/or larger private equity firms, we also include a measure of market concentration in some of our econometric specifications. The market share variable (Concentrate) that indicates the cumulative share of the public-to-private buyout market held by the private equity firms involved in a transaction is measured using the total value of all deals. The market is defined here as the segmented market, which focuses only on public-to-private transactions conducted by private equity firms and excludes other private and publicly traded companies, the estimates may overstate the degree of concentration for each transaction.[118]

Additionally, we included a number of control variables in the OLS and Probit ML models in attempt to explain the variation in the shareholder premium across transactions or—for the Probit model—the probability that an acquisition involves more than one private equity firm. These variables are related to the characteristics of the target company and/or the deal. As indicated in the body of this report, recent research suggests that private equity firms pay a higher premium for target companies with lower valuations, lower leverage, poorer management incentives (measured by management's ownership share), and less concentrated ownership among external shareholders. We include variables that capture these insights, as well as additional controls based on our audit work. Table 9 includes a listing of the primary variables included in the econometric models, ranging from company size (market capitalization) and financial leverage and liquidity ratios to indicators of a going concern opinion and variables thought to capture the potential for incentive realignment. As some of these variables may also be related to the club dummy variable, controlling for them along with the inverse Mills ratio from the first stage of the Probit model also enhances the internal validity of the OLS parameter estimates. We also include time period fixed effects and dummy variables for some industries in our principal specifications.

Table 9. Primary Variables in the Econometric Analysis

Variable	Description	Model used
PREMIUM	Log of the premium paid to the shareholders of the public company target calculated as logarithm of the final price offered by the acquiring firm(s) divided by the share price 1 day before the announcement or the share price 1 month before the announcement.	OLS
Club	Indicates whether a public-to-private buyout transaction is a club deal.	Dependent variable in PROBIT; independent variable in OLS
Concentrate	Percentage of the market (defined by deal value) held by the private equity firms involved in the transaction.	OLS
MCAP	Logarithm of target company's market capitalization.	OLS
DEALVAL	Logarithm of the value of the transaction.	PROBIT
BLOCK	Percentage of shares outstanding held by individuals and institutions holding 5 percent or more of the total shares outstanding before the buyout (beneficial ownership). Does not include managers and executives of the target company. Theory suggests that these shareholders have strong incentives to monitor company performance.	OLS
STAKE	Percentage of shares outstanding held by target company managers and executives before buyout (managerial ownership). Theory holds that these shareholders should have incentives aligned with outside shareholders.	OLS
FLOAT	Free public float. Calculated by subtracting beneficial and managerial ownership from the total shares outstanding. (Shares held by those not considered monitoring outside shareholders or inside shareholders).	OLS
CASHRATIO	Total dollar value of cash and marketable securities divided by current liabilities. The cash ratio measures the extent to which the target company can quickly liquidate assets and cover short-term liabilities.	OLS

Table 9. (Continued).

Variable	Description	Model used
DEBTEQUITY	Target debt-to-equity ratio calculated by dividing total liabilities by stockholders' equity. It indicates what proportion of equity and debt the company is using to finance its assets, the company debt capacity, and the ability of the buyout parties to reap tax benefits.	OLS
DEBTRATIO	Target debt ratio calculated by dividing debt by assets. The measure indicates the leverage of the target company along with the potential risks the company faces in terms of its debt load.	PROBIT
ACCRUALS	Measure of earnings quality calculated as cash flows divided by earnings.	OLS
FREECASH	Target company cash flows divided by its revenues. Ample free cash flow generation gives company management options in terms of uses of the cash, many of which can benefit equity shareholders.	OLS
GC	Indicates doubt about a company's ability to continue as a going concern was raised.	OLS, PROBIT
PRICE	A measure of stock market performance leading up to the transaction announcement. Measured as the ratio of the closing market price 1 month prior to the buyout announcement divided by the price 2 years before the transaction. This figure is divided by the equivalent ratio for the Russell 3000.	OLS
NONNYSE	Indicates whether the company's stock trades on NYSE.	PROBIT
MILLS	Inverse Mills ratio calculated from the parameters in the first stage Probit model to account for potential selection bias in club deal choice.	OLS
Year	Year dummy variables. The few observations occurring in early 2008 where coded as 2007 transactions.	OLS
Industry	Industry dummy variables (defined by two-digit NAICS codes).	OLS

Sources: GAO analysis of Dealogic, SEC, Audit Analytics, and LexisNexis data.

With the exception of the deal value (DEALVAL) and the market capitalization (MCAP), the variables are not highly correlated, minimizing our concern over multicollinearity (see table 10). While the correlation between the deal value and the market capitalization of the target company is roughly .97, none of the other correlations exceed .38 for variables we include simultaneously in a regression, and most fall below .20. (We of course do not include Float in regressions where Stake and Block are included since it is a linear combination of the other two variables.) The liquidity and debt ratios all show very little correlation in our sample.

RESULTS

We ran a number of different models with varied specifications as sensitivity tests. For brevity, we do not report all of the specifications in this appendix. The general OLS and two-stage OLS models run on 1998- 2007 and 2000-2007 data suggest that public-to-private club deals generally are not associated with lower premiums (see table 11). In fact, the coefficient on Club is positive in all specifications but is always insignificant in the primary models. Although not reported, we also found that share of the market held by the firms undertaking the transaction did not affect the size of the premium paid to shareholders of the target company. We also found evidence, consistent with the literature, that larger companies, companies with larger debt burdens, and companies with large beneficial and managerial holders of equity, received smaller premiums, while companies with poorer market-adjusted stock price performance received higher premiums. Moreover, shareholders of companies where doubt was raised about their ability to continue as a going concern received a lower premium over the 2000-2007 period. In all specifications reported we maintained a dummy variable for target companies only in the accommodation and food services sector, since the dummy variables for all other industries were insignificant.

The first-stage Probit model suggests that large companies, companies with lower debt ratios, and companies not trading on NYSE, controlling for size, have a greater probability of being taken private in a joint acquisition. Initially, we ran the first-stage Probit model with a larger number of independent variables but dropped those variables that were insignificant and then used the more parsimonious model represented in table 11 to estimate the inverse Mills ratio included in stage two. The insignificance of the Mills ratio for the 2000-2007 regression suggests that selection bias is not a problem given our control variables, while its marginal significance for the 1998-2007 regression indicates that selection bias is more likely an issue. To be conservative, we included the Mills ratio in the consequent regressions exploring the sensitivity of our results.

Table 12 presents the results of selected sensitivity models we employed to check the robustness of our main econometric results. We present the results of an alternative specification in which we drop the financial and leverage ratios to maximize the number of transactions included in the model. The results corroborate the findings of our less restrictive models suggesting that club deals are not associated with lower premiums paid to shareholders. Also, we estimated models where we considered only transactions with deal values greater than \$100 million and \$250 million. While some of the variables show instability, the club dummy remains positive and, in fact, becomes statistically significant at the 5 percent level in the 2000-2007 period for deals greater than \$100 million.

While our finding that the public-to-private club deals are not negatively associated with the premium, and the association is positive when small deals are excluded from the sample, is consistent with competitive behavior, one should not infer that these results provide definitive proof of competitive behavior given the modeling and data limitations. Accordingly, these results should be interpreted with caution. First, this is an aggregate analysis and, therefore, does not demonstrate that all shareholders of buyout targets receive a competitive price. Second, the nonexperimental, cross-sectional design we employ is among the weakest designs for the examination of causal relationships and, therefore, omitted

Table 10. Correlations Between Independent Variables

	1	2	3	4	5	6	7	8	9	10	11	12
1. MCAP	1.00											
2. DEALVAL	0.97	1.00										
3. BLOCK	-0.16	-0.15	1.00									
4. STAKE	-0.27	-0.26	-0.40	1.00								
5. FLOAT	0.39	0.38	-0.50	-0.59	1.00							
6. CASHRATIO	-0.04	-0.04	-0.05	0.08	-0.03	1.00						
7. DEBTEQUITY	0.04	0.04	-0.16	0.03	0.11	0.01	1.00					
8. CLUB	0.28	0.23	0.02	-0.18	0.15	-0.06	0.04	1.00				
9. PRICE	-0.01	-0.01	-0.08	0.02	0.05	-0.02	0.01	-0.05	1.00			
10. DEBTRATIO	0.00	0.06	0.23	-0.02	-0.18	-0.06	-0.09	-0.14	0.03	1.00		
11. ACCURALS	0.03	0.02	-0.16	0.06	0.08	0.02	-0.01	-0.05	-0.02	-0.04	1.00	
12. FREECASH	0.20	0.20	0.02	-0.09	0.07	-0.09	0.02	0.10	-0.02	0.04	-0.02	1.00

Sources: GAO analysis of Dealogic, SEC, Audit Analytics, and LexisNexis data.

Table 11. Multivariate Regression Analysis of Premium, 1998–2007

	1998-2007			2000-2007		
	OLS (1) N= 239	First-stage Probit (2) N= 288	Second stage OLS (3) N= 239	OLS (4) N= 215	First-stage Probit (5) N= 240	Second stage OLS (6) N= 215
C	0.3950 (4.33)*	-3.190 (-4.92)*	0.6906 (3.91)*	0.5405 (7.45)*	-2.8504 (-4.12)*	0.5812 (5.20)*
MCAP	-0.0337 (-3.33)*	- -	-0.0611 (-3.36)*	-0.0350 (-3.68)*	- -	-0.0390 (-3.21)*
DEALVAL	- -	0.4215 (5.65)*	- -	- -	0.4007 (5.11)*	- -
BLOCK	-0.2113 (-2.90)*	- -	-0.1735 (-2.33)**	-0.2238 (-3.03)*	- -	-0.2163 (-2.93)*
STAKE	-0.1625 (-2.09)**	- -	-0.1412 (-1.91)***	-0.1210 (-1.70)***	- -	-0.1181 (-1.66)***
CLUB	0.0259 (1.08)	- -	0.0161 (0.68)	0.0177 (0.7467)	- -	0.0160 (0.6577)
NONNYSE	- -	0.4474 (1.96)**	- -	- -	0.3797 (1.56)	- -
DEBTEQUITY	-0.0002 (-1.05)	- -	-0.0002 (1.23)	-0.0002 (-1.05)	- -	-0.0002 (-1.07)

PRICE	-0.0003 (-3.35)*	- -	-0.0003 (-2.89)*	-0.0003 (-2.37)**	- -	-0.0003 (-2.30)**
ACCURALS	-0.0003 (-0.54)	- -	-0.0001 (-0.26)	-0.0014 (-2.40)**	- -	-0.0013 (-2.25)**
FREECASH	0.0863 (1.59)	- -	0.0775 (1.38)	0.0706 (1.11)	- -	0.0699 (1.09)
CASHRATIO	-0.0076 (-5.37)*	- -	-0.0077 (-4.63)*	-0.0082 (-6.21)*	- -	-0.0082 (-6.03)*
DEBTRATIO	- -	-1.0488 (-2.86)*	- -	- -	-1.305 (-3.01)*	
GC	- -	- -	- -	-0.1090 (-3.03)*	- -	-0.1077 (-2.99)*
MILLS	- -	- -	-0.1157 (-1.82)***	- -	- -	-0.0175 (-0.42)
Dummy variables						
Time	Yes	Yes	Yes	Yes	Yes	Yes
industry	Food	No	Food	Food	No	Food
σe	0.1700	0.4415	0.1679	0.1549	0.4495	0.1552
R2	0.2491	-	0.2704	0.3715	-	0.3722
Adjusted *R2*	0.1840	0.1527	0.2034	0.3138	0.1595	0.3110
F-statistic (LR)	3.8244	50.774	4.0391	6.4368	45.330	6.0845

Sources: GAO analysis of Dealogic, SEC, Audit Analytics, and LexisNexis data.

Notes: T-statistics are in parentheses, and * indicates significance at the 1% level, **indicates significance at the 5% level, and *** indicates significance at the 10% level. T-statistics are based on White heteroskedasticity-consistent standard errors and covariance matrix in all specifications. LR denotes the Likelihood Ratio statistic for the Probit model.

Table 12. Multivariate Regression Analysis of Premium, Select Sensitivity Analyses

	1998-2007			2000-2007		
	>100 million (1) N= 203	>250 million (2) N= 159	Alternative specification (3) N= 284	>100 million (4) N= 183	>250 million (5) N= 144	Alternative specification (6) N= 236
C	0.5581 (3.80)*	0.6194 (3.95)*	0.7352 (4.54)*	0.5625 (5.28)*	0.5183 (5.17)*	0.6541 (5.56)*
MCAP	-0.0564 (-3.45)*	-0.0594 (-3.41)*	-0.0683 (-4.09)*	-0.0395 (3.26)*	-0.0384 (-3.07)*	-0.0473 (-3.74)*
BLOCK	-0.1368 (-2.07)**	-0.1268 (-1.79)***	-0.1963 (-2.88)*	-0.2030 (-3.27)*	-0.1814 (-2.90)*	-0.2190 (-2.91)*
STAKE	-0.1076 (-1.80)***	-0.2439 (-4.46)*	-0.1416 (-1.789)***	-0.1087 (-1.70)***	-0.2623 (-5.10)*	-0.1691 (-2.34)**
CLUB	0.038 (1.72)***	0.0316 (1.27)	0.0350 (1.48)	0.0441 (2.02)**	0.0443 (1.91)***	0.0362 (1.41)
DEBTEQUITY	-0.0002 (-0.95)	0.0030 (1.20)	- -	-0.0002 (-1.07)	0.0023 (0.78)	- -
PRICE	-0.0003 (-2.65)*	0.0049 (3.39)*	-0.0003 (-3.12)*	-0.0003 (-3.06)*	.00058 (5.726)	-0.0003 (-2.38)**
ACCURALS	- -	- -	- -	- -	- -	- -
FREECASH	0.0915 (1.68)***	0.0233 (0.35)	- -	0.0880 (1.54)	0.0188 (0.31)	- -
CASHRATIO	-0.0075 (-5.18)*	-0.0285 (-1.69)***	- -	-0.008 (-5.66)*	-0.0345 (-2.22)**	- -
GC	- -	- -	- -	.0038 (0.10)	0.0977 (2.61)*	-0.0833 (-2.27)**
MILLS	-0.0788 (-1.32)	-0.0977 (-1.60)	-0.1112 (-1.99)**	-0.0050 (-0.12)	-0.0187 (-0.53)	-0.0329 (-0.77)
Dummy Variables						
Time	Yes	Yes	Yes	Yes	Yes	Yes
industry	Food	Food	Food	Food	Food	Food
Other statistics						
σe	0.1443	0.1329	0.1825	0.1365	0.1156	0.1672
R2	0.3501	0.3577	0.2373	0.3832	0.4357	0.3035
Adjusted *R2*	0.2827	0.2699	0.1916	0.3155	0.3544	0.2560
F-statistic	5.1895	4.0744	5.1912	5.6613	5.3611	6.3904

Sources: GAO analysis of Dealogic, SEC, Audit Analytics, and LexisNexis data.

Notes:T-statistics are in parentheses, and * indicates significance at the 1% level, **indicates significance at the 5% level, and *** indicates significance at the 10% level. T-statistics are based on White heteroskedasticity-consistent standard errors and covariance matrix in all specifications.

variables bias remains a concern. Moreover, the Heckman-correction approach is imperfect, and some have raised concerns about the sensitivity of the parameter estimates to the distributional assumption that underlies the selection model. In that regard, we draw conclusions about the association, not casual relationship, between clubs deals and premiums. Additional data and in-depth case-by-case examinations of club deal transactions may allow for analysis to address the issue more completely or more validly. Third, we focused on public-to-private transactions given the availability of data on prices paid for target companies. We also focused solely on buyouts involving private equity firms since this sample provides the cleanest incremental test of the association between club deal private equity transactions and the premium paid. However, although our public-to-private sample exceeds the size of many of the samples used in similar studies, it should be emphasized that we have analyzed only a small sample of transactions involving club deals. Therefore, the results may not generalize to other deals involving other types of companies. Finally, we acknowledge the potential for error in the data collected on managerial and beneficial ownership. While the recording of these holdings was straightforward in most cases, it was difficult to distinguish the managerial holdings from the beneficial holdings in some cases. We took steps to validate our collection efforts, but some random errors may remain. Given that the model results are consistent with prior research, it appears that any errors are minor in the context of this performance audit.

Appendix XI: Comments from the Board of Governors of the Federal Reserve System

BOARD OF GOVERNORS
OF THE
FEDERAL RESERVE SYSTEM
WASHINGTON, D. C. 20551

RANDALL S. KROSZNER
MEMBER OF THE BOARD

August 25, 2008

Ms. Orice M. Williams
Director, Financial Markets and Community Investment
United States Government Accountability Office
Washington, DC 20548

Dear Ms. Williams:

The Federal Reserve appreciates the opportunity to comment on a draft of the GAO's report entitled "Private Equity--Recent Growth in Leveraged Buyouts Exposed Risks That Warrant Continued Attention." The large and episodic waves of leveraged buyouts of U.S. companies, the most recent of which slowed abruptly in mid-2007, raise a number of important questions about the potential microeconomic and macroeconomic effects of such deals. The GAO study provides a balanced and thoughtful review of the current state of knowledge of leveraged buyouts and their potential economic impacts, and it also offers a valuable and original analysis of the effects of "club" deals on the competitive structure of the leveraged buyout market.

In the report, the GAO recommends that "…federal financial regulators give increased attention to ensuring that their oversight of leveraged lending at their regulated institutions take into consideration systemic risk implications raised by changes in the broader financial markets, as a whole." This recommendation articulates for the leveraged lending market a broad and fundamental observation emphasized in a number of areas over the past year of financial market distress. Indeed, the need to ensure that regulatory and supervisory efforts take into account the systemic risk implications of changes in financial markets has been an important lesson learned across global and domestic markets, different types of financial institutions, and several financial products. The heightened awareness of systemic risk and the interconnectivity of markets and financial institutions are factoring into the Federal Reserve's approach to its activities and responsibilities, including the supervision and oversight of leveraged lending at our regulated institutions. Importantly, by making the recommendation to multiple U.S. regulators, the GAO recognizes that coordination among supervisors, along with each regulator's own targeted efforts and interaction with the private sector, are crucial to limiting potential systemic risks.

Several "lessons learned" exercises conducted by supervisors and policymakers over the past year have identified a number of risk-management weaknesses at major financial institutions. In addition to the exercise conducted by the President's Working Group on Financial Markets that is noted in the GAO report, similar efforts have been conducted by international supervisory groups, such as the Senior Supervisors Group and the Financial Stability Forum.[1] Together, these efforts--in which the Federal Reserve actively participated--have identified specific risk-management weaknesses in leveraged lending business lines along with the need for improvements in fundamental areas of firmwide risk management that, when addressed, will help mitigate the possibility that leveraged lending conducted at regulated institutions might either contribute to, or be affected by, systemic risk. Federal Reserve supervisors are monitoring efforts to remedy the risk-management weaknesses identified within specific institutions' leveraged lending business lines. These efforts include enhancements to leveraged lending underwriting standards, controls over leveraged loan pipeline exposures, and approaches in applying the originate-to-distribute model to leveraged lending. Our monitoring and review of institutions' remedial efforts, along with continued supervisory assessments surrounding leveraged lending at supervised institutions, will be used to determine the need for additional Federal Reserve or interagency guidance on leveraged lending and to ensure that any such guidance is sufficiently comprehensive.

From a broader perspective, the Federal Reserve, in coordination with other U.S. and international regulators, also is undertaking a number of supervisory efforts to address various firmwide risk-management weaknesses identified over the past year, initiatives that should help to better integrate leveraged lending risk exposures. Areas of particular importance include the need for global, systemically important institutions to enhance their firmwide stress testing and balance sheet management processes and to improve the comprehensiveness of their liquidity risk management and liquidity contingency planning. Enhancing these key elements of firmwide risk management will enable institutions to better manage their leveraged lending activities in coordination with other control functions and risk exposures of the firm and, thus, provide additional safeguards and shock absorbers in limiting the potential for leveraged lending activities to possibly contribute to systemic risk. Supervisory efforts also are under way to effect improvements in the counterparty credit risk-management practices of large institutions, including those practices used to manage exposures to hedge funds and private equity funds. These and other initiatives being undertaken by the Federal Reserve and other U.S. and international supervisors in response to market events over the past year illustrate steps toward a more systemwide focused approach to supervision. As pointed out in recent remarks by Chairman Bernanke, efforts to promote a systemwide focus in financial regulation using guidance and both targeted and horizontal on-site reviews of key financial institutions have significant potential for contributing to reducing systemic risk. This includes any such risks that may arise from, or may affect, leveraged lending--the topic of the GAO report.[2]

---

[1] See Senior Supervisors Group (2008), *Observations on Risk Management Practices during the Recent Market Turbulence* (New York: SSG, March); and Financial Stability Forum (2008), *Report of the Financial Stability Forum on Enhancing Market and Institutional Resilience*, interim and final reports (Basel: FSF, February 8 and April 7).

[2] Although not addressed by a GAO recommendation, market participants also have an important role to play in ensuring that various elements of the leveraged lending market do not contribute to the potential for systemic risk. To this extent, several industry groups, including the Counterparty Credit Risk Management Policy Group and the

3

A related issue is whether the overall structure of financial regulation and supervision in the United States could be changed in a way that would help mitigate systemic risk and improve efficiency. Indeed, as part of its *Blueprint for a Modernized Financial Regulatory Structure*, the Department of the Treasury proposed several legislative changes to the current financial regulatory structure to achieve these goals. The *Blueprint* is an important first step in the longer process of analyzing the broader issues of how financial market regulation and supervision may need to be changed to reflect developments in the markets and recent market turmoil. The Federal Reserve looks forward to working with the Congress as it considers these important issues.

Again, the Federal Reserve appreciates the opportunity to review and comment on the GAO's draft report entitled "Private Equity--Recent Growth in Leveraged Buyouts Exposed Risks That Warrant Continued Attention."

Sincerely,

Randall S. Kroszner
Board of Governors

Institute for International Finance, have issued industry-sponsored sound practices on counterparty credit risk, liquidity risk management, and other areas that, when implemented, should help limit the potential for leveraged lending to contribute to systemic risk in the future.

For a more general discussion of existing and potential methods for addressing systemic risks, see Ben S. Bernanke (2008), "Reducing Systemic Risk," speech delivered at "Maintaining Stability in a Changing Financial System," a symposium sponsored by the Federal Reserve Bank of Kansas City, held in Jackson Hole, Wyo., August 21-23.

APPENDIX XII: COMMENTS FROM THE SECURITIES AND EXCHANGE COMMISSION

CHRISTOPHER COX
CHAIRMAN

HEADQUARTERS
100 F STREET, NE
WASHINGTON, DC 20549

REGIONAL OFFICES
ATLANTA, BOSTON, CHICAGO,
DENVER, FORT WORTH,
LOS ANGELES, MIAMI, NEW YORK,
PHILADELPHIA, SALT LAKE CITY,
SAN FRANCISCO

UNITED STATES
SECURITIES AND EXCHANGE COMMISSION

August 27, 2008

Ms. Orice M. Williams
Director, Financial Markets and Community Investment
United States Government Accountability Office
Washington, DC 20548

Dear Ms. Williams:

We have received and reviewed the draft GAO report "Private Equity: Recent Growth in Leveraged Buyouts Exposed Risks that Warrant Continued Attention" (Report). This Report acknowledges that the leveraged loan market is a relatively small segment of the financial markets, and while leveraged loans are not, per se, systemically important, they nonetheless share similar characteristics to subprime mortgages and structured financial products that could contribute to a systemically significant event. In the Report, you recommend that federal financial regulators give increased attention to insuring their oversight of leveraged lending at their regulated institutions takes into consideration systemic risk implications raised by changes in the broader financial markets.

As you know, since 2004, the U.S. Securities and Exchange Commission has been the consolidated supervisor of certain investment bank holding companies. The Commission currently supervises the following U.S. securities firms on a group-wide basis: Goldman Sachs, Lehman Brothers, Merrill Lynch, and Morgan Stanley. For such firms, referred to as consolidated supervised entities (CSEs), the Commission oversees not only the U.S.-registered broker-dealer, but also supervises the holding company and all affiliates on a consolidated basis, including other regulated entities and unregulated entities such as derivatives dealers. The Commission's supervision of CSEs is primarily concerned with the risks that counterparties and market events potentially pose to the CSE firms and thereby to the regulated broker-dealers and other regulated entities. As such, in its daily oversight of CSEs the Commission is considering and monitoring developments or disruptions in one financial market for its implications for other financial markets and for supervised entities in particular.

In 2005, long before leveraged lending became a risk concern generally, the staff of the CSE program identified leveraged lending by investment banks as a risk concentration. In 2006, the CSE staff conducted an in depth review of leveraged lending practices and exposures at each of the CSEs. This work led to specific changes in certain risk management practices at some firms, and generated feedback on the range of practices that informed all CSEs in their efforts to improve control processes. Thereafter, the CSE staff monitored closely the terms and exposures of leveraged lending pipelines at each of the CSE for its impact on liquidity and funding. In this respect the Commission was diligent about the exposures and risk management of leveraged lending at CSEs.

CHAIRMANOFFICE@SEC.GOV
WWW.SEC.GOV

Ms. Orice M. Williams
Page 2

While the Commission daily endeavors to identify the potential transmission of risk by entities or by markets more broadly, it cannot do so alone. That is why the Commission participates in multilateral groups to identify and address the interconnections among markets and the potential cross currents of risk, some of which may be systemically significant. Specifically, the Commission is an active participant in: the President's Working Group (PWG); Senior Supervisor's Group (SSG); Basel Committee on Bank Supervision (BCBS) and Joint Forum (JF). We also work closely with our supervisory counterparts both domestically and abroad, including the Federal Reserve Board and Federal Reserve Bank of New York, the FDIC and OCC and UK FSA, to name a few.

We shall continue to work closely with our supervisory colleagues to identify and raise awareness about systemically important issues, both in leveraged lending and in the broader financial markets.

We appreciate the opportunity to comment on the draft Report.

Sincerely,

Chris Cox

Christopher Cox
Chairman

APPENDIX XIII: COMMENTS FROM THE OFFICE OF THE COMPTROLLER OF THE CURRENCY

Comptroller of the Currency
Administrator of National Banks

Washington, DC 20219

August 22, 2008

Ms. Orice M. Williams
Director, Financial Markets and Community Investment
United States Government Accountability Office
Washington, DC 20548

Dear Ms. Williams:

We have received and reviewed your draft report entitled, "Private Equity: Recent Growth in Leveraged Buyouts Exposed Risks That Warrant Continued Attention." Your report responds to a Congressional request for information concerning the oversight of private equity-sponsored leveraged buyouts (LBOs).

Among your conclusions, you found that recent credit events raised regulatory scrutiny about risk-management of leveraged lending by banks. You recommended that the federal financial regulators give increased attention to ensuring that their oversight of leveraged lending at their regulated institutions takes into consideration systemic risk implications raised by changes in the broader financial markets as a whole.

The OCC appreciates the importance of the issue raised by the GAO and the increasingly interconnected nature of the financial markets. As noted in the GAO report, this interconnectedness has been revealed by the financial market turmoil of the last year.

As the primary federal regulator for national banks, the OCC is responsible for ensuring national banks operate in a safe and sound manner. This is typically done by assessing risk relative to earnings and capital, and ensuring the quality of risk management systems are commensurate with the complexity and level of the banks' risk profile. Nevertheless, the OCC recognizes the need to monitor systemic risk issues resulting from financial innovation and the interconnectedness of risks and financial markets. Because systemic risk issues, by their very nature, span markets and national boundaries, no one regulator can effectively address systemic risk issues by itself. This is why the OCC is an active member and participant in the following groups: President's Working Group, Senior Supervisors' Group, Basel Committee for Bank Supervision, and Joint Forum. The OCC also collaborates closely with the Federal Reserve Board, and Federal Reserve Bank of New York, on matters that may cause concern to the U.S. financial system.

More specific actions the OCC has taken to address risks from leveraged finance activities conducted by national banks include the following:

- In February of this year, we issued our Leveraged Lending Handbook to bank CEOs and examining personnel. This handbook provided examiners with expanded examination procedures; reinforced existing regulatory guidance issued in 1988, 1999, and 2001; highlighted associated risks; and, provided risk rating and accounting guidance for leveraged lending. When applied consistently across the largest national banks that are the primary participants in the syndicated loan market, such regulatory policies serve to ensure leveraged lending is conducted in a prudential manner.
- In 2008, the OCC conducted a leveraged lending horizontal review at the largest national banks to identify emerging risk issues and risk management practices requiring attention.
- Prior to the commencement of the Shared National Credit (SNC) review for 2008, the OCC and Federal Reserve provided examination staff with clear guidelines that addressed risk identification and risk rating criteria with a focus on both deal performance and underwriting structure. We also worked with the Federal Reserve to promote a consistent risk identification approach to leveraged lending for the 2008 SNC review.
- In 2007 and 2008, the OCC and Federal Reserve collected underwriting data on leveraged syndicated loans reviewed during the annual interagency Shared National Credit review. This data collection provides the OCC and Federal Reserve with specific underwriting characteristics of leveraged loans originated for distribution.
- The OCC conducts and publishes an underwriting survey that, since 2005, has highlighted to industry participants and to examining personnel, weakening underwriting standards.

In summary, the OCC will continue to work closely with other regulators to better understand and address systemic risk issues in the leveraged loan market. As needed, the OCC will issue guidance to banks and examiners to ensure leveraged lending is conducted in a prudential manner across the national banking system.

We appreciate the opportunity to comment on the draft report.

Sincerely,

John C. Dugan
Comptroller of the Currency

-2-

BIBLIOGRAPHY

To analyze what effect the recent wave of private equity-sponsored LBOs has had on the acquired companies and their employment, we reviewed and summarized the following academic articles. Our review of the literature included academic studies of the impact of private equity LBOs, using data from industrialized countries, whose sample periods include

LBOs done from 2000 to the present. We do not include in our bibliography other studies that we reviewed and cited in connection with our other reporting objectives.

Amess, Kevin and Mike Wright. "The Wage and Employment Effects of Leveraged Buyouts in the UK." *International Journal of the Economics of Business*, vol. 14 (2007).

Amess, Kevin and Mike Wright. "Barbarians at the Gate? Leveraged Buyouts, Private Equity, and Jobs." Unpublished working paper (2007).

Andres, Christian, André Betzer and Charlie Weir. "Shareholder Wealth Gains through Better Corporate Governance: The Case of European LBOTransactions." *Financial Markets and Portfolio Management*, vol. 21 (2007).

Bargeron, Leonce, Frederik Schlingemann, Rene M Stulz and Chad Zutter. "Why Do Private Acquirers Pay So Little Compared to Public Acquirers?" National Bureau of Economic Research Working Paper, No. 13061 (2007).

Betzer, André. "Why Private Equity Investors Buy Dear or Cheap in European Leveraged Buyout Transactions." *Kredit und Kapital*, vol. 39, no. 3 (2006).

Cao, Jerry X. "A Study of LBO Premium." Unpublished working paper (Nov. 24, 2007).

Cao, Jerry and Josh Lerner. "The Performance of Reverse Leveraged Buyouts" National Bureau of Economic Research Working Paper, No. 12626 (2006).

Cressy, Robert, Federico Munari and Alessandro Malipiero. "Playing to Their Strengths: Evidence that Specialization in the Private Equity Industry Conveys Competitive Advantage." *Journal of Corporate Finance*, vol. 13 (2007).

Davis, Steven J., Josh Lerner, John Haltiwanger, Javier Miranda and Ron Jarmin. "Private Equity and Employment" in *The Global Economic Impact of Private Equity Report 2008*, ed. Anuradha Gurung and Josh Lerner (Geneva, Switzerland: World Economic Forum, 2008).

Gottschalg, Oliver. *Private Equity and Leveraged Buy-outs,* Study IP/A/ECON/IC/2007-25, European Parliament, Policy Department, Economic and Scientific Policy (2007).

Guo, Shourun, Edith Hotchkiss and Weihong Song. *Do Buyouts (Still) Create Value?* Unpublished working paper (2007).

Lerner, Josh, Morten Sørenson and Per Strömberg. "Private Equity and Long-run Investment: The Case of Innovation." in *The Global Economic Impact of Private Equity Report* 2008, ed. Anuradha Gurung and Josh Lerner (Geneva, Switzerland: World Economic Forum, 2008).

Levis, Mario. *Private Equity Backed IPOs in UK.* Unpublished working paper (2008).

Meuleman, Miguel and Mike Wright. "Industry Concentration, Syndication Networks and Competition in the UK Private Equity Market for Management Buy-Outs." Unpublished working paper (2006).

Renneboog, Luc, Tomas Simons and Mike Wright. "Why Do Public Firms Go Private in the UK? The Impact of Private Equity Investors, Incentive Realignment, and Undervaluation." *Journal of Corporate Finance*, vol. 13 (2007).

Strömberg, Per. "The New Demography of Private Equity" in *The Global Economic Impact of Private Equity Report 2008*, ed. Anuradha Gurung and Josh Lerner (Geneva, Switzerland: World Economic Forum, 2008).

References

[1] Although widely used, the term "private equity" investment has no precise legal or universally accepted definition. Some market participants and observers define private equity narrowly as LBOs; others define it more broadly to include venture capital and other investments. In this report, we focus on private equity funds engaged in LBOs because this activity has been at the center of the recent debate and is the focus of our congressional request.

[2] Typically, a private equity firm: (1) creates an entity, usually a limited partnership, (2) solicits capital from investors in exchange for limited partnership interests in the partnership, and (3) manages the limited partnership (commonly referred to as a private equity fund) as the general partner.

[3] See, e.g., Revlon, Inc. v. MacAndrews & Forbes Holdings, Inc., 506 A.2d 173 (Del. 1986), where the Delaware Supreme Court outlined directors' fiduciary duties under Delaware law in the context of a corporate auction.

[4] In general terms, a tender offer is a broad solicitation by a company or a third party for a limited period of time to purchase a substantial percentage of a company's registered equity shares.

[5] Act of Oct. 15, 1914, ch. 323, § 7A (as added by the Hart-Scott-Rodino Antitrust Improvements Act of 1976, Pub. L. No. 94-435, tit. II, § 201, 90 Stat. 1383, 1390). The required premerger notification and waiting period provides the Federal Trade Commission and Antitrust Division with the opportunity to evaluate the competitive significance of the proposed transaction and to seek a preliminary injunction to prevent the consummation of any transaction which, if consummated, may violate federal antitrust laws.

[6] We compiled a list of the largest private firms using various publicly available sources and had SEC staff verify which of the firms were registered as investment advisers or had affiliates that were registered as investment advisers.

[7] SEC supervision extends to the registered broker-dealer, the unregulated affiliates of the broker-dealer, and the broker-dealer holding company itself—provided that the holding company does not already have a principal regulator. In other words, SEC does not supervise any entities (such as banks, credit unions, or bank holding companies) that are a part of the consolidated supervised entity but otherwise are supervised by a principal regulator.

[8] Deal values were not available for all transactions. The median value is for transactions for which price information was available.

[9] According to Dealogic data, information on whether a private equity-sponsored LBO was hostile was available for 686 private equity buyouts done from 2000 through 2007; of these, none were reported to be hostile. In 299 of the transactions, the target company's board was reported "friendly" to the takeover; in the remainder, the board was reported as "neutral."

[10] A trade journal report recently discussed the possible reemergence of hostile deals. See "Hostile Bids Could Make a Comeback," *Private Equity Analyst,* Dow Jones & Company, Inc. (February 2008).

[11] McKinsey Global Institute, The New Power Brokers: How Oil, Asia, Hedge Funds, and Private Equity Are Shaping the Global Capital Markets (October 2007).

[12] Large syndicated loans may involve one or more lead banks.

[13] No standard definition of leveraged loans exists, but leveraged loans are distinguished from nonleveraged, or investment-grade, loans based on one of two criteria: (1) the borrower's credit rating or (2) the loan's initial interest rate spread over the London Interbank Offered Rate, or LIBOR (the interest rate paid on interbank deposits in the international money markets).

[14] In analyzing exits of LBOs by private equity funds, a recent study found that the most common strategies were sales to a strategic buyer, sales to a financial buyer (e.g., private equity fund), or IPOs. See Steven N. Kaplan and Per Strömberg, "Leveraged Buyouts and Private Equity," draft paper (March 2008).

[15] Our review of the literature included academic studies of the impact of private equity LBOs, using data from industrialized countries, whose sample periods include LBOs done from 2000 to the present. These studies include both published papers (5) and working papers (12), all written between 2006 and 2008. We excluded reports by trade associations, consulting firms, and labor unions in an effort to focus our review on independent research. We also note this review does not include research on the returns to investors (limited partners or general partners) in private equity funds. The studies of the impact of recent private equity-sponsored LBOs we reviewed are listed in the bibliography at the end of the report.

[16] See, for example, Bengt Holmstrom and Steven N. Kaplan, "Corporate Governance and Merger Activity in the United States: Making Sense of the 1980s and 1990s," *Journal of Economic Perspectives* 15, no. 2 (2001), and Mike Wright, Andrew Burrows, Rod Ball, Louise Scholes, Miguel Meuleman, and Kevin Amess, *The Implications of Alternative* Investment Vehicles for Corporate Governance: A Survey of Empirical Research, Report for the OECD Steering Group on Corporate Governance (2007).

[17] In other words, there can be "selection bias"—buyouts are not randomly assigned, as in controlled experiments, where causality is easier to determine. Some studies used statistical techniques to account for the nonrandom nature ("endogeneity") of buyout decisions, but these techniques are imperfect, and most studies do not attempt to account for this endogeneity. These techniques include instrumental variables and Heckmancorrection for sample selection.

[18] Due to similar levels of financial development, studies based on European data should be instructive for understanding U.S. buyouts, although there are some structural differences between the U.S. and European economies. In particular, differences in shareholder rights in continental Europe may lead to differences in LBOs.

[19] Robert Cressy, Federico Munari, and Alessandro Malipiero, "Playing to Their Strengths: Evidence That Specialization in the Private Equity Industry Conveys Competitive Advantage," Journal of Corporate Finance 13 (2007).

[20] These two studies are based on small samples (89 and 63 buyouts, respectively) of the post-buyout performance of private firms where accounting data were available. Shourun Guo, Edith Hotchkiss, and Weihong Song, *Do Buyouts (Still) Create Value?* (unpublished working paper, 2007), and Gottschalg, Oliver, *Private Equity and Leveraged Buy-outs*, Study IP/A/ECON/IC/2007-25, European Parliament, Policy Department, Economic and Scientific Policy (2007).

[21] Josh Lerner, Morten Sørenson, and Per Strömberg, "Private Equity and Long-run Investment: The Case of Innovation," in The Global Economic Impact of Private Equity *Report 2008*, ed. Anuradha Gurung and Josh Lerner (Geneva, Switzerland: World Economic Forum, 2008).

[22] Jerry Cao and Josh Lerner, "The Performance of Reverse Leveraged Buyouts," National Bureau of Economic Research Working Paper No. 12626 (2006).

[23] Highlighting the difference between first-day returns and the longer term performance of IPOs can differentiate initial under-pricing of the IPO from the long-run performance of the company. Mario Levis, *Private Equity Backed IPOs in UK* (unpublished working paper, 2008).

[24] Even after a public-to-private acquisition, a company may still make securities filings—for instance, if it has publicly traded debt securities.

[25] Strömberg, Per, "The New Demography of Private Equity" in *The Global Economic Impact of Private Equity Report 2008*, ed. Anuradha Gurung and Josh Lerner (Geneva, Switzerland: World Economic Forum, 2008).

[26] See, for example, Jensen, Michael C., "Agency Costs of Free Cash Flow, Corporate Finance, and Takeovers," *American Economic Review* 76, no. 2 (1986): 323-329, and Holmstrom and Kaplan (2001).

[27] Greater debt also provides tax benefits, via deductibility of interest payments, which should enhance value for firm owners but may not result in aggregate economic benefits because of the transfer of revenue from the government to the firm and the distortion of economic incentives for financing the firm with debt versus equity.

[28] In a perfectly competitive market, potential buyers would bid up to their willingness to pay for the target.

[29] Luc Renneboog, Tomas Simons, and Mike Wright, "Why Do Public Firms Go Private in the UK? The Impact of Private Equity Investors, Incentive Realignment, and Undervaluation," Journal of Corporate Finance 13 (2007).

[30] Concentrated external shareholders such as institutional investors should have incentives to monitor performance similar to internal managers with large equity stakes. See, for example, Jay C. Hartzell and Laura T. Starks, "Institutional Investors and Executive Compensation," *Journal of Finance* 58, no. 6 (2003). Betzer, André, "Why Private Equity Investors Buy Dear or Cheap in European Leveraged Buyout Transactions," *Kredit und Kapital* 39, no. 3 (2006). Christian Andres, André Betzer, and Charlie Weir, "Shareholder Wealth Gains Through Better Corporate Governance: The Case of European LBOtransactions," Financial Markets and Portfolio Management 21 (2007).

[31] The premium is measured relative to the share price on the day prior to the deal announcement. Jerry X. Cao, *A Study of LBO Premium* (unpublished working paper, Nov. 24, 2007).

[32] The premium is measured relative to the share price on the day prior to the deal announcement.

[33] However, default risk decreased for target firms whose debt was already poorly rated. "Default and Migration Rates for Private Equity-Sponsored Issuers," Special Comment, Moody's Investors Service (November 2006).

[34] One study of U.S. corporate ownership supports the view that private owners have a longer time horizon than public owners. In particular, the study found that private

equity funds have longer holding periods than "blockholders" (external shareholders in public firms who have more than a 5 percent stake), with 88 percent of blockholders selling after 5 years, but only 55 percent of private equity firms selling after 5 years. Gottschalg (2007).

[35] Andrew Metrick and Ayako Yasuda, "The Economics of Private Equity Funds," Wharton School, University of Pennsylvania (2007).

[36] Kevin Amess and Mike Wright, "The Wage and Employment Effects of Leveraged Buyouts in the UK," International Journal of the Economics of Business 14 (2007).

[37] See Steven Kaplan, "The Effects of Management Buyouts on Operating Performance and Value," *Journal of Financial Economics* 24 (1989) and Frank R. Lichtenberg and Donald Siegel, "The Effects of Leveraged Buyouts on Productivity and Related Aspects of Firm Behavior," Journal of Financial Economics 27 (1990).

[38] The authors describe establishments as "specific factories, offices, retail outlets and other distinct physical locations where business takes place." The lower job growth, relative to peers, results primarily from differences in layoffs, as new hiring is similar between private equity and nonprivate equity establishments. Steven J. Davis, Josh Lerner, John Haltiwanger, Javier Miranda, and Ron Jarmin, "Private Equity and Employment" in *The* Global Economic Impact of Private Equity Report 2008, ed. Anuradha Gurung and Josh Lerner (Geneva, Switzerland: World Economic Forum, 2008).

[39] Lower employment growth at private equity controlled firms may shift employment to other firms and sectors of the economy, rather than reducing the overall level of employment in the economy. However, economic theory suggests that a greater willingness to restructure firms could result in temporary "frictional unemployment," as people moved from job to job more often, or more permanent "structural unemployment," if rapid innovation increased the rate at which certain job skills became obsolete. One expert we interviewed suggested that the unemployment resulting from any job losses was likely to be temporary in nature.

[40] Furthermore, as one survey of the private equity academic literature noted, "it cannot be assumed that the pre-buyout employment levels would have been sustainable." Wright et al. (2007).

[41] Venture capital firms have long pursued a similar strategy. Venture capital firms are similar to private equity firms, but they typically invest in early stage companies (whereas private equity firms invest in more established companies) and acquire less than a controlling position (whereas private equity firms typically buy all of, or a controlling position in, the target company).

[42] One study rejects such "benign rationales" for club deals. See Micah S. Officer, Oguzhan Ozbas, and Berk A. Sensoy, *Club Deals in Leveraged Buyouts* (unpublished working paper, June 2008). The authors state that while club deals are larger on average than solesponsor LBOs, only about 19 percent of club deals are larger than the largest single-firm deal conducted by any of the club members in a 4-year window around the club deal announcement date. In addition, they state that club deal targets do not appear to be systematically more risky than target companies of single-firm deals. "These facts suggest that capital constraints or diversification returns are unlikely to be [the major] motivations for club deals." But, see also footnote 51, for a discussion of limitations of this study.

[43] The less common way, known as "proprietary" deals, is when the buyer and seller negotiate with each other on an exclusive basis. Such deals might arise, for example, from relationships developed between the parties over time. Private equity executives told us that they maintain regular contacts with companies of interest, even if the companies are not immediately available for sale. Through such contacts, a private equity firm might learn of a sale opportunity, and then pursue it with the target company.

[44] Although some auction deals have included go-shop provisions, they are more common with proprietary deals. There is some skepticism about the value of go-shop provisions; for a discussion, see Sautter, Christina M., "Shopping During Extended Store Hours: From No Shops to Go-Shops," *Brooklyn Law Review* 73, no. 2 (2008).

[45] For academic research describing this process, see Audra L. Boone and J. Harold Mulherin, Do Private Equity Consortiums Impede Takeover Competition? (unpublished working paper, March 2008). According to the authors' analysis, in takeovers in which a single private equity firm is the winning bidder, the target company, on average, contacts 32 potential bidders, signs confidentiality agreements with 13 potential bidders, receives indications of interest from roughly 4 bidders, receives binding private offers from 1.5 bidders, and receives formal public offers from 1.1 bidders.

[46] An econometric model seeks to mathematically examine relationships among variables and the degree to which changes in "explanatory" variables are associated with changes in a "dependent" variable, or variable under study—here, price paid for a buyout, as measured by premium paid over stock price. Explanatory variables are factors included in the analysis to adjust for differences among the subjects being studied. While an econometric model can measure associations between variables, it cannot by itself establish causation—that is, the extent to which changes in the explanatory variables cause changes in the variable under study.

[47] Our analysis is based on data compiled for approximately 325 public companies acquired by private equity firms from 1998 through 2007 for which premium information was available. The data also permitted us to include several transactions occurring in early 2008. The data are from Dealogic, Audit Analytics, and company filings with SEC. To address potential bias in our estimates due to differences between club deals and nonclub deals, we used Heckman's two-stage modeling approach. See appendix X for a more complete discussion of our econometric approach, including model specification, variables used, data sources, estimation techniques, and limitations. In focusing on prices paid for target companies, the analysis did not examine individual deals for specific evidence of anticompetitive behavior.

[48] Differences in the premium at different intervals before announcement may result from "information leakage." In general, the buyout premium may be lower closer to the date of the announcement because of speculation that a deal is imminent or word of a transaction has leaked out. In such cases, the stock price will adjust to reflect the takeover possibility. When a single private equity firm engages in a buyout, it may be easier to keep the transaction confidential until the time of the announcement. It may be harder to keep a transaction confidential when two or more private equity firms are involved. Because price leakage may be more likely for club deals, there may be greater variance in premium at the 1-month point before the announcement.

[49] The notable exception to this is our sensitivity test where we drop small deals from the sample. In these models, we find a positive statistically significant association between club deals and the premium.

[50] See, for example, Boone and Mulherin. The authors state: "A striking result…is that private equity consortiums are…associated with above-average levels of takeover competition. Indeed, the level of competition in deals in which private equity consortiums are the winning bidders is as great or greater than that for single private equity deals. Although the formation of a consortium would appear to arithmetically reduce the level of competition, the use of consortiums actually is associated with more bidding than the average deal. [T]he data indicate that consortiums are a competitive response by private equity firms when bidding for larger targets."

[51] See Officer et al. The sample studied included 198 private equity transactions, of which 59 were club deals. The authors find that 35 deals prior to 2006 drive the negative price impact. The authors selected club deals after identifying leading private equity firms through *Private Equity International* magazine and other sources. To the extent this selection method categorizes a significant number of private equity firms' buyouts—whether club deals or single-firm deals—as buyouts by other private firms, there could be measurement error introduced into the model. Also, because the study bases its selection of transactions on the activities of leading private equity firms, its sample is likely unrepresentative of the entire population.

[52] Our results also suggests—as relating to which target companies are more likely to be acquired through a club deal—that large companies, companies with lower debt ratios and, controlling for size, companies that do not trade on the New York Stock Exchange had a greater probability of being taken private in a joint acquisition.

[53] An "oligopoly" is generally defined as a market that is dominated by a small number of relatively large firms. A tight oligopoly is generally defined as a market in which four providers hold over 60 percent of the market and other firms face significant barriers to entry into the market.

[54] For example, if there were 10 companies in a marketplace, and each held a 10 percent share of the market, the index value would be 1,000—for an individual company, the market share of 10 percent, when squared, is 100; summing the values for all 10 participants would yield an index value of 1,000.

[55] See, for example, "Private-Equity Firms Face Anticompetitive Probe; U.S.'s Informal Inquiries Have Gone to Major Players Such as KKR, Silver Lake," *Wall Street Journal* (eastern edition), Oct. 10, 2006, A3, and "Merrill Arm Draws U.S. Questions In Informal Probe of Private Equity," *Wall Street Journal* (eastern edition), Nov. 6, 2006, A9.

[56] *See Pennsylvania Avenue Funds v. Borey*, No. C06-1737RAJ (W.D. Wash. Nov. 15, 2006); Murphy, et al. v. Kohlberg Kravis Roberts & Co. (KKR) et al., No. 06-cv-13210-LLS (S.D.N.Y. Nov. 15, 2006). *Murphy v. KKR* was voluntarily dismissed by the plaintiff. In *Pennsylvania Avenue Funds v. Borey*, the federal district court dismissed the antitrust claim for failure to state a claim under the Sherman Act. The court concluded that the plaintiffs had failed to make allegations from which the court could reasonably infer that the defendant private equity firms had market power, either in the private equity marketplace at large or more narrowly in the marketplace for acquiring the target company.

[57] *See Davidson v. Bain Capital Partners, LLC*, No. 07-CV-12388 (D. Mass. Dec. 28, 2007); *Dahl v. Bain Capital Partners, LLC*, No. 08-CV-10254 (D. Mass. Feb. 14, 2008). The two cases have been consolidated under No. 07-CV-12388.

[58] Some private equity funds are organized as limited liability companies and occasionally as corporations.

[59] Private equity funds typically rely on one of two exclusions from the definition of an investment company under the Investment Company Act of 1940 (Investment Company Act). First, section 3(c)(1) of the Investment Company Act excludes from the definition of investment company any issuer (1) whose outstanding securities (other than short-term paper) are beneficially owned by not more than 100 investors and (2) that is not making, and does not presently propose to make, a public offering of its securities. 15 U.S.C. § 80a- 3c(1). Second, section 3(c)(7) of the Investment Company Act excludes from the definition of investment company any issuer (1) whose outstanding securities are owned exclusively by persons who, at the time of acquisition of such securities, are "qualified purchasers" and (2) that is not making, and does not at that time propose to make, a public offering of its securities. 15 U.S.C. § 80a-3(c)(7). Qualified purchasers include individuals who own at least $5 million in investments or companies that own at least $25 million worth of investments. 15 U.S.C. § 80a-2(a)(51). Private equity advisers typically satisfy the "private manager" exemption from registration as an investment adviser under section 203(b)(3) of the Investment Advisers Act of 1940 (Advisers Act). This section exempts from SEC registration requirements investment advisers (1) that have had less than 15 clients during the preceding 12 months, (2) do not hold themselves out generally to the public as an investment adviser, and (3) are not an investment adviser to a registered investment company. 15 U.S.C. § 80b-3.

[60] *See* 15 U.S.C. § 80b-6. In 2007, SEC adopted a rule designed to clarify its ability to bring enforcement actions against unregistered advisers that defraud investors or prospective investors in a pooled investment vehicle, including a private equity fund. *See Prohibition of* Fraud by Advisers to Certain Pooled Investment Vehicles, 72 Fed. Reg. 44756 (Aug. 9, 2007) (final rule) (to be codified at 17 C.F.R. § 275.206(4)-8).

[61] Under the Securities Act of 1933, a public offering or sale of securities must be registered with SEC, unless otherwise exempt. To exempt from registration the offering or sale of partnership interests of private equity funds to investors, private equity funds generally restrict the sale of their partnership interests to accredited investors in compliance with the safe harbor conditions of Rule 506 of Regulation D. 15 U.S.C. § 77d and § 77e; 17 C.F.R. § 230.506 (2007). Accredited investors must meet certain wealth and income thresholds and include institutional investors such as banks, broker-dealers, insurance companies, and pension funds, as well as wealthy individuals.

[62] *See* 15 U.S.C. § 80a-2(a)(48). Generally, eligible portfolio companies are domestic companies that (1) are not investment companies under the Investment Company Act and (2) do not have their securities listed on a national securities exchange or have their securities listed on a national exchange and a market capitalization of less than $250 million. 15 U.S.C. § 80(a)(46); 17 C.F.R. § 270.2a-46 (2008).

[63] *See* 15 U.S.C. §§ 80a-55 – 80a-62. The Small Business Investment Incentive Act of 1980, Pub. L. No. 96-477, tit. I., 94 Stat. 2278, among other things, amended the Investment Company Act to establish a new system of regulation for business

development companies as a means of making capital more readily available to small, developing and financially troubled companies that do not have access to the public capital markets or other forms of conventional financing.

[64] McKinsey Global Institute, The New Power Brokers: How Oil, Asia, Hedge Funds, and Private Equity Are Shaping the Global Capital Markets (October 2007).

[65] Routine examinations are conducted based on the registrant's perceived risk. SEC staff seek to examine all firms considered higher risk once every 3 years. SEC staff select a random sample of firms designated as lower-risk to routinely examine each year. During a routine examination, SEC staff assess a firm's process for assessing and controlling compliance risks. Based on that assessment, examiners assign advisers a risk rating to indicate whether they are at higher or lower risk for experiencing compliance problems.

[66] We did not review two examinations because SEC staff did not prepare reports for these examinations, which covered one firm. According to SEC staff, the agency has staff monitoring that firm on an ongoing basis, but the staff do not prepare reports after completing their examination work.

[67] In a sweep examination, SEC staff probe specific activities of a sample of firms to identify emerging compliance problems. SEC staff conduct cause examinations when they have reason to believe something is wrong at a particular firm.

[68] SEC staff said that a separate report was not prepared for one of the sweep examinations, since it was part of a larger review.

[69] See Registration under the Advisers Act of Certain Hedge Fund Advisers, 69 Fed. Reg. 72087 (Dec. 10, 2004). In June 2006, a federal court vacated the rule. See *Goldstein v.* Securities and Exchange Commission, 451 F.3d 873 (D.C. Cir. 2006).

[70] GAO, Defined Benefit Pension Plans: Guidance Needed to Better Inform Plans of the Challenges and Risks of Investing in Hedge Funds and Private Equity, GAO-08-692 (Washington, D.C.: Aug. 14, 2008).

[71] IOSCO is an international organization that brings together the regulators of the world's securities and futures markets. IOSCO and its sister organizations, the Basel Committee on Banking Supervision and the International Association of Insurance Supervisors, make up the Joint Forum of international financial regulators.

[72] FSA stated that it is not just at the time a private equity transaction is arranged that access to inside information is an issue. Participation in the debt components of a leveraged finance structure can give access to significant amounts of data about the ongoing performance of the company—potentially price-sensitive information. According to FSA, trading in any related instruments could make them vulnerable to committing market abuse if price-sensitive information forms the basis of the decision to trade.

[73] Banks also may agree to provide bridge loans, which serve to provide temporary financing, until longer term financing can be put in place. For example, a private equity fund may use a bridge loan to help finance an LBO, until it can complete a bond offering.

[74] In addition to bank loans, private equity firms may use high-yield bonds or "mezzanine" debt to help finance their LBOs. High-yield bonds are debt securities issued by companies with lower-than-investment grade ratings. Mezzanine debt is a middle level of financing in LBOs—below bank debt and above equity capital.

[75] Dealogic defines leveraged loans as loans for borrowers rated BB+ or below by Standard and Poor's or Ba1 or below by Moody's. In the case of a split rating or unrated borrower, pricing at signing is used. Loans with a margin of (1) between and including 150 and 249 basis points over LIBOR are classified as leveraged and (2) 250 basis points or more in the U.S. market are classified as highly leveraged.

[76] The term "highly leveraged transactions" generally was defined as a type of financing that involves the restructuring of an ongoing business concern financed primarily with debt. In 1990, the Federal Reserve required banks to report data on their highly leveraged transactions, but the definition and reporting requirement were eliminated in 1992. According to federal banking regulators, the definition achieved its purposes of focusing attention on the need for banks to have strong internal controls for highly leveraged transactions and structure such credits consistent with their risks. The regulators said that they would continue to scrutinize the transactions in their examinations.

[77] OCC, Federal Reserve, the Federal Deposit Insurance Corporation, and Office of Thrift Supervision, "Interagency Statement on Sound Risk Management Practices for Leveraged Financing," April 9, 2001. Subsequently, in February 2008, OCC updated its handbook on leveraged lending, which summarizes leveraged lending risks, discusses how a bank can manage the risks, and incorporates previous OCC guidance on the subject.

[78] The Bank Holding Company Act of 1956, as amended, generally requires that holding companies with bank subsidiaries register with the Federal Reserve as bank holding companies. The act generally restricts the activities of bank holding companies to those that the Federal Reserve determined, as of November 11, 1999, to be closely related to banking. Under amendments to the act made by the Gramm-Leach-Bliley Act, a bank holding company that qualifies as a financial holding company may engage in a broad range of additional financial activities, such as full-scope securities, insurance underwriting and merchant banking.

[79] Loan covenants enable lenders to preserve and exercise rights over collateral value, initiate and manage appropriate courses of action on a timely basis, and provide lenders with negotiating leverage when the loans do not perform as expected. "Incurrence" covenants generally require that if a borrower takes a specified action (such as paying a dividend or taking on more debt), it must be in compliance with some specified requirement (such as a minimum debt-to-cash flow ratio). "Maintenance" covenants are more restrictive than incurrence covenants and require a borrower to meet certain financial tests continually, whether the borrower takes an action. If a borrower fails to comply with loan covenants, it would be in technical default on the loan.

[80] The Shared National Credit Program was established in 1977 by the Federal Reserve, Federal Deposit Insurance Corporation, and OCC to provide an efficient and consistent review and classification of any large syndicated loan. The program covers any loan or loan commitment of at least $20 million that is shared by three or more supervised institutions.

[81] Board of Governors of the Federal Reserve System, Joint Press Release: Shared National Credit Results Reflect Large Increase in Credit Commitment Volume, and Satisfactory Credit Quality (Sept. 25, 2007) at http://www.federalreserve.gov/newsevents/press/bcreg/20070925a.htm.

[82] OCC has been surveying the largest national banks (73 banks in 2006 and 78 banks in 2007) for the past 13 years to identify trends in lending standards and credit risk for the most common types of commercial and retail credits. The survey also includes a set of questions directed at the OCC Examiners-in-Charge of the surveyed banks.

[83] The Federal Reserve generally conducts the survey quarterly, which covers a sample selected from the largest banks in each Federal Reserve district. Questions cover changes in the standards and terms of the banks' lending and the state of business and household demand for loans. The survey often includes questions on one or two other topics of current interest.

[84] If a broker-dealer and its ultimate holding company consent to be supervised on a consolidated basis by SEC, the broker-dealer may use an alternative method of calculating its net capital requirement. See 17 C.F.R. § 240.15c3-1 (2007). Generally, this alternative method, the result of a recent amendment to the SEC net capital rule, permits a brokerdealer to use certain mathematical models to calculate net capital requirements for market and derivative-related credit risk. The amendments to SEC's standard net capital rule, among other things, respond to international developments. According to SEC, some U.S. broker-dealers expressed concern that unless the firms can demonstrate that they are subject to consolidated supervision that is "equivalent" to that of the European Union (EU), then their affiliate institutions located in the EU may be subject to more stringent net capital computations or be required to form a subholding company. *See Alternative Net* Capital Requirements for Broker-Dealers that Are Part of Consolidated Supervised *Entities*, 69 *Fed. Reg*. 34428, 34429 (June 21, 2004) (final rule). For a description of the CSE program, see SEC Holding Company Supervision Program Description at www.sec.gov/divisions/marketreg/hcsupervision.htm.

[85] GAO, Financial Market Regulation: Agencies Engaged in Consolidated Supervision Can Strengthen Performance Measurement Collaboration, GAO-07-154 (Washington, D.C.: March 15, 2007).

[86] Basel regulatory capital standards were developed by the Basel Committee on Banking Supervision, which consists of central bank and regulatory officials from 13 member countries. The standards aim to align minimum capital requirements with enhanced risk measurement techniques and to encourage internationally active banks to develop a more disciplined approach to risk management.

[87] The share of a syndicated loan held by a bank varies from deal to deal, but the major banks generally have a target of holding 10 percent or less of each leveraged loans they arrange and underwrite, according to regulators and bank officials.

[88] A collateralized loan obligation is an asset-backed security that is usually supported by a variety of assets, including whole commercial loans, revolving credit facilities, letters of credit, or other asset-backed securities. In a typical transaction, the sponsoring banking organization transfers the loans and other assets to a bankruptcy-remote special purpose vehicle, which then issues asset-backed securities consisting of one or more classes of debt. This type of transaction represents a "cash flow collateralized loan obligation."

[89] Syndicated leveraged loans issued to finance LBOs generally include a revolver, term loan A (amortizing term loan), and term loan B (a term loan that typically carries a longer maturity and slower amortization than term loan A). The revolver and term loan

A often are packaged together, called the pro rata tranche, and syndicated primarily to banks, as well as nonbank institutions. Term loan B, called the institutional tranche, is syndicated typically to nonbank institutions.

[90] In general, when a commercial bank funds a leveraged loan, it will record (1) the portion that it plans to retain as a loan held for investment and (2) the portion that it plans to sell as a loan held for sale. Held-for-investment loans are recorded at their amortized cost less any impairment. Held-for-sale loans are recorded at the lower of cost or market value. When an investment bank funds a leveraged loan, it generally will record the loan at fair value (such as based on a quoted market price). According to SEC staff, starting in the third quarter of 2007, as it became apparent that those commitments that had not yet closed would not be able to be distributed at par, the investment banks had write downs not only on the closed loans but also on the unfunded commitments.

[91] An analysis by Moody's found that LBOs sponsored by private equity firms generally were associated with an increase in default risk, but default risk decreased for target firms whose debt was already poorly rated. "Default and Migration Rates for Private Equity- Sponsored Issuers." Special Comment, Moody's Investors Service (November 2006).

[92] See President's Working Group on Financial Markets, *Policy Statement on Financial Market Developments* (March 13, 2008). PWG was established by Executive Order 12631, signed on March 18, 1988. The Secretary of the Treasury chairs PWG, the other members of which are the Chairpersons of the Board of Governors of the Federal Reserve System, SEC, and Commodity Futures Trading Commission. The group was formed in 1988 to enhance the integrity, efficiency, orderliness, and competitiveness of the U.S. financial markets and maintain the public's confidence in those markets.

[93] We identified club deals as private equity buyouts with at least two private equity firms participating in an acquisition, and with at least one of the two firms participating on an "entry" basis—that is, making an initial investment in the target company.

[94] IOSCO is an international organization that brings together the regulators of the world's securities and futures markets. IOSCO and its sister organizations, the Basel Committee on Banking Supervision and the International Association of Insurance Supervisors, make up the Joint Forum of international financial regulators.

[95] PWG was established by Executive Order 12631, signed on March 18, 1988. The Secretary of the Treasury chairs PWG, the other members of which are the chairpersons of the Board of Governors of the Federal Reserve System, SEC, and Commodity Futures Trading Commission. The group was formed in 1988 to enhance the integrity, efficiency, orderliness, and competitiveness of the U.S. financial markets and maintain the public's confidence in those markets.

[96] The Senior Supervisors Group is composed of eight supervisory agencies: France's Banking Commission, Germany's Federal Financial Supervisory Authority, the Swiss Federal Banking Commission, the Financial Services Authority, the Board of Governors of the Federal Reserve System, FRBNY, OCC, and SEC.

[97] GAO-08-692.

[98] We reviewed data from surveys of defined benefit pension plans conducted by three organizations: (1) Greenwich Associates, covering midsize to large-size pension plans with $250 million or more in total assets; (2) Pyramis Global Advisors, covering

midsize to largesize pension plans with $200 million or more in total assets; and (3) *Pensions & Investments*, limited to large plans that generally had $1 billion or more in total assets. Greenwich Associates is an institutional financial services consulting and research firm; Pyramis Global Advisors, a division of Fidelity Investments, is an institutional asset management firm; and *Pensions & Investments* is a money management industry publication. These data cannot be generalized to all plans.

[99] The figures reported by these surveys differ somewhat because they are based on different samples. Comprehensive data on plan investments in private equity are not available. The federal government collects information on investment allocations but does not require plan sponsors to report such information on private equity as a separate asset class.

[100] According to the Pension Benefits Guaranty Corporation, individual defined benefit plans with less than $200 million in total assets comprised about 15 percent of the total assets of all such plans in 2005.

[101] *Pensions & Investments* was the only survey GAO reviewed that reported the allocations of individual plans to private equity. Among the top 200 pension plans, ranked by combined assets in defined benefit and defined contribution plans, 133 were defined benefit plans that completed the survey and provided asset allocation information in 2007.

[102] Private equity firms can also receive other fees, such as monitoring fees for providing acquired companies with management, consulting, and other services, or transaction fees for providing acquired companies with financial advisory and other services in connection with specific transactions.

[103] Some private equity funds are organized as limited liability companies, but the tax characteristics of partnerships and limited liability companies can be the same.

[104] By contrast, income earned by a corporation is subject to two layers of federal income tax—once at the corporate level, and again at the shareholder level if dividends are paid.

[105] A related income and taxation issue is treatment of this initial grant of a "profits interest." Under current law, the grant of carried interest is not a taxable event, provided that certain conditions are satisfied. Under proposed Treasury regulations, a partnership and its partners could elect to use a safe harbor, under which the fair market value of a partnership interest that is transferred in connection with the performance of services is treated as being equal to liquidation value of the interest transferred. Thus, because the liquidation value of a profits interest on the date of its issuance is zero, the fair market value of carried interest at the time of its issuance would be zero.

[106] The discussion in this report of the tax treatment of private equity firms' compensation is summary in nature. For fuller discussion and analysis, see, *inter alia*: "The Taxation of Carried Interest," testimony of Peter R. Orszag, director, Congressional Budget Office, before the Committee on Ways and Means, U.S. House of Representatives, September 6, 2007; "Present Law and Analysis Relating to Tax Treatment of Partnership Carried Interests and Related Issues, Part I," prepared by the staff of the Joint Committee on Taxation, also for the September 6 hearing before the Committee on Ways and Means; "Two and Twenty: Taxing Partnership Profits in Private Equity Funds," working paper by Victor Fleischer, associate professor, University of Illinois

College of Law; and testimony of Eric Solomon, assistant secretary for tax policy, U.S. Treasury Department, before the Committee on Finance, U.S. Senate, July 11, 2007.

[107] A related, but separate, tax issue for private equity that has drawn criticism is deductibility of interest as a business expense. Interest payments are generally deductible as expenses, and critics, such as labor unions, say that given the significant amount of debt used to finance private equity buyouts, the interest deduction is a concern. We note, but do not address, this issue.

[108] Tax avoidance, which is legal, is distinct from tax evasion, which is not, whereby a taxpayer intentionally avoids true tax liability. Tax avoidance, while legal, is nevertheless a concern to some because it can lead to inefficiencies, as entities undertake transactions they would not otherwise make if not for the tax advantages.

[109] This bill would also make a number of changes across the tax spectrum, including modifying the standard deduction, reducing the top marginal tax rate for corporations, and eliminating the alternative minimum tax for individuals.

[110] Publicly traded partnerships are generally treated as corporations for tax purposes and are subject to the corporate income tax. The primary exception to this rule is that partnerships that derive at least 90 percent of their income from passive investments and which, therefore, are not required to register as investment companies under the Investment Company Act of 1940, do not pay the corporate tax.

[111] This approach would involve altering IRS Rev. Proc. 93-27.

[112] Although our analysis focuses on the 1998-2007 period, we also included several transactions occurring in early 2008 because such data was available in Dealogic.

[113] Because we hand-collected the data from company filings in the EDGAR database, and some companies report statistics differently, we discuss the possible impact of random error below.

[114] J. Heckman, "The Common Structure of Statistical Models of Truncation, Sample Selection, and Limited Dependent Variables and a Simple Estimator for Such Models," Annals of Economic and Social Measurement 5 (1976).

[115] The inverse Mills ratio is calculated (using the residuals from the Probit model) as the ratio of the probability density function (PDF) over the cumulative distribution function (CDF). The distributional assumption of the error term is the standard normal distribution; therefore, the ratio of the standard normal PDF and CDF applied to the residuals for each transaction in the data set is created. The inclusion of this quantity in the OLS regression mitigates the potential bias in estimates due to the absence of a variable that captures potential differences in the companies that would warrant a different premium even if multiple equity firms did not participate in some buyouts.

[116] For more information see J. Johnston and Dinardo, *Econometric Methods*, 4th edition, 447- 450. See also R. J. Willis and S. Rosen, "Education and self-selection," *The Journal of* Political Economy 87, no. 5 (1979).

[117] L. Renneboog et al. (2007) 609.

[118] This must be balanced against our treatment of clubs deals in the calculating of market shares for each firm—the total value of a given club deal was split equally among participating private equity firms. Apportioning deal value equally among private equity firms in a club deal may bias market share estimates downward because some participants in the joint transaction actually commit less capital than other private equity firms in some deals.

In: Private Equity and its Impact
Editor: Spencer J. Fritz, pp. 101-159

ISBN: 978-1-60692-682-6

Chapter 2

PRIVATE EQUITY'S EFFECTS ON WORKERS AND FIRMS, HEARING BEFORE THE COMMITTEE ON FINANCIAL SERVICES, U.S. HOUSE OF REPRESENTATIVES, MAY 16, 2007

U.S. Government Printing Office

The committee met, pursuant to notice, at 10 a.m., in room 2128, Rayburn House Office Building, Hon. Barney Frank [chairman of the committee] presiding.

Present: Representatives Frank, Waters, Maloney, Watt, Meeks, Moore of Kansas, Hinojosa, Clay, McCarthy, Baca, Lynch, Scott, Cleaver, Moore of Wisconsin, Davis of Tennessee, Klein, Wilson, Perlmutter, Boren; Bachus, Bak er, Pryce, Castle, Royce, Gillmor, Manzullo, Shays, Feeney, Hensarling, Barrett, Pearce, Neugebauer, Roskam, and Marchant.

The CHAIRMAN. This hearing of the Committee on Financial Services will come to order.

The subject of today's hearing is the question of private equity and specifically the effect that purchases of existing companies by private equity has on the workers and on the firms. There have been a number of concerns expressed about various new forms of activity in the economy, and this committee has had some hearings, and will have more, on the question of hedge funds.

Today, we are talking very specifically about private equity and one special area of concern. I will say, in general that I have not seen any argument that it is a matter for which public policy ought to be concerned as to whether people choose to own a company through a public shareholder method or privately. That seems to me to be a decision that ought to be left entirely up to the people who are making the investments, but we do have concerns about the impact on workers.

The committee, myself and many others, have been concerned for some time about increasing inequality in America. A year ago, we were debating the question about whether wages, real wages, were seriously lagging growth. We were debating inequality. That debate is largely over. There is general agreement that we have increasing inequality and that real wages have, in fact, lagged. There was a period earlier this year when they began to go up.

That is now once again in jeopardy. I find the situation in which this country prospers overall, but the increased wealth is enjoyed by a relatively small number of people, to be troubling. It is morally wrong because it takes the efforts of most people to produce that wealth, and it should be shared fairly. No one is talking about equality. We are talking about degrees of inequality. I believe that the case for being concerned about this excessive inequality goes beyond moral considerations.

There is a big debate in this country now about immigration. There is a debate about trade. We are engaged in the question about how welcoming we should be to foreign investment, direct foreign investment. As more and more Americans have become convinced that economic growth, globalization, and technological change do them very little good, and in some cases, harm, you have seen increasing resistance to the kind of public policies that many in the business community believe are in the interest of economic growth, and until we are able to diminish this trend of increasing inequality, I believe that resistance will grow.

Now, with regard to private equity, I assume that the market is rational and that the private equity method increases value. I do not think people make deals in large numbers for no good reason. The question we have is does any of that increased value accrue to the people who work for the companies. Conversely, there is the fear that, to the extent that private equity is accompanied by significant increases in debt in some cases, this may have a negative effect on workers.

Now, what goes into some of the other concerns we have had in terms of compensation—and we are talking here not about compensation paid by shareholders, which is a matter we dealt with elsewhere, but the compensation that some individuals get when a small number of individuals benefit from a particular deal in the tens and sometimes hundreds of millions of dollars, and, concurrently, workers are laid off. We have a situation which seems, to me, wrong. Now the question then is, well, what are we going to do about it?

It is not clear. There may or may not be public policy implications, but to the extent that there are public policies that have an effect on the private equity situation, some of which would come before this committee, some which would deal with taxation which would come before other committees, and to the extent that we see gross imbalances, then we are going to have to act.

As an example of that, I would ask to put into the record the article from today's New York Times with the headline, ''Unkind Cut For Janitors At Hilfiger,'' which says that one consequence of a $1.6 billion buyout of Tommy Hilfiger is that janitors making $19 an hour were fired to be replaced by janitors making $8 an hour. The Hilfiger Company was bought for $1.6 billion. Janitors show up to work, and they make $19 an hour, union wages. They are fired, and they are going to be replaced by people getting $8 an hour. Mr. Hilfiger got $66 million as the result of the sale and will get $14.5 million a year through 2010. Workers in their 40's and 50's have been laid off with 1 day's notice.

I do not know, as I said, whether public policy can do anything about that, but I do know that this is the sort of pattern that will make many of us determined to do something. So the point is a very simple one. If we have a situation, private equity, where enormous values are created, as apparently they are, and if only a few people get these large sums of money, and the workers are either no better off or worse off, then from a public policy standpoint that seems to me to be undesirable. Whether or not there are public policy remedies is the second question, but the first question I want to focus on today is whether there is such a pattern.

I must say, and let me say in closing, that in many of the areas of private equity, we are talking about hotel workers; we are talking about service employees in buildings; we are talking about janitors. These are not people who are competing with low-wage workers elsewhere. These are people serving in very low-wage capacities in a market that cannot move.

I think America can do better. Whether or not there should be a public policy response, we will find out, but we might find out with respect to policies involving unionization, taxation, and elsewhere. But the question remains, does the way in which private equity deals go forward exacerbate what is already an unfortunate trend in America for growth to go forward, for wealth to increase, but for inequality to increase even faster.

The CHAIRMAN. The gentleman from Alabama.

Mr. BACHUS. Thank you, Chairman Frank, for holding this hearing.

This is the second hearing the committee has held on alternative investment vehicles, and, of course, this hearing is on private equity industry. Private equity is not a new phenomenon. It has been used, at least with some frequency, since the 1960's. More recently, the industry has drawn attention, you could say scrutiny, because of several blockbuster transactions: earlier this week, DaimlerChrysler; and earlier than that, Clear Channel, Sallie Mae, and Equity Office Products, just to name a few.

In 2006 alone, U.S. private equity transactions totaled $406 billion and accounted for 27 percent of all U.S. mergers and acquisition activity. One telling barometer of the growth of the industry is that, in 2001, private equity firms purchased 324 companies. By 2006, that number had more than tripled to over 1,000 acquisitions.

Several factors appear to be driving the explosive growth in private equity. Institutional investors, including public and union pension funds and university endowments and foundations, are turning more and more to private equity investments to generate higher returns for their stakeholders. In addition, publicly traded companies face an environment in which burdensome or overly burdensome regulations result in frivolous shareholder lawsuits and demands of activist shareholder groups, and all of those things have made going private an increasingly attractive alternative. And I think the executive compensation legislation that we considered just a few weeks ago may even accelerate this trend towards private financing if it empowers activist shareholders even more.

Private equity can be a valuable tool for providing capital and expertise to underperforming companies or to companies struggling to generate quarterly growth and meet Wall Street expectations. The overwhelming majority of publicly traded companies are single-mindedly focused on one thing right now, and that is June the 30th, or the end of the next quarter, which is most usually June the 30th, with the second quarter. Are they going to meet or beat estimates? Has the market already accounted for the company's possible growth?

Additionally, taking a struggling public company private gives its managers the opportunity to address strategic concerns free of dayto-day competitive pressures. To improve corporate performance, private equity firms typically recruit top managers often drawn from the ranks of senior management at publicly traded companies and directly tie their compensation to long-term performance and growth, not to short-term stock price gyrations. Indeed, our former Treasury Secretary, John Snow, verified this trend when he described his firm's acquisition of Chrysler as providing ''management with the opportunity to focus on their long-term plans rather than pressures of short-term earnings expectations.''

We must, I think, support the continued growth of private equity and other alternative investments in our marketplace. An overly proscriptive, rules-based approach to regulation of private pools of capital could stifle the industry and drive private equity firms and their capital offshore or to investments in other countries, potentially compromising the competitive standing of our capital markets.

Concerns have been expressed about the treatment of workers at companies that are taken private, as the chairman did earlier. While I intend to carefully listen to the testimony of today's hearing on this point, it is at least not clear to me at this point that privately managed companies act any differently with respect to worker retention or compensation than publicly traded companies.

To conclude, we have heard anecdotal accounts of differences in workers' wages in private versus public companies—the chairman read one this morning—but we have yet to see any definitive empirical evidence in this area.

Further, we should not automatically concede the premise that taking action to increase efficiencies in a privately held company is always unfair, unwarranted, or not in the best interest of the company. The actions of new management may, in fact, restore a company to competitive health, preserving most workers' jobs that would otherwise be lost, maintaining pensions and providing other benefits.

We must also not lose sight of the fact that, according to a recent study, private equity created 600,000 jobs in the United States from 2000 to 2003. Given the increasingly competitive nature of the global economy, our policy should be to ensure that American public and private companies can survive.

So, in closing, Mr. Chairman, I will look forward to hearing the testimony of the witnesses and to learning more about the ways in which this committee can play a constructive role or if there are ways of enhancing the competitiveness and vitality of our U.S. capital market.

The CHAIRMAN. The gentleman from Massachusetts, Mr. Lynch.

Mr. LYNCH. Thank you, Mr. Chairman, and thank you for holding this hearing.

First, I would like to say I am pleased to notice that a constituent of mine is here today to testify, Mr. Jon Luther of Dunkin' Brands, a Canton, Massachusetts-based company, who probably, I think, will offer a positive example of private equity involvement.

I am also very pleased that we are exploring the impact of the growth of private equity firms on the U.S. economy and financial system. I think it is important that this committee has a solid and accurate understanding of the modern workings of private equity funds given the recent concerns about fund executive compensation, the treatment of capital gains tax benefits on their profits, and also their ability to exploit the debt market to make those profits, sometimes to the detriment of companies and their employees.

I am going to be interested in a number of questions, but one of those is related to the modern-day private equity investment framework and how does it differ from the corporate raiders and leveraged buyouts of the 1980's given that the same big names are still involved.

Also, I think this committee, which recently held a hearing regarding hedge funds, would like to know what the difference in investment strategies is between the two. That is the private equity firms—a more long-term strategy or a more short-term, such as the hedge funds have exhibited. I think the common connector seems to be making a profit, and there seems to be a lot of industry overlap these days.

The second issue that I will raise regards the pensions and benefits of the workers at the companies that are acquired by private equity firms. Yesterday's Wall Street Journal said that Cerberus, which has announced its takeover of DaimlerChrysler, has pledged to work with the UAW, and I am a former employee of the General Motors Corporation at their plant in Framingham, Massachusetts, so I have a particular interest there; but they have assured the UAW that the $18 billion owed to autoworkers, my brothers and sisters, in benefits will still be honored, and they refer to this deal as a watershed moment for the private equity industry in global finance dealings. I would like to have confidence in that, and perhaps the panelists can sort of expand on that concept if they are able to.

My third issue that I would raise is regarding the pension funds that invest in private equity firms. Mr. Lowenstein mentioned in his testimony that millions of retirees are benefiting from private equity investments through their pension funds, and that pension funds have at least $111 billion invested in private equity. I would like to hear a description of the allure in private equity investments and what are the benefits specifically to pension funds and being involved.

Those are the issues that I would like to raise in a general sense, Mr. Chairman, and with that, I yield back.

The CHAIRMAN. The gentlewoman from Ohio is recognized for 3 minutes.

Ms. PRYCE. Thank you, Mr. Chairman.

Thank you to our panel for being here today.

Already this year, 33 U.S. companies worth $160 billion have made equity buyout deals. The Chrysler deal serves as an example that private equity can go anywhere, even buying the most symbolic of American brands. Hitting close to my home, Limited Brands, based in Columbus, Ohio, announced yesterday that they would sell off their Express line to a private equity firm, Golden Gate Capital.

The timing of this hearing could not be more appropriate. Thank you, Mr. Chairman, for holding it. The maintenance of our capital markets is paramount to our continued economic growth.

I want to thank our witnesses for helping us demystify a market that has become an increasingly important source of funds for public firms seeking privatization, for companies in financial distress, for start-up enterprises, and for companies looking to spin off parts of their operations. There are often short-term losers with job losses tied to the public companies that had, for perhaps too long, delayed badly needed restructuring, but long term, a healthy, growing private company is better than a stagnant, underperforming public one, for the investors, the employees, and the economy.

Mr. Chairman, I think we should be focusing some of our energy on what is making it advantageous for these companies to go private or, to put it another way, what is making it disadvantageous for companies to be public. Going private frees companies from the short-term pressures of the stock market, and as the U.S. Chamber and others have pointed out, quarterly earnings per-share statements are a centerpiece to this problem. Companies often sacrifice, creating long-term value if it means missing quarterly earnings' projections. Even if they believe that the cuts are destroying business value over the long term, they are not investing in things in which they should be investing. We should be focusing on decreasing the regulatory burden on public companies, not increasing the burden on private equity.

I want to thank the witnesses once again and the chairman for having this hearing, and I yield back.

The CHAIRMAN. The gentleman from Louisiana is recognized for 5 minutes.

Mr. BAKER. Thank you, Mr. Chairman. I appreciate the interest in the matter in calling the hearing. Although there is really no clear definition of ''private equity,'' there are some characteristics of funds which I think are important to point out. Although sophisticated investors, those with a net worth in excess of $1 million, are certainly participants, it is financial institutions, insurance companies, mutual funds, and pension funds that provide the overwhelming bulk of the financial resources deployed by private equity. So, when we are contemplating regulatory constraint, we need to realize it is not just millionaires we are going after in this case, it is the CalPERS pensioners—by the way, CalPERS holds direct investment in private equity funds—and millions of others who, either through mutual fund investment or pension funds, have a share in the profits of private equity.

I was surprised to learn that in households with average annual incomes of $35,000 or less, 18 percent are invested in mutual funds—who would imagine?—and that if those families want to improve their quality of life, it will come through the democratization of investment opportunity.

As an example, Power Shares lists this morning in SmartMoney.com that they, by fall, may be a new ETF that will allow individuals to buy shares in an index that follows a benchmark of 30 traded private equity companies, companies that invest in private equities. This is similar in operation, I understand, to hedge funds, which offer the same opportunity to individual investors.

So, in the search to help working people, we need to be very careful about how fat we make this regulatory book. It may fall right on top of them and deny them the opportunity to share in economic growth. Well, how big is this thing? Private equity investment in 2006 was just over $400 billion. That compares with $1.1 trillion to hedge funds in a single period. Although big, the two together are the source of enormous liquidity in a highly competitive international marketplace.

Hedge funds are going to act very quickly. They are going to see imbalances in the market, whether overpriced or underpriced. They are going to move, bring about market discipline, and get out. The churn rate for hedge funds is typically about 9 months. Where private equities are different is that they buy into the company and bring in management sometimes, and it can be there for 2 or 3 years. For them to turn their profit, it means the underlying economic value must be improved, and the company itself must grow and prosper. This is not just about squeezing just a little inefficiency out; this is about providing jobs that otherwise might disappear. So, in engaging about concerns over workers' fate, often it is better to have a healthy company grow over time than it is to let a staggering company fall under the weight of its failed economic model.

So what happens if the U.S. rulebook is unreasonably fattened? There is a high probability that money will go elsewhere. The view that we are an economic island from which there is no escape is a very limited view of the world. London, Bombay, and Hong Kong are experiencing extraordinary growth. I have heard many members of this committee concerned about London's passing New York as the primacy trading location for securities. The private equity firms in India enjoyed a 21 percent rate of return on equity last year. India passed China with $1 trillion, $239 million of private equity investments last year, and they, India and China, are modifying their rulebook to make their investment world all the more attractive to potential investors from the United States.

So we need to be very careful about how we act here. The Dow Jones Index of India, called CNX, is up 42 percent year over year. This is not an illiquid, overregulated market from which people are saying to outside investors, ''Do not come.'' Instead, they are saying, ''Come on down. Bring your money and your suitcases. We will make you a nice hotel room offer, and you can stay here for as long as you like.''

How does that contrast with a market discussion where we are contemplating restricting the rules that enable smart people to deploy important resources to help grow our economy?

You know, we need to go slow. Maybe we need to go really slow, or maybe we do not need to go at all. Maybe we need to just watch for a while and make sure we understand market function before we unintentionally take it backwards in an enormous step. Said another way, sometimes in Washington, people see a profit.

So, first, they regulate it. If that does not stop it, then they tax it, and if that thing is still going, then they sue it. It is the three-step recovery plan to profit in America.

I think we need to get past that. I think we need to realize that working families, employed by companies, will change jobs, and new opportunities will come, but investing in the corporate growth for the long haul, not the next 10 minutes, is what grows value. That is what builds wealth in American families, and that is what American workers need.

The CHAIRMAN. The gentleman from California, for 4 minutes.

Mr. ROYCE. Thank you, Mr. Chairman.

Mr. Chairman, I also want to thank you for holding this hearing to examine the effect that private equity has on the U.S. economy.

Recently a great deal of attention has been focused on private equity due to the increased role that it is playing in the capital markets, and I understand the committee's interest in exploring this topic. I am very concerned, though, that statutory exclusions from Congress are unwarranted. It could be very dangerous for the economy, and I think we have had some very cogent arguments from Congressman Baker. I am going to add a few additional points to this that I think we should be concerned about.

If the goal of our hearing today is for Congress to have a better understanding of this recent boom that we are seeing in private equity, then we should be asking ourselves and we should review some of the failings of our public equity markets.

For example, what is driving money out of the public into the private equity markets? One is the Sarbanes-Oxley legislation, frankly, coupled with abusive shareholders' lawsuits, and that has created a terrible operating environment for many firms in this country. Companies have become more risk-averse, resulting in less investments and new business ventures. Of course, this means fewer opportunities for employees and an inefficient capital structure for investors.

In my view, private equity is playing an important role in our financial system. As we have seen in recent years, private equity firms provide stagnant corporations with a viable alternative to public markets in a public market right now that is beset with enormous costs when associated with Sarbanes-Oxley. Private equity provides growth capital to these corporations, which frequently results in a properly capitalized corporation, which frequently means more investments in employees, and usually means the development of new business lines for that company.

In conclusion, I believe the presence of private equity is an important component of our financial system, and any attempt to regulate the industry will be harmful to our capital markets and to our economy as a whole.

Again, Mr. Chairman, I would like to thank you for exploring this issue today, and I look forward to hearing from our witnesses.

The CHAIRMAN. I thank the gentleman.

We will get to the witnesses, but I do want to ask one more question.

People may hear something that sounds like the gavel. It will be my cast inadvertently knocking against the wall. If you do not see the gavel, ignore the noise.

With that, we will begin with our witnes ses. We will begin with Mr. Andrew Stern, president of the Service Employees International Union.

STATEMENT OF ANDREW L. STERN, PRESIDENT, SERVICE EMPLOYEES INTERNATIONAL UNION

Mr. STERN. Thank you, Mr. Chairman, and members of the committee. My name is Andy Stern, and I am president of the largest union, the Service Employees International Union, CTW, CLC.

The story of America's success is a story of work and working people. The greatness and promise of America has always been that if you work hard, you will have your work valued and rewarded. America's gift has been that every generation has done better than the previous one, but we are now at a moment when the promise of the American dream is in jeopardy.

A majority of Americans, sadly, say that they believe their children will actually be worse off than they are, and the facts are beginning to prove them right. People are working harder and harder for less wage increases. Opportunities are disappearing for access to jobs leading to the middle class. This is happening during an unprecedented period of prosperity in America. Some even have named it America's new, ''Gilded Age.'' We have the highest rate of income inequality in this country since the Great Depression. Productivity is up, but wages are down. Profits are up, but Americans have less healthcare, less savings, and less stock ownership than they had the year before.

Private equity, as Steven Pearlstein wrote today in the Washington Post about the Chrysler deal, has become, ''the most powerful force in business and finance.'' Today, private equity is buying and selling larger and larger companies and reshaping whole industries. It is engineering financial deals on a scale that, until a few years ago, seemed unimaginable. But the real story of private equity is the incredible wealth being created amongst its partners and the incomes being accumulated as a major contributor to the concentration of wealth amongst the top 1 percent of all Americans.

Private equity activity is raising significant concerns about the impact on workers, on companies, and on the financial markets. First, there is the increasing practice of quick flips and sell-offs that undermine the industry's claims that it seeks to promote longterm business growth. When private equity firms work with the managers and directors of companies that are targeted to buy and then offer those managers and directors ownership stakes in the new private company, it raises all kinds of questions of conflict of interest. And in discussing the conflicts between the banks and the private equity firms, the vice chairman of Morgan Stanley said, ''We are totally conflicted. Get used to it.''

We have seen the problems of the economic exuberance of Enron and high-tech industries in the past. As some of the experts have said, even if one major deal fails, there is very serious concern raised about its impact on the credit markets, on investors such as pension funds, and not least of all on the workers of the affected companies.

In terms of the workers, these risky deals at times put workers and companies at risk when high debt levels involved in buyout deals and high fees can create pressures to cut costs that are counterproductive to the stated goals of private equity firms to create long-term value and productivity. There are concerns about transparency and disclosure and concerns that, obviously, not everyone is sharing in the success of these deals.

For all of the hundreds of millions of dollars of fees and billions of dollars of profits taken out of these deals by private equity firms, the workers at most of these companies have seen no increases in benefits and no increases in wages. If we had just taken the $4.4 billion in fees paid to the private equity firms in the 10 largest buyout deals, just the 10 largest buyout deals in the last 2 years, we could have paid for family healthcare for over 1 million American workers. You do not have to take my word for it. As the chairman said, look at what financial leaders and experts are saying about the private equity economy.

But here is the opportunity. The opportunity is we are creating value. The question is, are we sharing in the value? For working people today in the private equity world, there have been far more misses than hits in the private equity buyouts. There have been far more fees raised than paychecks raised. It would be best if the industry made its changes itself and took steps to self-regulate to make sure that private equity did work for working people in the rest of the country.

For worker s in communities, the industry should also be expectedto play by the same set of rules as everyone else. We should eliminate the conflicts of interest. If unions exist at a company being bought, like Chrysler, they should be at the table as soon as possible, and if no union exists, the private equity firms should make sure that workers have the right to form unions. But the private equity firms will not self-regulate, Mr. Chairman, or take their own steps to change, and we think it is necessary that Congress legislate.

America has been at its best when a broad group of people have shared in the prosperity being created in the economy. We have gotten away from that in recent years. The greatest country on Earth can do much better to make sure that everyone shares in the success and in the prosperity that workers help create. There is more than enough wealth in the buyout business for private equity firms to continue to prosper, while also adapting their existing business model to expand opportunities for communities, workers and our country. The incredible wealth that exists in the private equity buyout industry presents an historic opportunity. It is an opportunity to repair the American dream.

Thank you, Mr. Chairman.

The CHAIRMAN. Thank you.

[The prepared statement of Mr. Stern can be found on page 55 of the appendix.]

The CHAIRMAN. Next is Jon Luther, the chairman and CEO of Dunkin' Brands, Inc.

STATEMENT OF JON L. LUTHER, CHAIRMAN AND CHIEF EXECUTIVE OFFICER, DUNKIN' BRANDS INC.

Mr. LUTHER. Thank you, Chairman Frank, and members of the committee.

As you mentioned, my name is Jon Luther, and I am the chairman and chief executive officer of Dunkin' Brands. Dunkin' Brands is the parent company of Dunkin' Donuts, Baskin-Robbins, and the sandwich brand out West called Togo's. I appreciate this opportunity to share with you the Dunkin' Brands' experience with private equity ownership.

Our talented team of executives and employees, together with our thousands of franchisees and licensees, predominantly small businesspeople, has built a $6.4 billion enterprise operating in 47 States and in 50 countries. Thanks to their effort and commitment, our brands are known and loved by consumers around the world.

When I joined Dunkin' Brands in January of 2003, we were owned by Allied Domecq, a publicly traded spirits and wine company headquartered in the United Kingdom. In November of 2005, Allied Domecq was acquired by Pernod Ricard, another spirits and wine company, based in France. Shortly thereafter, because Dunkin' Brands was perceived as a noncore asset of Pernod Ricard, Pernod put our company on the auction block for sale. In March of 2006, we were acquired by a consortium of three United Statesbased private equity firms: The Carlyle Group; Bain Capital Partners; and the Thomas H. Lee Partners.

During the period when we were an Allied Domecq subsidiary, we were considered, for lack of a better term, a ''cash cow.'' We were assigned yearly growth targets. We were usually last in line for attention, and certainly for capital to fuel our growth. Significant decisions required that I go to London. Our cash was swept every night, and our focus was usually on the next quarterly numbers.

Our acquisition by Carlyle, Bain, and Thomas H. Lee has liberated our company. Our new owners expressed confidence in our management team, our leadership, our strategies, our vision, and our values.

Our three goals are to take Dunkin' Donuts national over time, transform Baskin-Robbins into a neighborhood ice cream shop once again, and to expand internationally, but rather than tell us to change our goals and our plans to achieve them, our new owners ask how they can support and how they can fuel our growth. Finally, we had the attention and the resources that we needed to realize our goals. The benefits of our new ownership to our company have been enormous. Their financial expertise has led to a groundbreaking securitization deal that has resulted in very favourable financing at favorable interest rates. This has enabled us to make significant investments in our infrastructure and in our growth initiatives. In addition, they have helped us create new franchisee financing programs that provide flexible, convenient, and competitive financing options to our franchisees, those small businessmen and women of every size in all of our markets. They have opened the door to opportunities that were previously beyond our reach.

For example, they have introduced us to a real estate development firm that is assisting our Baskin-Robbins growth and are finding great real estate opportunities. They have done so well that we are now considering using them for our Dunkin' Donuts growth and development as well.

Our acquisition and the expansion plan for which we now have the resources have put us also in the national spotlight. Countless news stories about it have caused us to be sought out by many new potential franchisees, small businessowners, and also new employees who want to join our company.

As a result of our franchising efforts, the engine for our growth has taken off. We are a 100 percent franchised enterprise. Every Dunkin' Donuts, and every Baskin-Robbins, store represents the achievement of a dream for an entrepreneur somewhere in America. A new Dunkin' Donuts means approximately 25 to 30 jobs per store, and a new Baskin-Robbins means approximately 12 to 15 jobs. Over the next 15 years, because of this growth vehicle we now have, you can expect 250,000 jobs, jobs for young people, and jobs with good career paths in restaurant management, making it possible for others to achieve the American dream.

Our new owners have never asked us to cut costs or to reduce our head count. Any reductions in staffing that we have had over the past 4 years have been as a result of our efforts to be more productive and more efficient. This year we expect to divest of Togo's, our west coast brand, because it generated only $200 million in annual system sales, and this decision we had considered prior to our new ownership because we wanted—because of its size, we wanted it to have the same attention that we were getting from our new owners, and we could not do that while focusing on our two larger brands.

You know, recently I was asked by a Boston Globe columnist whether Dunkin' Brands would follow the path of many companies and move to a location where the cost of doing business would be lower. I was pleased to say, Mr. Chairman, that Massachusetts is our home. We are not going anywhere. I have 700 or 800 families who work for Dunkin' Brands who rely on us for their employment. We believe in those strong community roots, and last year, together with our franchisees, we established the Dunkin' Brands Community Foundation, and we have given $1 million to that foundation out of our pockets, with no resistance from our new owners.

The mission of our foundation is to support those who serve our communities, especially in times of crisis, and this mission is true to our brand heritage and the values of the entire system, employees, franchisees, and our customers.

In conclusion, as a result of our relationship with Carlyle, Bain, and Thomas H. Lee, our business has benefited. Our franchisees and employees have benefited, and wealth-creating opportunities have been spread among hundreds of entrepreneurs and careerists associated with Dunkin' Brands.

Thank you.

[The prepared statement of Mr. Luther can be found on page 51 of the appendix.]

The CHAIRMAN. Next is Mr. Lowenstein, who is the president of the Private Equity Council.

STATEMENT OF DOUGLAS LOWENSTEIN, PRESIDENT, PRIVATE EQUITY COUNCIL

Mr. LOWENSTEIN. Thank you, Mr. Chairman, and members of the committee.

The Private Equity Council represents 10 of the leading private equity firms in the world, and we are pleased to be invited to participate in the beginning of this dialogue with this committee on private equity.

Before addressing the issues that the committee has raised, I think it would be helpful to just take a brief second to demystify private equity, because private equity is about hundreds of thriving companies contributing to the economy in numerous positive ways. You just heard that if you get a cup of coffee at Dunkin' Donuts, you are interacting with private equity. When you see a movie produced by MGM Studios, and then buy pizza for your kids afterwards at Domino's, you are interacting with private equity. When you buy a new outfit at J. Crew, or you buy toys for your kids at Toys-R-Us, you are interacting with private equity. When you watch a movie or a sporting event at home, or when you use your cell phone, the chances are you are interacting with a semiconductor chip produced by a private equity-owned firm.

Furthermore, private equity investments directly and indirectly benefit tens of millions of Americans. As we have heard this morning, public and private pension fund foundations and university endowments have chalked up returns from private equity investments that far exceed those available from the stock market.

Between 1991 and 2006, private equity firms worldwide have distributed $430 billion in profits to these and other investors. That is $430 ''billion'' with a ''b.'' These returns translate into stronger public employee pension programs, more funds for college financial aid and scholarships, and more funds for research and other causes supported by charitable foundations. Private equity, indeed, is about a lot more than enriching a handful of people.

Let me turn briefly to address a few of the questions that the committee has asked about. First, do private equity firms invest in the businesses they own and operate? Well, we have some examples in our testimony which are, I think, quite typical of private equity practices.

Sungard, for example, the software maker, has invested in its business. R&D projects since the private equity firm took ownership are up from 10 to over 50 today, and employment has grown by 3,000 people since the acquisition by private equity. Axel-Tech, with a 37 percent job growth and a 16 percent sales growth since the private equity firm acquired the company and the company moved into a new line of business, builds suspension systems and axles for vehicles, and it moved into servicing the United States military, which needs heavier suspension systems for the heavily armored vehicles serving our troops in Iraq, and Axel-Tech was a maker/supplier of those suspension systems. ITC Holdings, a Michigan utility, has seen private equity help grow the business, with job growth from 28 at the time of acquisition to 230, and capital spending up from $10 million to $200 million annually.

These are not the exceptions in any of these examples. You must understand one central fact about private equity which often gets lost in all of the rhetoric and debate. They only succeed if they improve the performance and increase the value of the companies in which they invest. The entire business model rests on selling investments at a gain. Firing workers and stripping assets is hardly the best way to show future buyers that you built something of greater value.

The second question raised by the committee concerns the impact of private equity on working men and women. Aside from case studies, which I think are helpful evidence of the impact, and there are hundreds more like it, it is true—data on private equity investments' impact on employment in the United States is, in fact, anecdotal at this point, but research in Europe does suggest that private equity investments do, indeed, result in long-term job growth. A study by the international management consulting firm A.T. Kearney found earlier this year that private equity firms worldwide generate employment on average at a much faster pace than comparable traditionally financed firms.

That said, the simple truth is that, as with any other acquisition involving a public or private company, private equity transactions can and do sometimes result in layoffs. In some cases, the most affected employees are the management level, and in other cases they are not. In some cases, the layoffs may eventually be offset by new hires over the long term when business grows stronger. Nor should we lose sight of the fact that even when there are layoffs, the willingness of the private equity owner to even acquire and invest in a troubled firm probably results in the savings of jobs that might otherwise have been lost.

There is no one-size-fits-all pattern to private equity. There is no pattern of busting unions and laying off workers in private equity. It is simply not there. By the way, these limited partners are pension funds, public employee pension funds, and I ask you: Does common sense tell you that if they saw private equity firms gutting employees and gutting workers that they would really continue to support this asset class the way they have?

The final area of interest to the committee is the impact of private equity on income inequality. Undeniably there are those in private equity who do very well. Equally undeniable is the fact that we have an income inequality problem in this country. Private equity is not the reason American companies and workers are under pressure or why wages and benefits are stagnant; these are based on pervasive global forces at work. Private equity alone cannot and will not and should not redress the income disparity problem in this country. That requires national will and national policies, and we are prepared to be part of any effort to attack that problem cooperatively and creatively either with government or with the SIRU and others in organized labor.

At the same time, I believe that ensuring the firemen and teachers of the income they expect when they retire or that kids get scholarships to college they might not otherwise have gotten suggests that private equity does more than just distort income disparity at the high end. I noted earlier the $430 billion in profits to limited partners and how these flow to average Americans, but let me give you one very concrete example.

The excess returns generated by private equity investments by the Washington State Investment Board for over 25 years has been $26,000 per retiree. Put another way, these returns have fully funded retirement plans for 10,000 WSIB retirees.

In sum, private equity makes significant contributions to the American economy. It is innovative and flexible. It is not a silver bullet, but it is a part of the system, and it is a good part of the system.

Thank you, Mr. Chairman.

[The prepared statement of Mr. Lowenstein can be found on page 41 of the appendix.]

The CHAIRMAN. Dr. Robert Frank.

Statement of Dr. Robert H. Frank, Johnson Graduate School of Management, Cornell University

Dr. FRANK. Thank you, Mr. Chairman. I am grateful for the opportunity to speak to you today about the consequences of the broader inequality problem.

I am an economist at Cornell University. I have been writing about the causes and the consequences of rising income inequality for the past several decades in books, including ''The Winner Take All Society,'' ''Luxury Fever'' and, next month, ''Falling Behind: How Rising Inequality Harms the Middle Class.''

Much of the testimony you have already heard. I think private equity is part of a whole complex of forces that have made the U.S. economy much more competitive in the last several decades. One consequence of greater competition is that money tends to flow to the players that have the greatest impact on the bottom line. If you look at Jon Luther, he is a perfect case study of how high rewards at the top of the corporate ladder are not primarily, as many people seem to think, a result of corporate malfeasance, vivid cases to the contrary notwithstanding. Typically, somebody who is in charge of a big organization and who is making good things happen needs only to make 2- or 3 percent better decisions in a year's time in order to have an impact on the bottom line of tens of millions of dollars. So, if the economy is getting more competitive, the expectation is that the rewards will flow to individuals who can make that happen. That is just the way the market is.

The market produces a bigger pie. No economist ever claimed that the market guaranteed that a bigger piece of pie would automatically go to every person as a result of greater competition. Even though people in the middle have slightly higher incomes than they had before, one of the practical consequences—and here, I agree with Chairman Frank that we have to focus on the practical consequences of inequality rather than the moral ones if we want to see anything done about it—of higher incomes at the top is that people in the middle will have a much harder time meeting basic middle-class goals.

Let me describe quickly a process that I call ''expenditure cascades.'' People at the top have vastly more money than before. People of middle income do not seem offended by that. That is one of the nice things about the United States. People are not jealous of the success of the rich. People at the top are spending more because they have more money. People just below the top are influenced by their spending. Maybe it is now the custom to have your daughter's wedding reception in the home rather than in a rented club, so you need to build bigger. People just below those just below the top build bigger in response to that, and so on. Now the median house newly constructed in the United States is about a third bigger than it was in 1980.

The rub for the middle-class family, which has no more real income now than in 1980, is if you do not buy the median-priced house for your area, your children will go to below-average schools. That is the way it works. So the median family is forced to save less, work more, commute longer distances, and work longer hours, in short, to be squeezed on every margin in order to meet the minimal goal of sending their children to a school of average quality. There is no pretending that this is not a genuine burden on the middle class.

If we are to do something about this, it is a fool's error to castigate corporate pay boards for not showing individual restraint. There is no such thing as individual restraint in a perfectly competitive system. You pay the market rate, or you do not get the talent that you need to be able to compete successfully. The only lever we have is tax policy in this arena if we are not happy about the way income distribution changes have been going. Most countries that have rising inequality have attempted to lean against it by increasing tax rates on top earners and increasing benefits for those who have been failing to keep up.

For some reason in this country, we have moved in precisely the opposite direction by reducing tax rates at the margin for top earners and cutting the social safety net. This is a testament, I think, to the mysterious power of trickle-down theory, that if we cut the taxes on the top earners, we will somehow cause the economy to grow much more quickly. I do not have time to go into it in detail, but it has been widely discredited by economists of all political persuasions. Bruce Bartlett, in The New York Times last month, said that it is time for the supply-side economists to stop saying that tax cuts for the rich generate increases in tax revenues.

So, again, I think there is no indictment of the people who are reorganizing businesses to make them more competitive and generate expansions in profits, and there is nothing morally improper about their being paid the going rate. There is, however, something morally questionable about a society that allows people's fate to hinge solely on market outcomes. That has never been a prescription for a sound society. Societies that have tried that in the past have failed to prosper in the long run. Even the rich, the ostensible beneficiaries of tax policy in recent years if you reckon the consequences of those tax cuts, have actually been harmed by them.

The tax cuts have enabled the rich to build bigger houses. What we know now is that, when everybody builds a bigger house, that just redefines the standard for what constitutes an acceptable dwelling. So you have more money after taxes, and you build larger. No gain. It is not really a tax cut. It is a loan financed by borrowing from China, Japan, Korea, and other nations that will have to be repaid in full with interest. In the meantime, we have been cutting the Energy Department's project for rounding up loose nuclear materials in the former Soviet Union. We have been cutting back on a whole array of public services. This is not intelligent public policy. I think, in another 50 years, people will look back and say, ''What on Earth could they have been thinking to do that?''

[The prepared statement of Dr. Frank can be found on page 31 of the appendix.]

The CHAIRMAN.

Thank you.

Let me begin by asking Mr. Stern: There is a lot of top equity. We have talked about this, that there are acquisitions, office buildings, hotels, and places that employ a large number of workers. We are not competitive with manufacturing workers elsewhere. Dunkin' Donuts would be the same.

One of the things that concerns many of us has been the hostility to unions, and I am just wondering what your experience has been, and I would say people are ready to talk about it. I would say for many of us—and obviously, there is a difference between parties on this—but the unions do seem to be one way to deal with this without government intervention, collectively bargaining for chambermaids and janitors, and this is a new class of people. These are the people who sit in the lobbies of office buildings and make me show them my driver's license so that I will not blow up the building. I do not know if that works very well, but it does not pay a whole lot, and that is probably the best job we have had since the WPA.

What has been your experience in terms of trying to get collective bargaining agreements with these new owners?

Mr. STERN. Well, first of all, I should say in response to the broader question, there have only been three ways we have distributed wealth in America historically: one has been the market, which as Alan Greenspan is saying is no longer working; two has been the government; and three has been unions. You know, unions are just a way to distribute wealth and end inequality. So, when you see a purchase like Cerberus, as Congressman Lynch said, you are glad the union is at the table, because you wonder what would happen if they were not.

And so I do think there is an issue here of how, not through government regulation, but by private activity that goes on. I would say, you know, the private equity people have to make a decision of whether they are going to proceed in a way that too many employers have been proceeding as owners, which is to not let workers make a free and fair choice about whether they want to have an organization.You know, that is a conversation we would love to have with a new owner.

The CHAIRMAN. What has your experience been?

Mr. STERN. There have been no better than the private equity field, but there is now a growing—they are much more involved in the economy today, and so we are going to get to see again, you know, as they go from owner-distressed companies to very successful companies like Equity Office Properties or—you know, how they are going to behave as the new owners. Time will only tell, but so far there is no difference.

The CHAIRMAN. Let me ask you. I do want to make one comment, and that is that one of the things we hear is that, to the extent that, for instance, we did our executive compensation bill, and to the extent that there were concerns about the compensation of the CEOs of public companies, that becomes an incentive for them to go into private equity. I must say that is the most serious attack on the morals of those people that I have ever heard. What it says is that they are so concerned with their own pay that they will make a fundamental decision about the form of ownership. It is the notion that someone is running a public company with his or her obligations to the shareholders who says, ''I can make a lot more money if I sell out my shareholders and go to private equity,'' and that would be a motive for making a change. I am shocked that people would think so ill of these people.

Now let me ask Mr. Lowenstein. I agreed when you said that private equity did not cause this, but sometimes there are opportunities for the inequality, and I appreciate your acknowledging it. You say that private equity would be willing to participate in the dialogue. Let me ask, for instance, with regard to unionization, is there any general principle, is there any kind of general predisposition one way or the other? I must say, if we saw that there was some willingness to enter into those kinds of agreements, that would be relief for a lot of us.

Mr. LOWENSTEIN. Well, I think it is difficult, obviously, for me to speak in the context of, you know, hundreds of deals and transactions that are being done involving dozens and dozens of private equity firms.

My sense in the little time that I have been involved with this sector is that there is an openness to meeting and to talking with people from a variety of different stakeholder groups, including organized labor. There is no sort of antilabor, antiunion bias in private equity. There are plenty of private equity companies where union employees are a central part of the business, and those jobs have grown as part of the basic business plan. So, beyond that, I think it is difficult for me to generalize other than to, as we have in recent weeks, make clear that we are more than open to opening constructive and cooperative discussion with all stakeholders on these kinds of issues.

The CHAIRMAN. Well, I appreciate that. My time is up. I do think, from the standpoint of many of us workers, particularly, frankly, low-wage workers in some of these occupations, they are a particularly important group for stakeholders, and it does seem to be—you say you are prepared to enter a dialogue. Some concern for the workers sharing in this value created would be very helpful.

The gentleman from Alabama.

Mr. BACHUS. Thank you,

Mr. Chairman. Mr. Chairman, I saw and the members of the committee saw a ‘‘Dear Colleague’’ that the chairman sent out yesterday.

It says, ‘‘Dear Colleague, I appreciate the concern expressed by many about why my arm is in a sling. In order to avoid having to repeat the same conversation, I am sending out this ‘Dear Colleague.’ I ruptured a tendon in my left arm using a curling machine in the gym, and had it surgically repaired yesterday at Bethesda.’’

My staff went to that gym, found the curling machine, and found that it was manufactured by a private equity company. Now, we all know why we are here. His arm will be out of a sling in a week or 2, and we can maybe put the focus on something else.

Mr. LOWENSTEIN. Perhaps it was a stronger curling machine than one made by a nonprivate equity firm.

Mr. BACHUS. All right. Mr. Luther, I noticed as I was reading the history of Dunkin' Donuts that it seems like, since it has been taken private, the number of franchises has expanded. Has being owned by private equity investors been something that is financing that, or has there been a change in corporate policy?

Mr. LUTHER. Yes. Under the Allied Domecq regime, and shortly with the Pernod Ricard regime, they would sweep our cash every day to fuel their wines and spirits business. Our good cash generated —our good cash flow would go to them to build a Beefeater gin brand. For example, since private equity and since the ownership, they focus on our growth and enable us to go forward, meaning that they invest in infrastructure, which is something that we were not able to do before, meaning our IT systems and technology, so we can remain competitive with our competitive segment. Because of their brilliance in financing and the financial world, it has enabled us to put a program together, a franchisee financing program, which is more convenient for them to apply so they can build these stores to add the jobs and to get in these communities and do good work, and if it were not for their great expertise in that area enabling us to do that, our franchise system would be slower in growth, and that is important. Since we are 100 percent franchised, obviously that is the engine for our growth, and one of the most important attributes to our business growth.

Mr. BACHUS. So your private owner sponsors actually help finance these franchisees?

Mr. LUTHER. No. They have aided and abetted us to work with outside financial firms to get better favorable rates by their better understanding of financial aspects, and perhaps we get too close to it sometimes, but for this outside influence to come in and educate and coach us in those areas, it has benefited us greatly.

Mr. BACHUS. I will ask this to anyone on the panel. Back in the 1980's, we had corporate raiders, and we had the LBOs. As to private equity investments, how are they different from that, or is there a difference?

Mr. LOWENSTEIN. I will take the first crack at that. I think there are a number of differences today than 20 or 30 years ago. For one, in the early days of private equity, the lending typically would come from a single lender, the debt levels in a transaction would typically be at the 90 percent level, maybe even higher, and the transactions were much more tied to asset sales as a way to quickly repay the debt to make the leverage play work. Today, you have a lot of differences.

First of all, the typical debt level in recent years in private equity transactions has been hovering around 40 percent—I am sorry—equity levels are around 40 percent, so up considerably. There is a lot less leverage in the transactions. Secondly, the level of due diligence of private equity firms today compared to 20 years ago is quantumly farther along than it was then, and even the simple technology available to do effective analyses of the investments and so forth is far better. Sometimes it takes private equity firms 2 years before they actually make an acquisition, so they raise funds, but they are not investing all of their funds immediately.

I think you also have—the other critical point is that we are at the point where the way today that you make money in private equity is not by an asset sale, because, in a sense, everybody knows what the assets are, and they are priced into the deal. These are all auctions. They are competitive processes. If you are going to grow a firm, you have to grow it with operating improvements. That is a big change from the way it was 20 years ago, and so the value creation comes from investment, from growing, from improving operations in the management of the company. So I think those are some of the major changes.

Mr. STERN. I am not as familiar with all of the details, but I do want to read to you what the founder of The Carlyle Group says, which I know we talked a lot about value and decisionmaking, but he says, ''The fabulous profits that we have been able to generate for our limited partners are not solely a function of our investment genius, but have resulted, in large part, from a great market and the availabilities of an enormous amount of cheap debt. Frankly, there is so much liquidity in the world financial systems that lenders, even our lenders, are making very risky credit decisions,'' and I think that is a very big difference from the 1980's.

Mr. BACHUS. If they are paying top dollar, of course the shareholders are all benefiting from these sales, I would think, and then the private equity investors—I mean, if they pay top dollar, and they still make it work, that seems like a win-win situation.

Mr. LUTHER. Just to weigh in, my experience is that there has been a lot of equity put into our deal, so it is not leveraged quite as it was in the 1980's. I think a significant difference for me in being in this industry for a while, meaning my industry, the restaurant industry, and watching what happened in the 1980's as compared to today is the fact of Carlyle, Bain, and Lee. During our auction process, we were engaged with maybe 25 of these firms that were in the auction process. They looked at the leadership. They looked at the management. They looked at organic growth as opposed to ways to cut their way or to save their way to success. They looked at all of those organic pieces—management values. What kind of leadership values do we have? What do you give back to the communities? What kind of relationships do we have with communities and franchisees? That was a greater part of their due diligence than maybe 20 years ago—I am not sure—but in talking with all of the potential bidders for our company, they all had those questions and that curiosity rather than the 5-year plan or the numbers.

By the way, just for the record, in our case we were able to put our numbers together—the management team's and the management projections—in the bidding process. No one told us to put the numbers higher or lower or whatever. They left it up to us, and then the auction was based on that. So there was not this, ''Make it better than it is. Let us take this thing forward in a way so we win or lose.'' It was how do we do this the right way, and I think that is an important distinction, maybe, of the perceptions of the past.

Mr. BACHUS. Thank you,

Mr. Chairman. The CHAIRMAN. I would note that you got extra time for reading my ''Dear Colleague.'' The gentlewoman from California.

Ms. WATERS. Thank you very much, Mr. Chairman.

I want to thank our panelists for being here today to help us understand what has become a very, very important area as we look at our responsibilities here in this committee.

I would like to know from Mr. Lowenstein, I believe it is, if you can help me to understand what requirements are placed on the fund, the private equity funds, by the investors. For example, CalPERS in California has a $240 billion portfolio there, and if they invest in one of these funds, what do they ask of the fund? What do they say they want you to do if they are investing in funds so that the fund can be involved in these buyouts where we are concerned about the employers in the community? What kind of requirements do they place on the people they give the money to?

Mr. LOWENSTEIN. Congresswoman, I think that, in all candor, the question is probably better put to CalPERS and the investors, themselves. I am not part of those negotiations. I will say that there are very, very intensive negotiations that occur between the limited partners and the private equity firms in putting the partnerships together. These are very, very intensely negotiated funds over an extended period of time, and certainly, in that context, limited partners are able—

Ms. WATERS. But you do not know of any standard code of conduct that is being required? Let me ask Mr. Stern. Mr. Stern, does the union place any requirements on its money that it invests in these kinds of deals?

Mr. STERN. Well, I mean, most of the unions who are in the private sector are governed by fiduciary responsibilities that would not allow us to place particular kinds of requirements, you know, in terms of investment decisions other than the nature of the return that we would get on the investments. I think CalPERS' instructions, for better or worse, to the private equity firms are to make a lot of money.

Ms. WATERS. So public-employee pension funds and union funds could be investing in deals where people are going to get laid off? Mr. STERN. Yes, because, as I understand most of these limited partnerships, you know, they are called ''limited partnerships'' because they have a limited role in the decision-making process, and so part of the problem with some of the laws in our country today is that they do not allow investors to make what one might think are appropriate decisions about issues like that because it would be a breach of our fiduciary responsibility.

Mr. LOWENSTEIN. If I may just add to that, though, nobody is forcing any limited partner to invest in a private equity fund, so the best way to vote against companies that are not using your money in socially responsible ways that you care about is to not give them your money. As we said, CalPERS and many other limited partnerships' stakeholder pension funds are providing billions and billions of dollars to fuel this, in a sense, and then vote with their pocketbooks if they see a problem of how these transactions are being conducted.

Ms. WATERS. Well, let me just say this: For years, I was involved in a struggle in California to divest our pension funds from companies doing business in South Africa. We heard all of the fiduciary arguments, but we changed it, and we got involved in a divestment movement that helped to change the attitudes and create some social responsibilities, so it is something that we need to examine. I yield back the balance of my time.

The CHAIRMAN. Mr. Hensarling.

Mr. HENSARLING.

Thanks, Mr. Chairman. First, Mr. Stern, you spoke about income inequality, I believe, in your testimony. Does the janitor who cleans your office make the same income as you do?

Mr. STERN. No, sir.

Mr. HENSARLING. So can one say that you, yourself, are practicing income inequality?

Mr. STERN. No, sir.

Mr. HENSARLING. Why not?

Mr. STERN. Because I think what we are talking about here in terms of income inequality is the growing gap between the rich and the rest of the population—that 150,000 or 300,000 Americans now make as much as the other 150 million Americans. I think we are talking about a very drastic set of extreme circumstances that were raised in the colony of the Great Depression.

Mr. HENSARLING. So are you more offended by the income inequality of those who make less than you? It appears that maybe you have more concern for those who make more than you.

Mr. STERN. I am not concerned with people getting wealthy, but I am concerned that people who work every day cannot own a home, raise a family, and live the American dream. And I am very concerned about a country where my kids and grandkids will be the first generation in American history to do worse than their parents. I do not think that is America.

Mr. HENSARLING. Well, I happen to agree with you there, and that is, for one, why I am concerned that recently the House passed a budget that included the largest tax increase in American history that will impose an approximately $2,700 tax increase on all of the families back in the Fifth Congressional District of Texas. Dr. Frank, in your testimony, you talked about, I believe—I do not want to put words in your mouth—that we have been cutting the social safety net. Does that capture what you said in your testimony?

Dr. FRANK. Yes, sir.

Mr. HENSARLING. I have been reviewing figures for the Congressional Budget Office and the Office of Management and Budget, and by the figures I have seen since 2001, healthcare assistance has increased 40 percent at the Federal level; housing assistance, 27 percent; food assistance, 58 percent; cash and other assistance, 40 percent; and general anti-poverty spending at the Federal level has been 41 percent. The only major poverty program that I can find that has decreased is TANF. That is because the caseload is down about two-thirds due to work requirements. What have you discovered that CBO and OMB and everybody else who calculates these numbers haven't discovered?

Dr. FRANK. Well, part of what you have to understand, Congressman, is that the cost of a lot of the entitlement programs goes up for everyone, so we can provide that year by year. There have been cuts in the earned income tax credit programs. There have been cuts in the rate at which public transport has been supported. The public schools—

Mr. HENSARLING. I'm sorry, if I could interrupt. Where did you get your figures on the earned income tax credit? Because my figures show that it has increased at least 38 percent since 2001. Dr. FRANK. Relative to the cost of the middle- and low-income family meeting basic needs, those payments have not kept pace, Congressman.

Mr. HENSARLING. Let me ask you another question. I think you spoke of the need of tax policy changes to address income inequality. Is that a fair assessment of your testimony?

Dr. FRANK. Yes.

Mr. HENSARLING. From my figures, we have roughly 50 percent of the population that for all intents and purposes pay no income tax at the moment. Do your figures differ from that?

Dr. FRANK. No, they don't differ from that. Most of those people do, however, pay payroll tax.

Mr. HENSARLING. That they do, and if we don't reform our entitlement programs, they will pay more as well. My figures show that over the last 25 years, the top 20 percent of income earners have seen their percentage of Federal tax paid increase and 80 percent of the taxpayers have seen them go down. Do you have some other set of figures besides the ones that I viewed from the U.S. Department of the Treasury.

Dr. FRANK. No, sir, that is an expected consequence of the change in where the pretax income has gone. The more pretax income that goes to the top, of course the more tax will be paid by people at top.

Mr. HENSARLING. I see where the top, I believe, 5 percent of income earners pay almost 60 percent of Federal income taxes. What percentage would you have the top 5 percent pay?

Dr. FRANK. A higher percentage than that because we are currently borrowing $800 billion a year because we are not collecting as much in revenue as we are incurring in expenses. The tax increase —

Mr. HENSARLING. Maybe we need to do something on the spending side as well. I see my time is up.

The CHAIRMAN. Ms. Maloney.

Mrs. MALONEY. I would like to thank you, Mr. Chairman, for having this hearing, and to thank the panelists for attending. Many of you have touched on the widening gap between the haves and the have-nots in our country, which is a tremendous concern, I would say, of all Members of Congress. It is very troubling and has major ramifications. Last year, Steven Schwartzman, the chief executive of the private equity group Blackstone warned in an interview with The Financial Times that the widening gap between the lavish pay of executives and CEOs and middle America's stagnating wages may result in a backlash and in a political and social crisis in our country, and the best way to deal with this widening income inequality, according to Mr. Schwartzman, is for the middle class to do better.

So I would like to ask Mr. Lowenstein and Mr. Stern if you would comment and anyone else on my question. Mr. Lowenstein, can you tell us how the private equity deals where Mr. Schwartzman and his colleagues are reaping, literally, billions of dollars in fees and payouts, how are their private equity deals helping the middle class do better? Are the workers sharing in the increased profits of these private equity firms through increased wages or benefit packages? How are these deals helping middle America?

Mr. LOWENSTEIN. Well, I think as a general proposition, as I said in my testimony, we believe that private equity is strengthening companies, and making them more competitive. And by definition, if that is true, people who work for those companies have more secure jobs. And in many cases, as I also said in my testimony, the few examples we use there has been job growth in those companies.

And so, I think in that way that obviously supports middle income wage earners and so forth. As I also said, there is a range of indirect benefits. When you talk about private equity profits, 80 percent of the profit when an asset is sold goes to the limited partners. And those limited partners, as we discussed, have money that then flows back to retirees and many others in our community who benefit from that indirectly.

I would also suggest to you that there is another indirect benefit to the extent that private equity firms are allowing and strengthening businesses that are part of people's everyday lives—Dunkin' Donuts and Domino's Pizza and J. Crew and other places that people shop on a regular basis. That is also helping people acquire the necessities of everyday life.

So I think there are various ways that these transactions promote value and growth and flow through to lots of individuals.

Mr. STERN. The Census Bureau reports that America has had its fifth straight year in a row that Americans did not get a raise, the longest period of economic stagnation in the history of our country. And it is all about that we are creating wealth, but it is not being distributed. I don't think private equity per se—maybe indirectly, but not directly, has done anything to help rebuild the middle class. There used to be a joke about when people were creating new jobs, they would say there are 10 million new jobs and I got 3. I think that is a lot of what we are seeing here.

We are not necessarily creating the middle-class jobs that we saw in the plants in Massachusetts, where there were union jobs, and jobs where people could own a home and raise a family. And I am not saying that private equity is the cause of it. I am just saying that I don't think they are the solution to it either, so far.

Mrs. MALONEY. Would you like to comment, Dr. Frank, or anyone else, on this?

Dr. FRANK. Again, I don't think that attacking the competitive forces is the lever that you want to pull. I think the lever that you want to pull—you do have to cut spending where possible, but the government we elected last time campaigned as an opponent of government waste. You cut what you can. Yet one of the programs they cut was the Energy Department's program to round up loosely guarded nuclear materials in the former Soviet Union. We just don't have the revenue to do the things that we need to do, and I think that is where your focus should be.

Mrs. MALONEY. Mr. Luther?

Mr. LUTHER. Yes, my experience might be a microcosm of the overall economy, but in our case when private equity acquired, the opportunity for many of our employees who worked for Dunkin' Brands, not our franchise organizations, we distributed some of that wealth to them in the form of stock and options to over 150 people in our organization; that is 15 percent of our company that now has some opportunity perhaps for their children to go to college without borrowing money or whatever.

Our goal is to continue to distribute those stock options and equity opportunities into our organization deeper and deeper, so we distribute the wealth in that regard.

Our franchise communities create the jobs and create management jobs within our restaurants and multi-unit jobs that hopefully can enable those employees to continue to grow their experiences and their careers so that they can compete in the middle-class environment, so we try hard to make sure we do that.

The CHAIRMAN. We will take Mr. Castle and then we will break for the votes and come back immediately. There is apparently only one 15-minute vote.

Mr. Castle. And then we will break and come right back.

Mr. CASTLE. Thank you, Mr. Chairman. This is an interesting plight and tug of war going on here.

Mr. Stern, let me ask you a question. I read your paper and listened to what you had to say and you are concerned, as you should be, with working people and the status and how they have gone. My question or concern here is, frankly, I am not sure how private equity has impacted that directly. You do have some comments in there and some anecdotal evidence of some things. But my question to you is—or to anyone else who really knows the answer—is there any empirical or statistical evidence with respect to private equity in terms of their investments and what has happened to the employees either in losing jobs or losing benefits, be it healthcare or pensions or whatever? And has any of that been laid up against what might have happened otherwise? That is, what is happening with corporations today in America? I am trying to get the gist of whether private equity has had a negative impact on that or not.

Mr. STERN. I don't think there is it enough data or studies really yet to make those decisions. And we all can cite anecdotal situations and claim that they sort of represent the macro level, but I think we are all watching what happens. I think there is a huge opportunity here as private equity does receive, as the Congresswoman said, money from lots of public sources, you know, and that has helped make them incredibly successful, to think differently about what is their social responsibility as we would expect any business in America.

And we are hoping that, given the source of their capital particularly, you know, from public pension funds and other places, that there could be a dialogue about doing as we saw with the deal in Texas, where environmentalists and people tried to work something out that was reasonable and rational for everybody.

Mr. CASTLE. Does anybody else know if there is any real study or statistical evidence, and not just your conjecture on it.

Mr. LOWENSTEIN. There is data in Europe. It is not perfect data, but there have been studies done in Europe that show that private equity tends to result in net job growth and more investment in R&D, and other sort of measures of economic growth. There has been very little research here, so I think that is a gap that we are looking to fill.

Mr. STERN. If you don't mind, there is one study that I think is important that shows that the private equity companies pay a lower premium to the public shareholders than other strategic reinvestors pay for the same companies. This is where Chairman Frank was asking questions about conflicts. It is not yet known whether that is true, but we are seeing the private equity pay a lower premium to shareholders in public companies than other strategic investors.

Mr. CASTLE. This is an unanswerable question, I guess. Mr. Lowenstein to you, with the news of the Cerberus capital management takeover of DaimlerChrysler, or of Chrysler at least, I have a concern. I am from Delaware and we have a Chrysler plant there that has already been notified that they are going to lose a number of those jobs—not this year, but in the next couple of years.

With respect to private equity type takeover, my question is what will happen to those employees—I am not suggesting we can wave a magic wand and get them reinstated—but with respect to their pension and healthcare plans, what has been the approach of private equity with respect to the rights of employees in circumstances such as the private equity takeover of a public corporation?

Mr. LOWENSTEIN. As I said, with respect to the Chrysler particulars, I am really not in a position to discuss that. As a general proposition, as I said in my opening statement, I am certainly not aware of any pattern or consistent effort on the part of private equity firms to raid pension funds or do a variety of things that are anti-worker, anti-pension, or anti-benefit. As I said, the long-term business strategy is growth and you need to have a motivated and viable workforce to do that.

Mr. CASTLE. I don't think Cerberus is under your direct jurisdiction, but again, on the automobile or perhaps any large investments —they have already made investments in the auto industry to a degree and my concern is that is a very capital-intensive business. And do they have the ability to be able to make the investments in equipment technology, research, and some of the other things that are going to be needed to restore the American automobile industry to where it was before or is this a temporary investment on the way to making a profit someplace shortly down the road?

Mr. LOWENSTEIN. Let me answer that two ways: One is—I can't say what they will or won't do in the long run—I do believe that as all private equity funds the intent here is to grow and add value to the company. Chrysler is a difficult case study because obviously it has been operated as a public company, and it is hard to argue that it has been operated successfully as a public company in recent years. They announced 16,000 layoffs recently, as you know. I think as to exactly how that transaction plays out, we will just have to wait and see.

But again, as an overall business proposition, there is nothing I have been exposed to in my conversations with private equity firms that suggests that they have sort of an anti-worker or anti-growth bias in the business model, and in fact, quite the opposite in my experience.

Mr. CASTLE. Thank you. Thank you, Mr. Chairman.

The CHAIRMAN. I thank the gentleman. Now, Mr. Watt informed me that I was too optimistic. Apparently this is a motion to adjourn and then there is going to be 10 more minutes of debate and a couple of votes. We will be gone for 45 minutes. Can the witnesses stay? If they can, we will reconvene at 12:15 p.m.. We will have time to do whatever, and we will be back in 45 minutes. So we are in recess for 45 minutes.

[Recess]

The CHAIRMAN. Another vote has been called. I am going to end the hearing. I apologize. You sat around for nothing. I wish—you got caught in the crossfire of a parliamentary dispute. It is another adjournment vote.

I appreciate you having put up with this. I am apologetic. I was misinformed and I would not have held you here. I thank you for coming and we will not hold you here any further.

If any of the witnesses wish to submit anything for the record, please feel free to do so.
[Whereupon, at 12:45 p.m., the hearing was adjourned.]

APPENDIX

May 16, 2007

30

Congressman Kenny Marchant
5-16-07 FSC-- Private Equity hearing

I'd like to thank Chairman Frank for holding this hearing on private equity. Private equity is an industry that I feel is much misunderstood and undeservedly maligned. I am happy that the Chairman has given the industry this stage to educate us on this subject matter.

Private equity has been grabbing headlines lately with larger and larger profile deals. The latest—Cerberus's deal to buy Chrysler—even involves one of the Big Four automakers. It is because of deals like these and others like it that the private equity industry has stepped into the public eye. Unfortunately for them, they are a victim of their own success because now they have to come educate Congress on their industry.

I have the utmost confidence that once we take a closer look, everyone will see that there is absolutely nothing sinister about this industry. In my opinion, this is capitalism in one of its most innovative and efficient forms.

I look forward to the testimony of the witnesses and thank the Chairman again for scheduling this timely hearing.

31

Falling Behind: How Rising Income Inequality Harms the Middle Class
Testimony by Professor Robert H. Frank[1] before the House Financial Services Committee
May 16, 2007

Economic inequality has been growing rapidly in the United States. Congress must soon decide whether to make permanent recent changes in tax policy that will increase it further. In this testimony I will review the causes and consequences of rising income inequality and explore possible policy remedies for it.

The Historical Context

At the end of World War II, income inequality was lower in the United States than at any time since the 1920s. During the ensuing three decades, incomes grew briskly and at about the same rate—almost 3 percent per year—for households up and down the income ladder.

That pattern began to change in the 1970s. Since 1979, for example, the incomes of families in the bottom 80 percent of the income distribution have grown by less than 1 percent each year, and only households in the top 20 percent have enjoyed income growth comparable to that in the earlier period. For a small group at the very top of the economic ladder, however, incomes have been growing explosively. The top tenth of one percent of earners, for example, now earn four times as much as in 1980.

The gains have been larger still for those even higher up the income ladder. For more than 25 years, *Business Week* has conducted an annual survey of the earnings of chief executive officers of the largest U.S. corporations. In 1980, those executives earned 42 times as much as the average American worker, a ratio larger than the corresponding ratios for such countries as Japan and Germany even today. By 2000, however, American CEOs were earning 531 times the average worker's salary.

But the biggest winners of all have been top earners in the financial services industry. Thus, according to Institutional Investor's *Alpha* magazine, James Simons, a hedge fund manager, earned $1.7 billion last year, and two other hedge fund managers made more than $1 billion. The combined income of the top 25 hedge fund managers was over $14 billion in 2006.

Why Has Inequality Grown?

In the standard textbook account, the salary a person commands in the labor market is proportional to his or her stock of human capital—an amalgam of talent, experience, education, training, and other factors that affect productivity. Armed with this perspective, many economists have argued that the recent growth in inequality has been the result of an increase in the rate of return to education and other forms of human capital. Yet we observe essentially the same pattern of inequality growth among college graduates as in the population as a whole. The least prosperous college graduates have struggled to stay even, those in the middle have made only modest gains, while those at the top have done spectacularly well. Among college graduates, the return to education has been higher in some fields than in others. For example, the earnings of computer science graduates grew more rapidly during the last two decades than those of English majors. But even among English majors, those at the top have enjoyed spectacular earnings growth.

Others have argued that inequality has increased in the United States because globalization has put unskilled American workers in competition with low-wage workers from other lands. Yet the basic pattern of inequality growth has been the same even among dentists, who are largely immune from foreign competition. Most dentists today earn little more than their counterparts from 1979, but the best paid dentists earn almost three times as much.[2]

The human capital story directs our attention to the worker rather than the job. Yet a person who embodies a certain level of human capital will realize its full value only if placed in a position with adequate scope and opportunity. For example, whereas the value of having a slightly more talented salesperson may mean little if the task is to sell children's shoes, it will mean a great deal if the task is to sell securities to the world's largest pension funds.

Philip Cook and I have argued that an important contributor to increased inequality has been the spread and intensification of reward structures once confined largely to markets for sports and entertainment.[3] In conventional labor markets, reward is proportional to absolute performance. Thus, in the classic piece-rate scheme, a worker who assembles 101 widgets in a week gets paid one percent more than a coworker who assembles only 100. In contrast, we define a winner-take-all market as one in which small differences in performance often translate into enormous differences in economic reward.

---

[1] Henrietta Johnson Louis Professor of Management and Professor of Economics, Johnson Graduate School of Management, Cornell University, Ithaca, NY 14853. Contact: www.robert-h-frank.com.
[2] For a discussion of increased inequality among different groups, see Frank and Cook, 1995, chapter 5.
[3] See Frank and Cook, 1995.

32

2

The winner-take-all perspective urges us to look first to the nature of the positions people hold, rather than to their personal characteristics. An economist under the influence of the human capital metaphor might ask: Why not save money by hiring two mediocre people to fill an important position instead of paying the exorbitant salary required to attract someone unusually good? Although that sort of substitution might work with physical capital, in does not necessarily work with human capital. Two average hedge fund managers or CEOs or novelists or quarterbacks are often a poor substitute for a single gifted one.

The result is that for positions for which additional talent has great value to the employer or the marketplace, there is no reason to expect that the market will compensate individuals in proportion to their human capital. For these positions—ones that confer the greatest leverage or "amplification" of human talent—small increments of talent have great value, and may be greatly rewarded as a result of the normal competitive market process. This insight lies at the core of our alternative explanation of growing inequality.

Technology has greatly extended the power and reach of the planet's most gifted performers. The printing press let a relatively few gifted storytellers displace millions of village raconteurs. Now that we listen mostly to recorded music, the world's best musicians can literally be everywhere at once. The electronic newswire has allowed a small number of syndicated columnists to displace a host of local journalists. And the proliferation of personal computers enabled a handful of software developers to replace thousands of tax accountants.

For present purposes, a key feature of winner-take-all markets is that participants' rewards depend on relative, not just absolute, performance. Whereas a farmer's pay depends on the absolute amount of wheat he or she produces, and not on how that compares with the amounts produced by other farmers, a software developer's pay depends largely on her performance ranking. In the market for personal income tax software, for instance, once the market reached consensus on which among the scores or even hundreds of competing programs was the most comprehensive and user-friendly, the lesser-ranked programs quickly disappeared. And although Intuit's *TurboTax* may have been only slightly better than its nearest rivals, the rewards to its developer were enormously greater.

Of course, the dependence of economic reward on performance ranking is nothing new. What is new is the rapid erosion of the barriers that once prevented the top performers from serving broader markets. In the music industry, the driving force was the arrival of breathtakingly lifelike pre-recorded music. Changes in physical production technologies have been important in other industries as well, but these changes often explain only a small part of the picture.

Of central importance in other cases has been the emergence of the so-called information revolution. In the global village, there is unprecedented market consensus on who the top players are in each arena, and unprecedented opportunity to deal with these players. A company that made the best tire in Akron was once assured of being a player in at least the northern Ohio tire market. But today's sophisticated consumers increasingly purchase their tires from only a handful of the best tire producers worldwide.

Before there can be large and concentrated rewards in a winner-take-all market, the top performers must not only generate high value, but there must also be effective competition for their services. Yet in many markets, a variety of formal and informal rules traditionally prevented such competition.

Most major sports leagues, for example, once maintained restrictive agreements that prevented team owners from bidding for one another's most talented players. It was major league baseball's reserve clause, for example, that made players the exclusive property of the teams that drafted them. Even though the introduction of nationally televised games in the 1950s increased the economic leverage of baseball players enormously, the ensuing decades saw little real growth in their salaries. In the wake of Andy Messersmith's successful court challenge the reserve clause in 1975, however, player salaries began to grow explosively, now averaging almost $3 million per year. Similar salary trajectories have ensued as players have won at least limited free agency rights in all the major professional team sports.

Unlike the owners of professional sports teams, the owners of businesses were never subject to formal sanctions against bidding for one another's most talented employees. But there were often informal norms that seemed to have virtually the same effect. Under these norms, it was once the almost universal practice to promote business executives from within, which often enabled companies to retain top executives for less than one-tenth of today's salaries.

The anti-raiding norms of business have recently begun to unravel, in part perhaps because managerial talent is has in fact become more fungible in the new environment. It once would have been unthinkable for a computer giant to hire a former tobacco executive as its CEO. But IBM's decision to hire RJR Nabisco CEO Louis Gerstner is now widely viewed as a move that ensured IBM's survival.. In the interim, inter-firm and inter-industry boundaries have become increasingly permeable, and business executives are today little different from the free agents of professional sports. Firms that fail to pay standout executives and investment managers their due now stand to lose them to aggressive rivals.

With corporate malfeasance much in the news in recent years, there is little doubt that at least some of the spectacular corporate pay packages were not won on merit. But it is a mistake to view corporate malfeasance as the only, or even the most important, cause of rising pay disparity. Despite the well-publicized cases of late, corporate corruption is almost certainly a less important problem today than it was several decades ago. Interlocking directorates, for example, are less common today, and shareholder activists backed by multibillion dollar pension funds simply did not exist several decades ago. Pay disparities have increased because new technologies have increased the leverage of key players in every arena, and increased competition has translated that additional leverage into higher pay.

Do Growing Pay Disparities Matter?

Technologies that extend the reach of top performers have greatly benefited consumers. But they have also led to increased inequality. Thus, as noted, the incomes of middle-income families are now slightly higher in real absolute terms than they were two decades ago, but substantially lower, in relative terms.

I will consider two possible ways in which this rise in inequality might have made things worse for these families. First, I will examine how the capacity of material goods to deliver satisfaction, in purely psychological terms, depends heavily on the context in which those goods are consumed. I will then discuss a variety of more tangible ways in which a family's economic welfare might be adversely affected by the spending of others.

The Psychological Costs of Inequality

Most of us were taught from an early age not to worry about how our incomes compare with the incomes of others. This sensible advice stems from the observation that since there will always be others with more, focusing closely on income comparisons can't help but generate reasons to feel unhappy.

But suppose you were faced with a choice between the following hypothetical worlds:

World A: You earn $110,000 per year, others earn $200,000

World B: You earn $100,000 per year, others earn $85,000.

The income figures represent real purchasing power. Thus your higher income in World A would enable you to purchase a house that is 10 percent larger than the one you would be able to afford in World B, 10 percent more restaurant meals, and so on. No matter which world you choose, your relative position will not change in the future. Confronting a once-for-all choice between these two worlds, which one would you choose?

Much of neoclassical economic theory rests on the premise that World A is the uniquely correct choice. This theory assumes that people derive satisfaction primarily from the absolute quantity of goods and services they consume. On that measure, World A is better because it offers higher absolute consumption for every citizen. That fact notwithstanding, however, a substantial proportion of people confronted with this choice say they would opt for World B.[4]

Many economists appear reluctant to take seriously the concerns that might lead people to make this choice. On its face, this is a curious position for a profession whose practitioners often warmly endorse Jeremy Bentham's dictum that a taste for poetry is no better than a taste for pushpins. If most people say they'd prefer World B, a genuine commitment to consumer sovereignty would appear to rule out any categorical claim that World A is necessarily best for all.

Modern disciples of Adam Smith have nonetheless been extremely reluctant to introduce the purely psychological costs of inequality into discussions of economic policy. Yet as Smith himself recognized, experiencing such costs is a basic component of human nature. Writing more than two centuries ago, he introduced the important idea that local consumption standards influence the goods and services that people consider essential (or "necessaries," as Smith called them). In the following passage, for example, he described the factors that influence the amount an individual must spend on clothing in order to be able appear in public "without shame."

> By necessaries I understand not only the commodities which are indispensably necessary for the support of life, but whatever the custom of the country renders it indecent for creditable people, even of the lowest order, to be without. A linen shirt, for example, is, strictly speaking, not a necessary of life. The Greeks and Romans lived, I suppose, very comfortably though they had no linen. But in the present times, through the greater part of Europe, a creditable day-labourer would be ashamed to appear in public without a linen shirt, the want of which would be supposed to denote that disgraceful degree of poverty which, it is presumed, nobody can well fall into without extreme bad conduct. Custom, in the same manner, has rendered leather shoes a necessary of life in England. The poorest creditable person of either sex would be ashamed to appear in public without them.[5]

---

[4] See, for example, Solnick and Hemenway, 1998.

[5] Smith, 1937.

34

4

The absolute standard of living in the United States today is of course vastly higher than it was in Adam Smith's 18th-century Scotland. Yet Smith's observations apply with equal force to contemporary industrial societies. Consider, for instance, *The New York Times* correspondent Dirk Johnson's account of the experiences of Wendy Williams, a middle-school student from a low-income family in a highly prosperous community in Illinois.[6] Both of Wendy's parents are employed at low-wage jobs, and the family lives in Chateau Estates, a trailer park at which her school bus picks her up each morning.

> Watching classmates strut past in designer clothes, Wendy Williams sat silently on the yellow school bus, wearing a cheap belt and rummage-sale slacks. One boy stopped and yanked his thumb, demanding her seat.
>
> "Move it, trailer girl," he sneered.
>
> It has never been easy to live on the wrong side of the tracks. But in the economically robust 1990's, with sprawling new houses and three-car garages sprouting like cornstalks on the Midwestern prairie, the sting that comes with scarcity gets rubbed with an extra bit of salt.
>
> ....
>
> To be without money, in so many ways, is to be left out.
>
> "I told this girl: 'That's a really awesome shirt. Where did you get it?'" said Wendy, explaining that she knew it was out of her price range, but that she wanted to join the small talk. "And she looked at me and laughed and said, 'Why would you want to know?'"
>
> A lanky, soft-spoken girl with large brown eyes, Wendy pursed her lips to hide a slight overbite that got her the nickname Rabbit, a humiliation she once begged her mother and father to avoid by sending her to an orthodontist.
>
> For struggling parents, keenly aware that adolescents agonize over the social pecking order, the styles of the moment and the face in the mirror, there is no small sense of failure in telling a child that she cannot have what her classmates take for granted.
>
> "Do you know what it's like?" asked Wendy's mother, Veronica Williams, "to have your daughter come home and say, 'Mom, the kids say my clothes are tacky,' and then walk off with her head hanging low."

An adolescent in 18th-century Scotland would not have been much embarrassed by having a slight overbite, because not even the wealthiest members of society wore braces on their teeth then. In the intervening years, however, rising living standards have altered the frame of reference that defines an acceptable standard of cosmetic dentistry. On what ground might we argue that inequality's toll on individuals like Wendy Williams is unimportant because it occurs in psychological rather than explicit monetary terms?

More Tangible Costs of a Widening Income Gap

Increased spending at the top of the income distribution has not only imposed psychological costs on families in the middle, it has also raised the cost of achieving many basic goals. It has done so by means of a process I call expenditure cascades.[7] Expenditure cascades have been launched by the large growth in purchasing power at the top of the income ladder.

Consumption generally tracks income. When the incomes of the wealthy rise, they eventually spend more on houses, cars, clothing and other goods, just as others do. Upon learning that someone at the top has built a 60,000-square-foot house or purchased a new Ferrari Scaglietti, most people in the middle quintile feel no inclination to alter their own spending. But among those just below the top, such purchases have an impact. They subtly change the social frame of reference that defines what kinds of houses and cars seem necessary or appropriate. Additional spending by top earners thus leads others just below them to spend more. And when they do so, others just below them are affected in the same way, and so on, all the way down the income ladder.

In short, burgeoning incomes at the top have launched expenditure cascades that have put financial pressure on the middle class. An expenditure cascade in housing, for example, helps explain why the median size of a newly constructed house in the United States, which stood at less than 1,600 square feet in 1980, had grown to more than 2,100 square feet by 2001.[8] During the same period, the median family's real income increased by less than 15 percent—not nearly enough to comfortably finance so much larger a house.

---

[6] Johnson, 1998, p. A1.

[7] See Frank and Levine, 2007.

[8] http://www.census.gov/prod/2003pubs/02statab/construct.pdf; http://www.census.gov/hhes/income/histinc/f03.html.

The steep rise in median house prices is one of the most important sources of the middle-class economic squeeze. It is an indirect consequence of the higher incomes and spending of top earners. Although it might seem that a family could escape the squeeze by just buying a smaller house, that option would in fact entail a significant cost. The problem is that there is a strong link between the price of a house and the quality of the corresponding neighborhood school. Failure to buy a house near the median price for the area means having to send one's children to below-average schools, a cost that most parents seem unwilling to bear. The upshot is that despite a modest increase in their incomes, middle-class families must now work longer hours, borrow more, save less, and commute longer distances in order to continue sending their children to schools of just average quality.

Increased spending at the top has also imposed other costs on those below. Middle-class families who buy a typical 3,000-pound sedan will incur risks that didn't exist in the 1970s, since they must now share the roads with 6,000-pound Lincoln Navigators and 7,500-pound Ford Excursions. In self-defense, they may want to spend more for a heavier vehicle.

Consider, too, how increased spending at the top affects how much one must spend on a professional wardrobe. Placement counselors have always stressed the importance of dressing well for job interviews. But dressing well is a relative concept. To look good means to look better than other candidates. Because top earners have more money, they spend more on clothing, which has led those just below them to spend more, and so on. So to look good for a job interview, the median earner must spend more than before. Of course, if one job candidate is clearly much better qualified than others for a given position, the clothing he or she wears during job interviews is unlikely to make any difference. But competition is stiff for jobs that pay well and offer opportunities for advancement, and there are typically many well-qualified candidates for such jobs. Under the circumstances, candidates are prudent to take whatever steps they can to gain an edge.

Even the gifts that middle-income families feel compelled to give are have been affected by the greater affluence of top earners. Top earners have been spending a lot more on gifts because they have a lot more money. And as in the examples just considered, their extra spending has launched an expenditure cascade. When others spend more for gifts at weddings, anniversaries, birthdays, and other special occasions, the rest of us must follow suit, or else risk being seen as people who just don't care.

The Educational Arms Race: Another Costly Burden for the Middle Class

Because the pay gap between top earners and others has grown sharply in every field, there is much more intense competition than before for top positions. The employers that post openings for such positions typically receive résumés from hundreds or even thousands of applicants, more than they can possibly interview. Increasingly, a candidate's educational credentials have become the most important criterion in the screening process. Many employers now limit their interviews to applicants from a small handful of top-ranked schools. As expected, this change has fueled explosive growth in demand for elite educational credentials.

For the sons and daughters of the middle class, it was always more difficult than for the children of the wealthy to gain admission to the nation's leading universities. The growing demand for elite credentials has made access even more difficult. It has also made higher education more expensive and made it less likely that financial aid will be awarded on the basis of need.

In response to the increased demand for elite credentials, a growing number of institutions have moved aggressively to acquire the resources that confer elite academic status. But because elite status is an inherently relative concept, the primary effect has been to bid up the prices of these resources. The resulting "positional arms races" help explain why tuitions at both public and private university have risen sharply.[9] At public universities, for example, tuitions more than tripled between 1980 and 2004, and rose at nearly the same rate in private universities.[10] At some elite private schools, the annual cost of tuition, room, and board now exceeds $45,000.

Even as tuition and other college costs have been rising, the amount of financial aid available to middle-income and poor families has been dwindling. Because the average SAT score of entering freshmen is itself an important index of an institution's academic status, schools aspiring to elite status have little choice but to bid aggressively for top-scoring students. And hence the growing tendency for merit-based financial aid to displace need-based financial aid. The upshot is that for students from middle- and low-income families, the net cost of receiving a college education has risen dramatically.

At the same time, the economic payoff from a college degree has not kept pace. Indeed, the median salary of college degree holders has actually fallen during the last three decades. Among young male wage and salary workers, for example, the median earnings of those holding a bachelor's degree or higher was $52,087 in 1972 but only $48,955 in 2002 (both figures in 2002 dollars).[11]

---

[9] For a discussion, see Frank and Cook, 1995, chapter 8.
[10] College Board, 2004.
[11] U.S. Department of Education, 2004.

For the millions of students who have been unable to attend college because of the economic squeeze on the middle class, things are even worse. For although the payoff to a college degree has declined in absolute terms, it has increased relative to the payoff of having only a high school diploma. For those with only a high school diploma, median earnings was $42,630 in 1972 but only $29,647 in 2002 (again, both figures in 2002 dollars).

So even the slight income gains received by median earners in recent decades are illusory in a broader economic sense. The real hourly pay rates for most individuals in this group are lower now than they were 25 years ago. Their small gains in total family income are the result almost entirely of greater labor force participation of married women.

Consequences of the Financial Squeeze

If the real incomes of middle-class families are little larger than before, how have these families financed their higher levels of consumption and larger tuition payments? In part by working longer hours, but mainly by saving less, borrowing more, and doing without things that were once considered essential. American families with at least one credit card, for example, now carry an average of more than $9,000 in credit card debt, and before recent changes in the laws governing bankruptcy, personal bankruptcy filings were occurring at seven times the rate they did in 1980. The national personal savings rate, always low by international standards, has fallen sharply since the 1980s and have been negative for the past two calendar years (the first time that has happened since The Great Depression). One in five American families has zero or negative net worth. Some 45 million Americans now have no health insurance, 5 million more than in the early 1990s.[12]

In brief, the data support popular press accounts portraying widespread and genuine economic distress among middle class families. The difficulties confronting these families are not the result of exploitation by employers with market power. Rather, they stem in large part from the growing inequality in income and wealth that has resulted from ordinary market forces. Modern technology has greatly amplified the economic leverage of the best performers in every domain. By all indications, it will continue to do so. If future income gains continue to be captured disproportionately by top earners, as the winner-take-all perspective suggests, things will get worse. Luxury spending will continue to grow briskly, launching additional expenditure cascades that will raise the price of admission to the middle class still further.

Income Inequality Also Distorts Occupational Choice

Consumers clearly gain when modern technology and increased mobility allow the most talented people to serve broader markets. Once the world's hospitals are linked by high-speed data transmission networks, for example, the world's most gifted neurosurgeons can assist in the diagnosis and treatment of patients thousands of miles away—patients whose care would otherwise be left to less talented and experienced physicians. And we should count as a benefit that the most talented executives are now more likely to manage the most important companies.

Yet the lure of the top prizes in winner-take-all markets has also steered many of our most able graduates toward career choices that make little sense for them as individuals, and still less sense for the nation as a whole. In increasing numbers, our best and brightest graduates pursue top positions in law, finance, consulting, and other overcrowded arenas, in the process forsaking careers in engineering, manufacturing, civil service, teaching, and other occupations in which an infusion of additional talent would yield greater benefit to society.

One study estimated, for example, that whereas a doubling of enrollments in engineering would cause the growth rate of GDP to rise by half a percentage point, a doubling of enrollments in law would actually cause a decline of three-tenths of a point.[13] Yet the number of new lawyers admitted to the bar each year more than doubled between 1970 and 1990, a period during which the average standardized test scores of new public school teachers fell dramatically.

One might hope that such imbalances would fade as wages are bid up in underserved markets and driven down in overcrowded ones, and indeed there have been recent indications of a decline in the number of law school applicants. For two reasons, however, such adjustments are destined to fall short.

The first is an informational problem. An intelligent decision about whether to pit one's own skills against a largely unknown field of rivals obviously requires a well-informed estimate of the odds of winning. Yet people's assessments about these odds are notoriously inaccurate. Survey evidence shows, for example, that some eighty percent of us think we are better than average drivers; and that more than 90 percent of workers consider themselves more productive than their average colleague.

Psychologists call this the "Lake Wobegon Effect," and its importance for present purposes is that it leads people to overestimate their odds of landing a superstar position. Indeed, overconfidence is likely to be especially strong in the realm of career choice because, in addition to the usual motivational biases that support it, there is also

[12] http://www.nchc.org/facts/coverage.shtml
[13] See Murphy et al., 1991.

the fact the biggest winners are so conspicuous. The seven-figure NBA stars appear on television several times each week, whereas the many thousands who fail to make the league attract little notice. Similarly, the handful of hedge fund managers with 10-figure salaries are far more visible than the legions of aspiring hedge fund managers who never made the final cut. When people overestimate their chances of winning, the number who forsake productive occupations in traditional markets to compete in winner-take-all markets will be larger than what could be justified on traditional cost-benefit grounds.

The second reason for persistent overcrowding in winner-take-all markets is a structural problem that economists call "the tragedy of the commons." This same problem helps explain why we see too many prospectors for gold. In the initial stages of exploiting a newly discovered field of gold, the presence of additional prospectors may significantly increase the total amount of gold that is found. Beyond some point, however, additional prospectors contribute very little. Thus, the gold found by a newcomer to a crowded gold field is largely gold that would otherwise have been found by others.

Consider a man who must choose whether to work in a factory for $10,000 a year or to become a prospector for gold. If the two activities are equally attractive apart from the matter of pay, he should become a prospector only if he expects to find at least $10,000 worth of gold a year. Suppose he expects to find $11,000 in gold, and that $9,000 of that gold would have been found by others if he had worked in the factory. It will still be worth his while to go prospecting, even though his presence in the gold field increases the total amount of gold found by only $2,000. Yet society's total income would have been $8,000 higher had he instead gone to work in the factory.

Similarly misleading incentives confront potential contestants in winner-take-all markets. Beyond some point, for example, an increase in the number of aspiring hedge fund managers produces much less than a proportional increase in the amount of commissions on managed investments. One MBA student's good fortune in landing a position in a leading hedge fund is thus largely offset by his rival's failure to land that same position.

To be sure, even those who fail to win the biggest prizes often go on to earn comfortable incomes. But career choices must be measured not in terms of absolute pay, but relative to what might have been. Contestants for the top prizes in finance are highly talented people who could have held interesting jobs at high pay in other fields. Those who end up as account managers in small banks may not starve, but neither do they realize their full potential.

The externality that leads too many people to shoot for the top positions in law and finance is similar to the one that caused trouble in the case of prospectors for gold: Just as individual prospectors take no account of the fact that most of the gold they might find would otherwise be found by others, so also do aspiring superstars tend to ignore the fact that their presence makes other contestants less likely to win.

So for both informational and structural reasons, overcrowding in winner-take-all markets is not likely to be a self-correcting problem.

Inequality Is a Public Problem

Some have castigated organizations for their lack of restraint in curbing runaway salaries at the top. But to the extent that competitive forces have driving these salaries, it is quixotic to expect that they might be attenuated by individual restraint. A slightly more talented CEO or hedge fund manager can boost a large organization's annual bottom line by hundreds of millions of dollars or more. An organization that fails to bid aggressively for its top candidates all but ensures they will end up working for rivals.

The point is not that talented individuals are too lazy to work hard unless they are paid multimillion-dollar annual salaries. Rather, it is that most highly talented people, like others, tend to choose the employer that makes the best offer. Evidence suggests that if all salary offers were cut by half, the most talented individuals would work just as hard as before. But individual organization control only the amounts they pay, not the amounts paid by other organizations. If society wants to slow the rate of growth of income inequality, tax policy is the only available lever.

When market forces cause income inequality to grow, public policy in most countries tends to push in the opposite direction. In the United States, however, we have enacted tax cuts for the wealthy and cut public services for the needy. Cynics explain this curious inversion by saying that the wealthy have captured the political process in Washington and are exploiting it to their own advantage.

This explanation makes sense, however, only if those in power have an extremely naïve understanding of their own interests. A careful reading of the evidence suggests that even the wealthy have been made worse off, on balance, by recent tax cuts. The private benefits of these cuts have been much smaller, and their indirect costs much larger, than many recipients appear to have anticipated.

On the benefit side, tax cuts have led the wealthy to buy larger houses, in the seemingly plausible expectation that doing so would make them happier. As economists increasingly recognize, however, well-being depends less on how much people consume in absolute terms than on the social context in which consumption occurs. Compelling evidence suggests that for the wealthy in particular, when everyone's house grows larger, the primary effect is merely to redefine what qualifies as an acceptable dwelling.

So, although the recent tax cuts have enabled the wealthy to buy more and bigger things, these purchases appear to have had little impact. As the economist Richard Layard has written, "In a poor country, a man proves to his wife that he loves her by giving her a rose, but in a rich country, he must give a dozen roses."

On the cost side of the ledger, the federal budget deficits created by the recent tax cuts have had serious consequences, even for the wealthy. These deficits will exceed $1 trillion over the next six years, according to projections by the Congressional Budget Office. The most widely reported consequences of the deficits have been cuts in government programs that serve the nation's poorest families. And since the wealthy are well represented in our political system, their favored programs may seem safe from the budget ax. Wealthy families have further insulated themselves by living in gated communities and sending their children to private schools. Yet such steps go only so far.

For example, deficits have led to cuts in federal financing for basic scientific research, even as the United States' share of global patents granted continues to decline. Such cuts threaten the very basis of our long-term economic prosperity. As Senator Pete Domenici, Republican of New Mexico, said: "We thought we'd keep the high-end jobs, and others would take the low-end jobs. We're now on track to a second-rate economy and a second-rate country."

Large deficits also threaten our public health. Thus, despite the increasing threat from micro-organisms like E. coli 0157, the government inspects beef processing plants at only a quarter the rate it did in the early 1980's. Poor people have died from eating contaminated beef but so have rich people.

Citing revenue shortfalls, the nation postpones maintenance of its streets and highways, even though doing so means having to spend two to five times as much on repairs in the long run. In the short run, bad roads cause thousands of accidents each year, many of them fatal. Poor people die in these accidents but so do rich people. When a pothole destroys a tire and wheel, replacements cost only $63 for a Ford Escort but $1,569 for a Porsche 911.

Deficits have also compromised the nation's security. In 2004, for example, the Bush administration reduced financing for the Energy Department's program to secure loosely guarded nuclear stockpiles in the former Soviet Union by 8 percent. Former Senator Sam Nunn now heads a private foundation whose mission is to raise private donations to expedite this effort. And despite the rational fear that terrorists may try to detonate a nuclear bomb in an American city, most cargo containers continue to enter the nation's ports without inspection.

Large federal budget deficits and low household savings rates have also forced our government to borrow more than $800 billion each year, primarily from China, Japan and South Korea. These loans must be repaid in full, with interest. The resulting financial burden, plus the risks associated with increased international monetary instability, fall disproportionately on the rich.

At the president's behest, Congress has already enacted tax cuts that will result in some $2 trillion in revenue losses by 2010. According to one recent estimate, 52.5 percent of these cuts will have gone to the top 5 percent of earners by the time the enabling legislation is fully phased in.

With the economy already at full employment, no one pretends these cuts are needed to stimulate spending. Nor is there any evidence that further cuts would summon outpourings of additional effort and risk taking. Nor, finally, does anyone deny that further cuts would increase the already high costs associated with larger federal budget deficits.

Moralists often urge the wealthy to imagine how easily their lives could have turned out differently, to adopt a more forgiving posture toward those less prosperous. But top earners might also wish to consider evidence that their own families would have been better off, in purely practical terms, had it not been for the tax cuts of recent years.

The nation's recent fiscal policy choices provide striking testimony to the incredible staying power of trickle-down theory. This largely discredited theory's claim that lower taxes on the rich will spur economic growth has animated the push for less progressive taxes for almost two decades. Trickle-down theorists are quick to object that higher taxes would cause top earners to work less and take fewer risks, thereby stifling economic growth. In their familiar rhetorical flourish, they insist that a more progressive tax system would kill the geese that lay the golden eggs. On close examination, however, this claim is supported neither by economic theory nor by empirical evidence.

The surface plausibility of trickle-down theory owes much to the fact that it appears to follow from the time-honored belief that people respond to incentives. Because higher taxes on top earners reduce the reward for effort, it seems reasonable that they would induce people to work less, as trickle-down theorists claim. As every economics textbook makes clear, however, a decline in after-tax wages also exerts a second, opposing effect. By making people feel poorer, it provides them with an incentive to recoup their income loss by working harder than before. Economic theory says nothing about which of these offsetting effects may dominate.

If economic theory is unkind to trickle-down proponents, the lessons of experience are downright brutal. If lower real wages induce people to work shorter hours, then the opposite should be true when real wages increase. According to trickle-down theory, then, the cumulative effect of the last century's sharp rise in real wages should have been a significant increase in hours worked. In fact, however, the workweek is much shorter now than in 1900.

Trickle-down theory also predicts shorter workweeks in countries with lower real after-tax pay rates. Yet here, too, the numbers tell a different story. For example, even though chief executives in Japan earn less than one-fifth what their American counterparts do and face substantially higher marginal tax rates, Japanese executives do not log shorter hours.

Trickle-down theory also predicts a positive correlation between inequality and economic growth, the idea being that income disparities strengthen motivation to get ahead. Yet when researchers track the data within individual countries over time, they find a negative correlation. In the decades immediately after World War II, for example, income inequality was low by historical standards, yet growth rates in most industrial countries were extremely high. In contrast, growth rates have been only about half as large in the years since 1973, a period in which inequality has been steadily rising.

The same pattern has been observed in cross-national data. For example, using data from the World Bank and the Organization for Economic Co-operation and Development for a sample of 65 industrial nations, the economists Alberto Alesina and Dani Rodrick found lower growth rates in countries where higher shares of national income went to the top 5 percent and the top 20 percent of earners. In contrast, larger shares for poor and middle-income groups were associated with higher growth rates.[14] Again and again, the observed pattern is the opposite of the one predicted by trickle-down theory.

The trickle-down theorist's view of the world is nicely captured by a Donald Reilly cartoon depicting two well-fed executives nursing cocktails on a summer afternoon as they lounge on flotation devices in a pool. Pointing to himself, one says angrily to the other, "If those soak-the-rich birds get their way, I can tell you here's one coolie who'll stop" working so hard.

This portrait bears little resemblance to reality. In the 1950s, American executives earned far lower salaries and faced substantially higher marginal tax rates than they do today. Yet most of them competed energetically for higher rungs on the corporate ladder. The claim that slightly higher tax rates would cause today's executives to abandon that quest is simply not credible.

Now, our growing understanding of the incentive problems created by winner-take-all markets poses an even more decisive challenge to trickle-down theory. Society's highest incomes accrue to the top performers in winner-take-all markets, which, as noted, persistently attract too many contestants. To the extent that economic incentives matter at all (and it is the cornerstone of trickle-down theory that they do), the effect of higher taxes on top earners would be to cause fewer of our most talented people to compete for limited slots in winner-take-all markets. Moreover, the people most likely to drop out would be those whose odds of making it into the winner's circle were smallest to begin with. Thus, the value of what gets produced in winner-take-all markets would not be much reduced if higher taxes were levied on winners' incomes; and any reductions that did occur would tend to be more than offset by increased output in traditional markets.

The optimistic conclusion is that a more progressive tax structure may produce not only greater equality of incomes, but also higher economic growth.

Better Still: A Progressive Consumption Tax

Advocates of consumption taxes have stressed their positive impact on savings, their ability to capture revenue now lost to the underground economy, and their relative simplicity. These are important advantages, to be sure. Yet they pale in comparison to the advantages of using consumption taxes to counteract the inefficiencies that arise from winner-take-all markets.

For instance, a progressive tax on consumption, like a progressive income tax, would reduce the effective rewards of landing a superstar position. Like a progressive income tax, it would thus reduce overcrowding in winner-take-all markets.

A progressive consumption tax would also pay another dividend—namely, it would free up hundreds of billions of dollars of resources that are largely wasted through mine-is-bigger consumption arms races. Consider, for instance, a wealthy family's decision to build an 8,000-square-foot house. It does so not just because spacious living quarters are desirable in some absolute sense, but also because houses that size have become the norm for their income bracket. To have a smaller or less well appointed house than one's peers would entail social embarrassment. Yet, if *all* wealthy families had smaller houses (as indeed most do in cities like Manhattan and Tokyo), no one would be embarrassed in the least.

The standards that define acceptable wardrobes, cars, and a host of other important budget items likewise depend strongly on the amounts other people spend on them. This means that if others were to spend less, we, too, could spend less without any real loss in satisfaction.

Thus, if a consumption tax led wealthy families to buy 5,000-square-foot houses instead 8,000, and Porsche Boxsters instead of Ferraris, no one would really be worse off, and several hundred thousand dollars of resources per family would be freed up for more pressing purposes—deficit reduction, medical research, capital investment, job

[14] See Alesina and Rodrick, 1992.

40

10

training, school lunches, drug treatment programs, time for family and community, whatever. The elegant hidden feature of the progressive consumption tax is this ability to create resources virtually out of thin air.

Opponents of progressive consumption taxes will caution that such taxes will cause unemployment, citing the layoffs in the shipbuilding industry that followed imposition of a luxury tax on yachts in 1991. But that was a tax with a glaring loophole that exempted boats purchased outside the country. A general progressive tax on consumption would shift employment from some activities to others, to be sure, but that is precisely the objective. Full employment for carpenters can be achieved by the construction of small number of mansions for the well-to-do, or by the construction of a larger number of smaller houses for people with more modest incomes.

Proposals to tax consumption also raise the specter of citizens having to save receipts for each purchase, of politicians and producers bickering over which products are to be exempt, and so on. Yet a system of consumption taxation need entail no greater complexity than the usual systems of income taxation. Indeed, with the strategic elimination of certain deductions and loopholes, it could easily be made to entail less.

The need to keep receipts, for example, can be avoided by exploiting the simple accounting identity that a person's income is the amount she spends plus the amount she saves. This permits us to calculate overall consumption as the difference between current income, which must be reported under the current tax system, and current savings, which would document in much the same way that we currently document contributions to 401(k) retirement accounts. There is simply no need to add up the value of each item purchased.

The need to debate which, if any, consumption categories ought to be exempt can be avoided by having a large standard deduction—by making the first, say, $30,000 of each family's annual consumption expenditures exempt from taxation. This feature would serve two purposes: it would shield necessities like food, health care, basic clothing, shelter, and transportation-- from taxation; and it would make the tax progressive. Further progressivity could be achieved by having tax rates that rise with consumption, just as we now have tax rates that rise with income. The so-called "Unlimited-Savings-Allowance" proposal by Senators Nunn and Domenici in the mid-1990s, was a tax with all these features.

The so-called "flat tax" favored by many conservatives is itself a consumption tax, and that is a point in its favor. Yet its adoption would move us in precisely the wrong direction. By reducing the tax rates on top earners by more than half, it would steer even more of our best and brightest students into winner-take-all markets that are already overcrowded. By giving the top earners much more disposable income, it would also fuel the growth of wasteful consumption expenditures, both by the rich and by others who emulate them. And most important, it would worsen the social strains of income inequality.

The nation's current tax policies rest on an outmoded understanding of the forces that allocate both talent and reward in a winner-take-all society. These forces suggest that equity and growth are more likely to be complements than substitutes. This is a hopeful conclusion, indeed, for it means that the very same policies that promote both fiscal integrity and equality are also likely to spur economic growth.

References

Alesina, Alberto and Dani Rodrick. "Distribution, Political Conflict and Economic Growth: A Simple Theory and Some Empirical Evidence," in A. Cukierman, Z. Hercovitz and L. Leiderman (eds.), *The Political Economy of Business Cycles and Growth*, M.I.T. Press, Cambridge, MA, 1992.

College Board, "Trends in College Pricing 2004," http://www.collegeboard.com/prod_downloads/press/cost04/041264TrendsPricing2004FINAL.pdf.

Frank, Robert H. and Philip Cook. *The Winner-Take-All Society*, New York: The Free Press, 1995.

Frank, Robert H. and Adam Levine. "Expenditure Cascades," Cornell University mimeograph, 2007.

Johnson, Dirk. "When Money Is Everything, Except Hers," *New York Times*, October 28, 1998: A1.

Murphy, Kevin M., Andrei Shleifer, and Robert W. Vishny. "The Allocation of Talent: Implications for Growth," *Quarterly Journal of Economics*. CVI, May, 1991: 503-530.

Smith, Adam. *The Wealth of Nations*, New York: Random House, 1937.

Solnick, Sara J. and David Hemenway. "Is More Always Better? A Survey on Positional Concerns," 37 *Journal of Economic Behavior and Organization*, 373, 1998.

U.S. Department of Education, National Center for Education Statistics, The Condition of Education 2004, Indicator 14, Table 14-1. http://nces.ed.gov/programs/coed/2004/pdf/14_2004.pdf.

41

Testimony of Douglas Lowenstein
President, the Private Equity Council
Before the House Financial Services Committee
Washington, DC
Wednesday, May 16, 2007

Mr. Chairman and members of the committee: Good morning. My name is Douglas Lowenstein and I am president of the Private Equity Council, a new organization that represents ten of the leading private equity investment firms in the United States.[1]

Thank you for providing us the opportunity to be part of this Committee's effort to better understand the role of the private equity industry in the U.S. economy. This hearing marks the Private Equity Council's first presentation to a congressional committee, and we hope it represents the start of a continuing dialogue on issues of mutual interest.

Before addressing the issues the Committee has raised, I think it would be helpful to take a moment to demystify private equity. While some have a perception that private equity is a form of black box finance practiced by a small cadre of New York investors, the truth is that private equity is about hundreds of thriving companies contributing to the economy in numerous positive ways. When you buy coffee in the morning at Dunkin' Donuts, you're interacting with private equity; when you see a movie produced by MGM Studios and buy your kids ice cream at Baskin-Robbins afterwards, you're interacting with private equity. When you shop at Toys R Us for the hottest new video game or the latest "must have" doll, or when you buy a new outfit at J. Crew, you're touching private equity. When you buy pet food and supplies for your dog or cat at Petco, that's private equity, too.

Private equity is not just about household brand names. When you make online plane and hotel reservations for your vacation, you may be relying on private equity. Many of us work in office buildings owned by private equity firms, and drive cars and fly in airplanes that rely on parts and equipment made

[1] Apollo Advisors, Bain Capital, The Blackstone Group, The Carlyle Group, Kohlberg, Kravis & Roberts, Hellman & Friedman, T. H. Lee Company, Providence Equity, Silver Lake Partners, and TPG Capital.

by private equity-owned firms; even the power that lights our homes in some parts of the country is delivered by private equity companies.

Further, private equity investments directly and indirectly benefit tens of millions of Americans. Public and private pension funds, foundations and university endowments have chalked up returns from private equity investments that far exceed those available from the stock market. Between 1991 and 2006, private equity firms worldwide created more than $430 billion in net value for these and other investors. These returns translate into stronger public employee pension programs, more funds for college financial aid and scholarships, and more funds for research and other causes supported by charitable foundations.

Private equity is intrinsic to American capitalism. Venture capital, for example, is a form of private equity used at the start-up phase of a business. By contrast, the transactions under review by this Committee are more typical for companies in later stages of their development. These transactions may take many forms. They may involve the acquisition of a private company with the intent of providing its founders the capital necessary to take its performance to the next level. They may involve the acquisition of a division of a large company, with the purpose of offering the newly independent business the management focus and resources needed to achieve a new mission. They may involve "privatizing" a public company in an effort to undertake improvements that would be difficult to achieve with the short-term earning focus of the public markets.

Academics and business leaders have recognized for years that the public markets sometimes distort the incentives for companies to put in place sound long-term business strategies. Because the managers of publicly-owned companies are forced to keep a close eye on quarterly earnings to maintain their stock price, they sometimes are hesitant to make the often substantial investments in new processes, personnel or equipment required to drive strong, long-term growth, but that can depress earnings and lower share prices in the short term.

Private equity firms, on the other hand, can take a longer view. Without the pressures from outside public shareholders looking for short-term gains, owners and managers can focus in a laser-like way on what is required to improve the medium to long-term performance of the company. This structure also makes it far easier to align the interests of owners with those of managers who also have a direct stake in the success of the company.

Ultimately, the mangers of private equity firms understand that they must improve the underlying value of the companies they own over time to continue to attract the capital they need. By better aligning owner-manager interests and by instituting a nimbler operating style that fosters greater innovation and long-term investment, private equity owners are leaders in spurring improved productivity and competitiveness.

Private equity is not a silver bullet, nor is it the right solution for every company. In the end, it is nothing more than a flexible form of ownership that, in appropriate circumstances, can create a successful operating environment for companies at different stages and in different conditions.

The Committee has asked that we address three issues: first, whether firms acquired through private equity make the investments in technology, capital equipment, and research essential to long run productivity growth; second, do workers find themselves disadvantaged through financial or other restructuring, and third, what are implications of private equity profits for growing income inequality in this country.

Private Equity and Growth

It is important to understand one central fact about private equity: private equity firms seek to improve the performance and increase the value of the companies in which they invest. Any other approach would defy common sense, because the entire business model rests on selling investments at a gain. That's why those who claim that private equity is all about asset stripping are missing the point: it is rather difficult to strengthen an underperforming business if you first vaporize the assets and the workforce. Bear in mind that after a private equity fund returns a company to public ownership, it usually maintains a very substantial equity stake in the company. In other words, if it adopts a short-term mentality, it takes money out of its own pocket by undermining the value of its own long term investment.

There has been much discussion about the degree to which private equity firms use debt as a tool in their transactions, and this is the premise for the Committee's question about private equity's commitment to long-term growth. In today's intensely competitive environment, the use of efficient capital structures remains important. Adding debt does promote fiscal discipline, discouraging wasteful spending on things like "country club" corporate headquarters. However, a strategy of simply adding more debt to an "underleveraged" balance sheet – which once might have sufficed to allow private equity firms to recognize substantial gains with only modest performance improvements – no longer works.

In the leveraged buyout wave of the 1980s, financing was often 90 percent or more debt and 10 percent or less equity. Since 2002, PE deals average in the range of 60 to 66 percent debt, though there have been more recent deals with higher debt levels due to the unusually low interest rate environment we've enjoyed the past few years.

In any event, regardless of the debt levels, to succeed today, a private equity firm needs to bring much more to the table than financial creativity. The PE firm must add new capabilities to the company it buys (by adding new products), increase competitiveness (by reducing waste and improving operations) and grow revenues (by entering new markets or finding new customers) in order to make any money for itself or its investors. And it needs to develop, implement and successfully execute a compelling strategy to do so. The best private equity firms today must bring to the table much more than capital. They deliver deep expertise in the sector in which the investment is being made; managerial and functional (IT, for example) capabilities; a performance culture that rewards entrepreneurship and results; and an ownership structure that allows even the toughest decisions to be made quickly.

A recent analysis by McKinsey & Company of more than 220 transactions using primary data collected from firms in the U.S. and Europe that were held by PE firms for three and one-half years or more showed that PE fund performance is disproportionately driven by the very best and the very worst transactions in each fund. And for these outlier transactions, company performance is the main factor driving returns. In the very best transactions (with annualized returns of more than 60 percent), 70 percent of the value created came from improving company performance. In those that did not produce significant returns, the failure was caused by the general partner's inability to make fundamental improvements to the company's operations.

Consider the private equity acquisition of SunGard, a major software developer and vendor which was under tremendous pressure from public shareholders to increase its earnings. SunGuard CEO Cristobal Conde has said that under private equity ownership, the company plans to complete 53 new research projects in 2007, up from about 10 annually pre-PE acquisition. Under the new ownership, SunGuard's common services architecture program is thriving, covering 60 SunGard products, compared to four before the private equity acquisition. The firm is annually training about 800 programmers, up from 50 prior to the transaction, as part of a focused effort to streamline software development and distribution and reduce the cost of rolling out products and make it easier to integrate SunGard software with other vendors' products.

Or take The Carlyle Group's 2005 acquisition of a company called AxleTech International Holdings, Inc., which designs and manufactures drive train components for growing markets in the military, construction, material handling, agriculture and other commercial sectors. AxleTech was a solid business, but it was focused on the low-margin, low -growth commercial segment of the market. Under Carlyle's strategic direction, AxleTech undertook a concerted business development initiative to offer its axle and suspension solutions to military vehicle manufacturers in need of heavier drive train equipment to support the heavy armored vehicles required to protect American soldiers in Iraq and Afghanistan. At the same time, AxleTech expanded its product and service offerings in its high-margin replacement parts business while continuing to grow its traditional commercial business. Since Carlyle's acquisition, AxleTech sales have increased 16 percent annually and employment has increased by 37 percent, from 425 to 568. New jobs were created in AxleTech's facilities in Troy, MI, Oshkosh, WI, and overseas. AxleTech is one of the very few U.S. automotive-related companies that are growing in today's challenging industry environment. AxleTech's job growth does not take into account the ripple effects on AxelTech's suppliers who are experiencing new hiring and capital investments.

Finally, KKR's acquisition of ITC Holdings, an electric power transmission company in Michigan, offers a third case study of how private equity firms invest in the long-term health of their companies. When KKR acquired the company, it had a capital budget of $10 million and 28 direct employees; since being acquired, ITC has invested $400 million to rebuild and upgrade the transmission grid in its service area of southeast Michigan. ITC's annual capital budget is now $200 million, and employment has grown to 230 direct employees. In January, 2007 Michigan Governor Jennifer Granholm commended ITC for its "commitment to enhancing electric reliability" and for "investing in our electric transmission infrastructure to ensure that electricity will be delivered to millions of Michigan citizens as well as customers in other Midwest states."

Private equity is not perfect, nor does it always deliver the results predicted for its portfolio companies. Sometimes, firms do add too much leverage; sometimes, management cannot deliver successful growth strategies. But there are literally hundreds of positive stories similar to the ones I have described here. And overall, in the most thorough research on the impact of private equity to date, a study by the British Venture Capital Association found that PE companies in the UK grew sales faster than public firms and that their investment and R&D outlays grew at an average annual rate of 21 percent, results I expect are replicated here in the U.S.

Perhaps the best indicator that private equity firms build stronger businesses is revealed in research by Harvard Business School's Josh Lerner. In a recent study, Lerner found that the stock prices of companies operated by private equity firms for more than a year outperform the stock prices of industry peers that remained in public ownership. In other words, if we believe that the public markets reward the best-run companies, the Lerner study offers undisputed evidence that private equity creates significant value in the companies they owned.

Private Equity and Workers

The second question raised in the Committee notice regards the impact of private equity on working men and women. While data on private equity investment's impact on employment in the U.S. is anecdotal, a void the PEC hopes to fill in time, research in Europe suggests that PE investments do indeed result in long term job growth. A study by the international management consulting firm A.T. Kearney found earlier this year that PE firms generate employment, on average, at a much faster pace than comparable, traditionally-financed firms. Research by the BVCA on both venture and private equity portfolio companies found that during the last five years, businesses backed by private equity increased employment an average of nine percent per year compared to one to two percent for public companies. Earlier this year, the Financial Times studied the 30 largest European private equity transactions in 2003-04 and reported that "overall, jobs were more likely to have been gained than lost as a result of private equity- backed buys." I cannot say definitively that the same outcomes occur in the U.S., but there is little reason to think differently.

That said, the recent increase in private equity activity is part of a larger and pervasive domestic and international economic wave that is driving changes across all classes of American companies, regardless of their capital and ownership structure. Profound forces unrelated to private equity are reshaping the American economy. In his work on the New Democratic Network's Globalization Initiative, economist Rob Shapiro has noted that while we have been in a period of sustained economic growth since the 2001 recession, as measured by GDP and productivity rates, wages for American workers have been flat or declining when adjusted for inflation. At the same time, job creation is occurring at a lower rate than after prior recessions.

I am not here to analyze the reasons for these unusual trends, nor am I qualified to do so. I raise it because it is important to understand the larger context in which private equity operates, and not to view it in a vacuum as if it can be isolated from these larger forces. Private equity is not causing these economic changes; but neither can it operate in a business environment isolated from them. The simple truth is that, as with any other acquisition involving public or private companies, private equity transactions can result in layoffs. In other cases, they may be short term layoffs until job growth over the long term increases as the business grows stronger. In still other cases, they may involve immediate employment growth. Even when some layoffs are essential, private equity has probably preserved hundreds or thousands of jobs that might have otherwise been lost by underperforming or failing businesses. In the end, this much I know: there is no evidence that private equity firms are more likely to cut jobs than any other form of ownership.

In fact, in the last months, we have read about a stream of layoffs at companies not involved in private equity acquisitions of any kind: Ford Motor Company, Circuit City and Citicorp, to name a few. Of course, if you're a worker, a lost job is no less painful regardless of the cause. And the point I am making is that demonizing private equity as a uniquely causative factor for job losses in this country is not just inaccurate, it diverts us from developing a more comprehensive national economic policy to deal with the evolving world in which we live. And as I said earlier, the entire business model of private equity is predicated on increasing value, not destroying it.

Private Equity and Income Disparity

The final area of interest to the committee is the impact of private equity on income inequality in this country. Undeniably, there are those in private equity who are doing very well. Fundamentally, this reflects the fact that they are good at what they do and that they have built significant value in their own businesses and in the companies that they acquire. Their personal success is directly tied to whether they in fact acquire companies, grow them, increase their value, and sell them for a gain. If they fail to do so, their access to investors' capital would dry up and they would be out of business. Moreover, there is no guarantee they will succeed, and the landscape is littered with private equity firms that crashed and burned precisely because there are real risks in PE investing. Not everyone does it well.

Equally undeniable is the fact that we have an income inequality issue in this country. But I submit to this Committee that the forces contributing to this go far beyond private equity, as do the solutions. Private equity is not the reason American companies are being pressured to lower costs, restructure, and employ new strategies to better compete with China, India and other emerging economies. And private equity alone cannot confront the forces contributing to the growing income disparity. But the members of the Private Equity Council are prepared to be part of a national dialogue about how to reverse this trend.

At the same time, it is important to point out how private equity is benefitting Americans from all walks of life. While the impact of PE on jobs is one important measure of its worth, it is not the only measure of private equity's impact on both workers and other Americans inside and outside the companies acquired. The beneficiaries of private equity include tens of millions of Americans whose retirements are made more secure by the very strong returns earned by public, private and union pension funds that invest in private equity ventures; they include the thousands of young people who obtain financial aid or scholarships to public and private colleges because of the high returns earned by university endowments investing in private equity; and they include those of us who may one day benefit from research to cure or treat a disease funded by a foundation generating above-average returns from private equity.

In fact, public pension funds, university endowments, and leading foundations accounted for one-third of all capital allocated to private equity in 2006. The 20 largest public pension funds for which data is available[2] - including the California Public Employees Retirement System, the California State Teachers Retirement System, the New York State Common Retirement Fund, and the Florida State Board of Administration - currently have some $111 billion invested in private equity on behalf of 10.5 million beneficiaries.

These investors seek out private equity because the return on investments made in private equity funds far outstrips that delivered by many other investment opportunities, including the public markets. Between 1980 and 2005, top-quartile private equity firms, on average, delivered to pension funds and other limited partners annualized net returns of 39 percent. During the same period, the S&P 500 posted returns of 12.3 percent. In the past five years, returns on investments made in companies by top quartile private equity firms averaged 20 percent, compared to seven percent for the S&P 500.

Let me give you a concrete example of what these numbers mean to real people. The Washington State Investment Board, which is responsible for more than $75 billion in assets in 16 separate retirement funds that benefit more than 440,000 public employees, teachers, school employees, law enforcement officers, firefighters and judges, has been a major private equity investor for 25 years. In that time, the WSIB has realized profits on its private equity investments of $9.71 billion. Annual returns on private equity investments made by the board since 1981 have averaged 15 percent, compared to 10.1 percent for the S&P 500. Put another way, the excess returns generated by private equity investments during that period are worth $26,000 per retiree; or expressed another way: these returns have fully funded retirement plans for 10,000 WSIB retirees.

---

[2] California Public Employees Retirement System, the California State Teachers Retirement System, New York State Common Retirement Fund, Florida State Board of Administration, New York City Retirement System, Teacher Retirement System of Texas, New York City Teachers Retirement System, New York State Teachers Retirement System, State of Wisconsin Investment Board, New Jersey State Investment Council, Washington State Investment Board, Regents of the University of California, , Ohio Public Employees Retirement System, Oregon State Treasury, State Teachers Retirement System of Ohio, Oregon Public Employees Retirement Fund, Pennsylvania Public School Employees Retirement System, Michigan Department of Treasury, Virginia Retirement System, Minnesota State Board of Investment.

Overall, between 2000 and 2006, private equity firms distributed $181 billion in profits to their limited partners in the U.S. alone. A corollary benefit from these exceptional returns is that dozens of states have been able to avoid budget cuts or tax increases that would have been required to meet their legally-mandated pension obligations to retirees who have devoted their careers to public service.

The bottom line:

Private equity makes significant contributions to the American economy. Through superior investment returns, it delivers important financial support for universities, research institutions and pension funds that benefit tens of millions of Americans. With infusions of capital, talent and strategy, private equity firms improve the productivity, performance and financial strength of the companies in which they invest. Private equity is not a silver bullet, neither is it a dark force. It is an innovative, flexible financial tool that has proven very successful in responding to the global challenges faced by American businesses today.

STATEMENT OF JON L. LUTHER, CEO OF DUNKIN' BRANDS, INC BEFORE THE COMMITTEE ON FINANCIAL SERVICES OF THE HOUSE OF REPRESENTATIVES, MAY 16, 2007

Chairman Frank and Members of the Committee, my name is Jon L. Luther. I am chairman and chief executive officer of Dunkin' Brands, the parent company of Dunkin' Donuts, Baskin-Robbins, and Togo's. I appreciate this opportunity to share with you Dunkin' Brands' experience with private equity ownership.

Our talented team of executives and employees—together with our thousands of franchisees and licensees, predominantly small businesspeople—has built a $6.4 billion enterprise operating in 47 U.S. states and 50 countries. Thanks to their effort and commitment, our brands are known and loved by consumers around the world.

When I joined Dunkin' Brands in January 2003, we were owned by Allied Domecq, a publicly traded spirits and wine company headquartered in the U.K. In November 2005, Allied Domecq was acquired by Pernod Ricard, a spirits and wine company based in France. Shortly thereafter, because Dunkin' Brands was not a core asset, Pernod put our company up for auction. In March 2006, we were acquired by a consortium of three U.S.-based private equity firms: The Carlyle Group, Bain Capital Partners LLC, and Thomas H. Lee Partners, L.P.

During the period in which we were an Allied Domecq subsidiary, we were considered a "cash cow." We were assigned yearly growth targets. We were usually last in line for attention and certainly for capital. Significant decisions required that I go to London. Our cash was swept every night and the focus was usually on the next quarter's numbers.

Our acquisition by Carlyle, Bain and Thomas H. Lee liberated our company. Our new owners expressed confidence in our management team, our strategies, and our vision. Our three key goals are to take Dunkin' Donuts national, transform Baskin-Robbins, and expand internationally. Rather than tell us to change our goals and our plans to achieve them, our new owners asked how they could support us. Finally, we had the attention and the resources we needed to realize our goals.

The benefits of our new ownership to our company have been enormous. Their financial expertise led to a ground-breaking securitization deal that resulted in very favorable financing at favorable interest rates. This has enabled us to make significant investments in our infrastructure and our growth initiatives. In addition, they have helped us to create a new franchisee financing program that will provide flexible, convenient and competitive financing options to franchisees of every size in all markets.

They have opened the door to opportunities that were previously beyond our reach. For example, they introduced us to a real estate development firm that is assisting our Baskin-Robbins franchisees in finding attractive real estate opportunities. Initial results have been so successful that we are now looking at using their services to support our Dunkin' Donuts development.

Our acquisition and the expansion plan for which we now have the resources have put us in the national spotlight. Countless news stories about us have caused us to be sought out by many potential employees and franchisees.

As a result, our franchising efforts, the engine of our growth, have taken off. We are a 100%-franchised enterprise. Every Dunkin' Donuts and Baskin-Robbins store that opens represents the achievement of a dream for an entrepreneur somewhere. A new Dunkin' Donuts means approximately 25 new jobs, and a new Baskin-Robbins approximately 12 jobs.

Over the next fifteen years, we would expect to add 250,000 jobs--jobs for young people, and jobs with good career paths in restaurant management, making possible for thousands the achievement of the American dream.

Our new owners have never asked us to cut costs or reduce our headcount. Any reductions in staffing that we've had over the past four years have been a result of our efforts to be more productive and less bureaucratic. This year, we also expect to divest of Togo's, our California sandwich chain, which generates approximately $200 million in annual revenues.

This decision, which our management team had considered prior to our being put up for auction, was finally made last summer. The decision was a function of Togo's size relative to our entire organization, and our inability to give it the kind of attention it required versus our two, much larger brands.

Recently, I was asked by a *Boston Globe* columnist whether Dunkin' Brands would follow the path of many companies and move to a location where the costs of doing business would be lower. I was pleased to say that Massachusetts is our home. We're not going anywhere.

54

We believe in strong community roots. Last year, together with our franchisees, we established our Dunkin' Brands Community Foundation. The mission of our Foundation is to support those who serve our communities, especially in times of crisis. This mission is true to our brand heritage, and the values of our entire system: employees, franchisees, and our customers.

As a result of our relationship with Carlyle, Bain and Thomas H. Lee, our business has benefited, our franchisees and their employees have benefited, and wealth-creating opportunity has been spread among hundreds of entrepreneurs and careerists associated with Dunkin' Brands.

# # #

Statement of
Andrew L. Stern
President
Service Employees International Union, CTW, CLC
To the U.S. House of Representatives Committee on Financial Services
"Private Equity's Effects on Workers and Firms"
May 16, 2007

Mr. Chairman and members of the Committee, thank you for the opportunity to appear before you today to discuss this critical issue facing our nation.

My name is Andy Stern and I am President of the Service Employees International Union (SEIU). With 1.8 million members, SEIU is America's largest union of health care workers, property services workers, and the second largest union of public services workers. A top priority of SEIU members is to unite working families, business leaders, community leaders, policy-makers, and other unions to find solutions to the challenges facing workers and our nation as our economy undergoes the most rapid transformation in history.

As the private equity buyout industry grows in size and influence, the impact of its practices on American workers, industries, the financial markets, communities and the nation as a whole must be examined more closely and I applaud the Chairman and this Committee for taking on these issues.

Today's economy and its impact on workers

The story America's success is a story of work and working people. The hard work of nurses, teachers, janitors, food service workers, home health and care workers, and millions in other professions have made our economy into the most successful, productive, innovative, and prosperous in the history of the world.

The greatness and promise of America has always been that, if you work hard, you will have your work valued and rewarded. You will be able to provide for your family, have a decent home, access to affordable health care, a secure retirement and time to spend with your family. You will have the opportunity to achieve the American Dream.

And throughout our history, this promise has driven millions to our shores. Every generation has done better than the last. But we are now at a moment in our history when the promise of the American Dream is in jeopardy.

Today, a majority of Americans say they believe their children will actually be worse off than they are, according to recent polling by Lake Research, which also found that an astounding 65 percent of working Americans now feel negative or uncertain about the American Dream.

Survey after survey tells us that Americans of all political persuasions think the nation is headed in the wrong direction. One poll last month conducted on behalf of *NBC News* and *The Wall St. Journal*, found that 66 percent of Americans feel this way.

Today's economy is simply not working for working people.

- More than 46 million Americans do not have health insurance. Tens of millions more are underinsured. More than 9 million American children have no health care coverage.
- Pensions are disappearing and retirement security is becoming a thing of the past.
- Schools are crumbling and failing our children—and not only in low-income communities, but in middle class communities too.
- Wages for working Americans are stagnant. In 2006, private sector wages dropped to 43 percent of national income, the lowest level in more than half a century.
- We have the highest rate of income inequality in this country since 1928. According to a recent study by the economists Thomas Piketty and Emmanuel Saez, the top 300,000 Americans have almost as much income as the bottom 150 million Americans combined.

People are working harder and longer for less. Opportunities that have always been there for Americans who work hard and build the value of our economy are disappearing.

But what is so puzzling to working people is that this is all happening during a time of unprecedented prosperity in America, a time that some are calling America's new "Gilded Age."

- Productivity is continuing to rise
- Corporate profits have more than doubled since 2000. In 2006, profits as a share of national income were at their highest level ever.
- The five largest companies in the world, Wal-Mart, General Motors, Exxon Mobil, Royal Dutch/Shell, and BP are each financially larger than all but 24 of the world's nations.
- CEO salaries are at record levels—the average CEO makes more than 431 times the amount of compensation of the average worker, a gap that has been growing steadily.

Productivity is up, but wages are not. Profits are up, but business investment is not. This is an economy that is not lifting all boats—just the luxury liners—and that's not good for our country.

Private equity is at the center of the today's economy

Private equity is a major driver of this economy. And while there are a number of private investment vehicles in the financial markets, including venture capital and hedge funds, today Mr. Chairman I am addressing the issues surrounding private equity leveraged buyouts.

Today, private equity is buying and selling larger and larger companies and reshaping whole industries. The buyout industry, armed with more than a half-trillion dollars of capital, is today engineering financial deals on a scale that until a few years ago seemed unimaginable.

- There were a record $197 billion worth of private equity mergers in first quarter of 2007.
- In the last five years, the volume of private equity deals has grown 600 percent—from $42 billion to $250 billion.
- The biggest five private equity deals together are larger than the annual budgets of all but 16 of the world's nations.
- The annual revenue of the largest private equity firms and their portfolio companies would give private equity four of the top 25 spots in the Fortune 500.
- Private equity firms control companies that employ more than 5 million workers. If the industry continues to grow at just half the rate it has grown in the last five years, by 2012 one out of every eight private sector workers – more than 15 million Americans—could work for a company owned by a private equity firm.

But the story of private equity is the incredible wealth being created for the small number of individuals at the top of the industry. As leveraged buyouts worth billions become more and more commonplace, private equity firms are extracting fees of hundreds of millions of dollars from the companies they buy and often generating profits of 20 percent or more.

In short, the income being accumulated by private equity is a major contributor to the concentration of wealth among the top 1 percent of Americans.

Private equity executives claim that while they are doing well, the wealth they are generating is helping fund retirement benefits for millions of public employees, university endowments, and foundations that support worthy causes. That is true. But make no mistake, there is more than enough money in the booming private equity industry for the firms to continue to do very well, for pension funds to continue to benefit, but also to make sure workers share in the economic opportunities being created by private equity.

Concerns about private equity

Against the backdrop of this record accumulation of wealth, private equity's practices are helping drive forces that raise significant concerns about their impact on workers, companies, and the financial markets.

Risky Deals Put Workers and Companies at Risk

A cornerstone of private equity is the corporate restructuring that follows a typical buyout. The industry claims it creates efficiencies in companies and helps turn around underperforming operations, building the long-term value of these companies and increasing the overall productivity in the economy. But the manner in which these restructurings are often undertaken raises serious concerns for workers and the companies themselves.

The high degree of leverage involved in buyout deals can create significant pressures to cut costs that are counter-productive to the stated goals of private equity firms and investors to create long-term value and productivity in the companies they buy.

In a highly leveraged buyout of a nursing home chain or hospital company for example, increased debt payments could squeeze capital expenditures necessary to maintain and update vital medical equipment. And what happens to operating budgets that go toward maintaining the staffing levels necessary to provide quality patient care? As private equity buys the market leaders in major service industries such as health care, the impact of private equity restructurings may create a ripple effect creating downward pressure on standards of care and potentially harming the long-term value and productivity of whole industries.

Another example is the case of the Bain Capital buyout of KB Toys, which was featured in SEIU's recent report "Behind the Buyouts: Inside the World of Private Equity." [Report available at www.BehindtheBuyouts.org] In 2000, Bain Capital purchased KB Toys in a highly leveraged buyout worth nearly $300 million. Bain's $18.1 million in equity accounted for only about 6 percent of the cost of the purchase—the rest was financed by loans and IOUs.

In 2002, Bain engaged in the increasingly common practice of a leveraged recapitalization of KB Toys. The company added additional debt to KB Toys—in order to pay Bain and several KB Toys executives a special dividend worth $120 million. Such dividend recaps increase a company's vulnerability to potential operational fluctuations or external changes that could result in either bankruptcy or restructuring.

In the case of KB Toys, the result was a bankruptcy filing in January 2004. As a result, more than 4,000 employees lost their jobs and 600 stores closed, the harsh result of a risky debt-driven business strategy.

Despite the cautionary tale of KB Toys, leveraged recaps increased from $3.9 billion in 2002 (the year Bain used the strategy at KB Toys) to $40.5 billion in 2005, according to Standard & Poor's. That's a lot of risk private equity is putting on these companies to pay themselves special dividends.

As we have seen most recently from the results of job cuts at Circuit City, layoffs are not the panacea many corporate managers would like them to be. Instead of viewing workers exclusively as a line-item on a balance sheet, or a cost to be cut, private equity must view workers first as the women and men who build the value of their companies and are the backbone of economic and civic life in their communities.

Private Equity "Exuberance"

The economy today has a case of buyout fever. Private equity firms raised $215 billion in 2006— the most ever. The total exceeds the amounts raised during the last private equity bubble, in 2000. With all this capital being raised, it increases the competition for deals, adding to the likelihood some firms will overpay for deals or do deals that are far more risky. A significant downturn in the public equity markets would severely impair the ability of private equity to exit deals that were poorly conceived, highly leveraged, or overvalued.

If even one major deal fails, very serious concerns have been raised about its impact on the credit markets, on investors such as pension funds, and not least, the workers at the affected company.

Quick Flips and Sell-Offs

The industry advertises its ability to achieve long-term business growth, free of the scrutiny of the public markets. But in recent years, private equity has sought to increase its funds' investment returns by liquidating part or all of their investment more quickly than the traditional time period of three to five years. To accomplish this, firms engage in "quick flips," relisting companies within a year or two of taking them private, with more leverage, but few if any operational improvements.

In the case of the buyout of Hertz car rental by the firms Carlyle Group, Clayton Dubilier & Rice, and Merrill Lynch, Hertz was taken public less than a year after being bought by the private equity firms. The Initial Public Offering for Hertz raised $1.3 billion, more than 95 percent of which paid for special dividends for the firms, which recouped more than half the equity they invested. Far from producing long-term growth, Hertz reported a 2006 decline in net income of two-thirds and this year announced an initiative to eliminate more than 1,500 jobs.

Conflicts of Interest

The managers and directors of a public company owe a fiduciary duty to maximize returns to shareholders. But when private equity invites those same managers or directors to participate in a leveraged buyout, their interest shifts to helping the private equity group get the lowest price possible for the company.

This conflict of interest, which unfortunately is all too common in buyout deals today, raises significant questions about the deals that are being put together and whether or not the companies being bought are being adversely affected over the long term. It has been suggested by more than one commentator that management participation in buyouts should be prohibited.

For example, in the proposed $6.1 billion Cerberus buyout of Affiliated Computer Services, questions are being raised about the role of ACS Chairman Darwin Deason's role in the offer. Cerberus has an exclusive agreement with Deason to negotiate a take-private transaction of the company, which has led ACS's lead director to raise questions about how competitive a bid can be.

At the very least this is a matter that requires much more study, as private equity buyouts occur with larger and more prominent companies that serve important public interests.

Transparency and Disclosure
Unlike publicly traded companies that are subject to securities laws, it is well known that private equity buyout firms operate out of the public eye, with little oversight. With the pressures of high debt levels and the increasing practice of quick flips and sell-offs, it is critical that the industry provide more transparency and disclosure so that the people who might be affected by a given deal—workers, community members, shareholders and others—are aware of the potential impact on their lives.

Though the list may vary depending on the circumstances, a given private equity firm could disclose at the time of a deal and then periodically thereafter, information such as total debt, employment levels, management or other fees, any potential conflicts of interest, and/or major business decisions they plan on making at the company.

This would be a step in the right direction for workers who now have almost no voice in the deals, little information about their new employers, and no say about the plans that could negatively impact their lives.

Missed opportunities
Perhaps most importantly, buyout deals present real opportunities for our country. For all the hundreds of millions of dollars in fees and billions in profits taken out in these deals by the private equity firms, the workers at most of the portfolio companies receive no increases in pay or benefits—not even a more generous 401(k) contribution. The same goes for the contract workers—the janitors, security officers, food service workers, and others—who provide valuable services. Their jobs are controlled by these companies, but they are paid mostly poverty-level wages and more often than not have no affordable health care, sick days, or retirement benefits of any kind.

Take for example the Blackstone Group's recent $39 billion buyout of Equity Office Properties, the nation's largest office landlord. Less than a month after the deal had closed Blackstone had sold $21 billion worth of the Equity portfolio.

It is easy to see how Blackstone benefited from the deal—but what about the tens of thousands of property services workers—janitors and security officers—who work hard every day and build the value of these properties—but who may be struggling to provide for their families.

The $360 million in transaction fees from the Equity deal could have provided health insurance for one year for more than 150,000 property services workers.

The $4.4 billion in fees paid to private equity firms in the 10 largest buyout deals of the last two years would pay for family health plans for 1 million American workers.

I would ask you Mr. Chairman and the members of the Committee to imagine the economic impact on families, on hard-hit neighborhoods and whole cities if these billion-dollar private equity deals were structured in such a way to ensure that workers and communities shared in the economic benefits of deals involving companies they helped to make successful.

Private Equity: The Opportunity

When it comes to private equity buyouts there have been both hits and misses. But for working people, there unfortunately have been far more misses than hits.

We could argue over a lot of issues, including whether or not private equity creates more total jobs than it destroys. The fact is there is not enough reliable information to make that determination across the board.

A better question for today, perhaps, is what kind of jobs are being created by private equity? In this economy, too often the jobs created are part time with low wages and no benefits. These are jobs with no future that cannot support families.

There is no argument, however, over the correlation between unions and good jobs and good jobs and increased opportunity for American families.

It would be best if the industry made changes itself and took steps to ensure that private equity works for working people and the rest of the country.

- That means making sure workers and communities that are impacted have a voice in the deals and benefit from their outcome.
- It means the industry should play by the same set of rules as everyone else and provide for more transparency and disclosure.
- It means they should eliminate conflicts of interest.
- It means that unions, if one exists at a company being bought, should be at the table as soon as possible when a buyout deal is being put together.
- If no union exists, private equity firms should see to it that they and their new portfolio company remain neutral on the question of unionization and allow workers to choose to form a union using the majority sign-up process.

But if private equity firms will not take steps to change, Mr. Chairman, Congress should legislate.

America has been at its best when a broad group of people have shared in the prosperity being created in the economy. We've gotten away from that in recent years.

It is ridiculous in America that everyone cannot share in the success and prosperity they helped create.

There is more than enough wealth in the buyout business for private equity firms to continue to prosper while also adapting their existing business model to expand opportunities to benefit workers, communities, and the nation. Everybody can win if we set our sights on that goal.

Improving the jobs of millions of Americans whose companies are involved in leveraged buyouts will have an impact on reducing the income inequality that is weakening our country, undermining our democracy, and harming the long-term sustainability of our financial markets.

The incredible wealth that exists in the private equity buyout industry presents a historic opportunity. It's time to repair the broken promise of the American Dream.

I thank the Chairman and the members of the Committee for their time.

###

The New York Times

ABOUT NEW YORK
Metropolitan Desk; SECTB

Unkind Cut For Janitors At Hilfiger

By JIM DWYER
792 words
16 May 2007
The New York Times
Late Edition - Final
1
English

On Thursday, Gloria Coreas took the subway from Jackson Heights, Queens, to 23rd Street, then a crosstown bus to the western edge of Manhattan, and spent her usual eight hours cleaning the office at the Tommy Hilfiger company.

At the end of the day, she was called to the fifth floor, along with the eight other men and women who make the daily mess disappear.

''A supervisor said, 'I'm going to give you bad news,' '' Ms. Coreas said. ''The job was ending.''

Nine people, who came by subway and bus to scrub Tommy Hilfiger's toilets, mop his floors, dust his shelves, were out of work. They made about $19 an hour, union wages. The Hilfiger operation found a new company to provide these services for about $8 an hour, said Chuck Santiago, one of the people who lost his job and tried to get hired by the new cleaning contractor.

Yesterday, black Town Cars lined up in the fine spring sunshine outside the Hilfiger office on West 26th Street to collect young designers and executives while their former cleaning women and men handed out fliers and accepted condolences from people on smoke breaks.

Gustavo Aguinaga said: ''Thursday night, they tell us the job is over on Friday. They tell us they're coming the next day to pick up the tools.''

''No notice,'' Ms. Coreas said. ''We were in shock.''

The Hilfiger company sells clothes around the world stamped with variations on Tommy Hilfiger's name; last year, the company was bought for what was reported to be $1.6 billion by a private equity company called Apax Partners. (What is $1.6 billion? Here's a scale: One million seconds is about 11 days. One billion seconds is about 32 years.)

Besides cashing in his own stake of $66 million, Mr. Hilfiger will be paid a minimum of $14.5 million a year through 2010, then receive a share of the sales.

For workers in their 40s and 50s, a job that pays $8 an hour was a nightmare. ''Rent in Jackson Heights is unbelievable now,'' Ms. Coreas said. ''It's more than a thousand dollars.''

''We're not asking for raises,'' Mr. Santiago said. ''We're not asking for anything, except to let us work.''

As they spoke, Andy Hilfiger, the brother of Tommy, stepped outside. ''I think they came with the building,'' he said of the laid-off cleaning people. No, he was told, the cleaners had moved with Hilfiger to 26th Street from offices a few blocks away. ''Oh, they did?'' he said. ''I'll try to find out something.'' He got on a cellphone, then drifted away.

Yesterday, Marybeth Schmitt, speaking for the people who own the Hilfiger name, called.

''I have a statement,'' she said.

Hold on.

Had her space been cleaned satisfactorily, the bathroom tidy, and so on?

''I would have to get back to you on that,'' she said.

64

Couldn't she say whether her trash can had been properly emptied? Without conferring with other executives?

"I don't think this is personal," she said. "This is a corporate matter."

Sigh.

Before getting to the statement, it's worth noting that on its Web site, Hilfiger says that garment manufacturers who work under contract for the company must treat their workers fairly.

Hilfiger used a contractor, Shepard Industries, to clean its space in Manhattan, and Ms. Schmitt's initial statement seemed to blame Shepard for the loss of jobs, saying the contractor had "ended its relationship with Tommy Hilfiger USA Inc."

That leaves out an important detail. "We have not been paid by Tommy Hilfiger for the last six months," said Joan Taylor, the director of operations for Shepard. "We have paid our employees."

So Tommy Hilfiger, a name owned by the global private equities firm Apax with $20 billion in assets under management, did not pay the company that paid the people who cleaned its bathrooms?

Asked about this, Ms. Schmitt said yes, it was true that Hilfiger had stopped paying the cleaning contractor in December, but only because it reduced its office space by half in November and disputed the contractor's bills. Hilfiger "is currently seeking a union employer to take up this contract," she said.

The first contractor contacted by Hilfiger, IBS Services Group, did not respond to inquiries.

On Friday morning, Gustavo Aguinaga and Gloria Coreas and the others came to work. At day's end, their tools were hauled away: buffing machines, vacuums, brooms, dusters, rags, Windex, Fantastik, degreaser, carpet shampoo.

"We packed it all up," Mr. Aguinaga said.

Why?

"They asked us," he said.

E-mail: dwyer@nytimes.com

Document NYTF000020070516e35g0003m

INDEX

C

D

E

F

G

N

O

P

Q

R

S

T

U

V

W

Y